ROMAN CLASSICS

NOTES

SUMMARIES AND CONCISE COMMENTARIES ABOUT THE
MAJOR WORKS OF CLASSIC ROMAN WRITERS, INCLUDING

Plautus • Terence • Cicero • Julius Caesar

Lucretius • Catullus • Virgil

Horace • Ovid • Plutarch • Suetonius

Tacitus • Apuleius • St. Augustine

and others

Mary Ellen Snodgrass, M.A.
University of North Carolina

INCORPORATED

LINCOLN, NEBRASKA 68501

Editor

Gary Carey, M.A.
University of Colorado

Consulting Editor

James L. Roberts, Ph.D.
Department of English
University of Nebraska

ABOUT THE AUTHOR

Mary Ellen Snodgrass earned her B.A. in British and classical literature from the University of North Carolina at Greensboro, her M.A. in English from Appalachian State University, and certification in gifted education from Lenoir-Rhyne College. A member of the American Classical League, Virgilian Society, Phi Beta Kappa, AFT, NCTE, and IRA, she taught English and Latin at Hickory High School for twenty years and has served as chairman of the English department, coordinator of language arts for the Hickory City Schools, reader for the North Carolina Textbook Commission, and writer, editor, and consultant for major textbook publishers. Her published works include Cliffs *Teaching Portfolios* as well as articles for *Islands* magazine, the Presbyterian Center, ERIC, and other professional groups. She was contributing editor of *The Short Story and You* (National Textbook) and *The Great American English Handbook* (Perma-Bound).

ISBN 0-8220-1152-2
© Copyright 1988
by
C. K. Hillegass
All Rights Reserved
Printed in U.S.A.

Cliffs Notes, Inc.   Lincoln, Nebraska

CONTENTS

THE SILVER AGE (14–117 A.D.)

THE LATE EMPIRE (117–395 A.D.)

৵

ROMAN CLASSICS

Augustus Caesar; bronze
British Museum, London

The genius of the Roman civilization, like other eras of greatness, came about from an auspicious amalgam of talent, pluck, raw material, and more than a pinch of good fortune. That a semi-barbaric village on the Tiber could have lasted over twelve hundred years, from 753 B.C. to 476 A.D., is not unlikely, but that it could develop into a world power of cultural and historical significance lasting into the modern age is indeed impressive. What, we ask ourselves, was the nature of this mongrel nation that gave it longevity? Why did this city spawn massive architectural monuments, military might, administrative acumen, and literary greatness when other, older parts of the known world merely survived?

Fortunately for the modern reader, there are plenty of answers in the writings of the Romans themselves. A careful perusal of plays, letters, speeches, poems, epigrams, laws, histories, and commentaries leaves no doubt that the cosmopolitan nature and strategic location of Rome nurtured natural inclinations toward conquest and expansion. The characteristic practicality of the Romans, symbolized by their road system, was the fiber which bound it all together and kept it whole through invasions from without and corruption within.

Although for most of its existence Rome lacked the refined tastes and philosophical depth of earlier civilizations, the Romans managed with hand-me-downs. They made judicious, pragmatic use of imported ideas—education, art, drama, language, literature, medicine, and architecture from Greece and Egypt; an alphabet, boat-building and business skills from Phoenicia; coins, food, and raw materials from all parts of the Mediterranean as well as from northern Europe and the Far East; and religion from Greece, Egypt, and, ultimately, Palestine.

A glance at Rome's minor spokesmen reveals a startling versatility of minds, from the didactic essays of Quintilian to the biographical sketches of Cornelius Nepos; from the amusing fables of Phaedrus to the Christian orthodoxy of Apollinaris; from the sober, self-appraising record of Augustus Caesar to the droll and seamy underworld depicted by Petronius Arbiter. Rome gathered in from the far corners of the Empire the creative minds that had something to contribute to its fundamental eclecticism. Josephus, a Palestinian, offered a binocular view of Rome's struggle against the Jews. Martial, from Spain, at the other end of the Mediterranean, gave Rome a glimpse of itself, its foibles, its inherent absurdities.

From the Italian peninsula came the two Plinys, natives of Como in the Alps, who channeled their energies into the world's first encyclopedia and an eyewitness account of Italy's most terrifying natural disaster, the eruption of Vesuvius in 79 A.D. To the northeast was the birthplace of Catullus and Virgil, poets of genius and vision, and St. Jerome, father of the Latin Bible. The land at the end of the Apennine Mountains offered the intellectualism and refined odes of Horace and the theatrical skills of Ennius, Pacuvius, and Livius Andronicus. From the city itself came Julius Caesar, consummate military strategist, demagogue, and orator; Lucretius, master scientist; and Marcus Aurelius, beneficent emperor and spokesman for stoicism.

An understanding of Rome's literature requires a nodding acquaintance with its three governmental systems. Evolving from a primitive monarchy in 753 B.C., the Republic, founded in 509 B.C., rose from the courageous heroism and selflessness of semi-legendary heroes to its culmination in the godlike Julius Caesar. After his death in 44 B.C., Rome agonized through a period of self-purgation, a cataclysmic living hell for some of its most incisive critics, its most gifted lyricists, notably Cicero, Livy, Ovid, and Virgil.

Reborn in the person of Julius Caesar's nineteen-year-old nephew, Octavian, Rome took on new and resilient life as an Empire. Naming himself Augustus, "venerable one," and adopting his uncle's cognomen (Caesar), the first emperor ruled for forty-five years, stabilized the nation's economic and governing systems, and launched a new era of peace and growth. Through the worst and best of successors, Rome survived, conquered, grew, shrank, and ultimately collapsed, a victim of a wave of invasions by less sophisticated, but more energetic peoples.

The record speaks for itself. Within the pages of Rome's literary canon lie facts, suppositions, music, praise, condemnation, and advice. By familiarizing ourselves with these long-dead voices, we of the

modern world can learn the methods by which people make themselves great, by which nations become superpowers. And, to the
betterment of human life, we can contemplate the internal elements
of destruction that festered long before the end and search for them
in ourselves.

EARLY ROMAN LITERATURE

- **Plautus**

PLAUTUS

- *Menaechmi*
  (The Twin Menaechmi)

- *Captivi*
  (The Captives)

- *Aulularia*
  (The Pot of Gold)

- *Amphitryon*

PLAUTUS

LIFE AND BACKGROUND

The exuberant punster and chief comedy writer of ancient Rome, Titus Maccius Plautus (ca. 254–184 B.C.) lived in that gray era before Romans recorded biographical information. Consequently, the minute bits of biographical information that survive, such as his military career and business ventures, are highly suspect. He was probably born in Sarsina, Umbria, inland about twenty miles from San Marino. His name may be a pseudonym, possibly derived from "Maccus," the stereotypical clown in comedies. In *Attic Nights*, Aulus Gellius relates that Plautus came to Rome as a youth to seek his fortune in stage productions, but that he lost his earnings in some unwise mercantile investments. While working as a laborer in a flour mill, Plautus supposedly struck it rich by composing three successful comedies.

Critics agree that Plautus had firsthand knowledge of the theater and possibly learned comic roles from his own stage experience as Maccus. Only two of his original works can be dated with certainty—*Stichus*, which was featured at the plebeian games of 200 B.C. and *Pseudolus*, acted at the dedication of the temple of the Magna Mater on the Palatine in 191 B.C. Estimates of the number of plays attributed to Plautus' quarter century as a playwright range from forty to a hundred and thirty, the lower figure, according to ancient critics, coming closer to an accurate total. Of these comedies, only twenty survive along with fragments.

Plautus' works are described as *fabulae palliatae*, or comedies dressed in Greek garb. His chief source, the New Comedy of such Greek playwrights as Menander, Diphilus, and Philemon, dates around 320–250 B.C. Yet, Plautus cannot be called an imitator in the fullest sense because Plautus' characters speak the Latin idiom with rollicking familiarity. The stylistic details, also sprung from genuine Italian sources, include local jests, arias, dances, caricatures, skits, and folk celebrations.

The standard ploys of Plautus' comedies are slapstick, farce, inno-cent boy meets sweet young girl, deception, mistaken identity, wily counterplotting, and emotional revelations of long-lost relatives. Cer-tainly there were crowd-pleasing contrivances, for Plautus enjoyed the national notoriety of a master of entertainment and was awarded Roman citizenship. At times, his humor broaches the limits of good taste, often sacrificing plot for a good belly laugh.

The Roman theater-going public showed their preference for Plautus' brand of humor throughout his lifetime, into the late Republic, and again in the second century A.D. His influence enjoyed a revival on the Renaissance stage – in particular, Molière's *L'Avare* and *Amphi-tryon,* Shakespeare's *Comedy of Errors,* and later, John Gay's *Beggar's Opera.* Other playwrights, notably Ben Jonson, Thomas Heywood, and Jean Giraudoux, found in Plautus fresh ideas for their own time.

——*MENAECHMI (THE TWIN MENAECHMI)*——

If imitation is any proof of success, Plautus' *Menaechmi* must surely be his greatest comedy. Filled with rollicking good fun, this comedy of errors, from which Shakespeare took his own *Comedy of Errors,* tickled the funny bone of audiences in antiquity with its con-fusion of a set of twins. The play opens with a parody of a prologue, studded with puns and one-liners, warming up the audience for the guffaws that are to follow.

The unnamed speaker, who stands in a street in Epidamnus before the houses of Menaechmus (a young married man) and Erotium (a courtesan), welcomes the spectators and explains how Plautus has adapted the Greek comedy:

> The action always takes place in Athens, they say; that way, the setting will seem to be Greek to you all the more. But from me, you'll hear the truth – where it actually happened. The plot of the play, to be sure, is Greek, but not of the Attic variety; Sicilian, rather.

The speaker promises that he will divulge not a peck nor a bushel of plot, but a whole barnful.

A merchant of Syracuse, he explains, took one of his seven-year-old identical twins to market in Tarentum. The boy was lost in the crowd and carried off by a rich Epidamnian merchant. After the father died of grief, the boy's grandfather renamed the remaining twin with the missing twin's name – Menaechmus. Years afterward, the kidnapper drowned, and the stolen twin inherited the kidnapper's wealth. Now, this Sicilian twin, Menaechmus II (the "II" added to avoid confusion with the Menaechmus introduced earlier), has arrived in Epidamnus, searching for his brother.

Act I opens with a short monologue from Peniculus, or "Brush," a parasite who is known to "sweep the table clean." Before he can knock at Menaechmus' door, the master comes out, concealing a dress under his cloak and aiming a volley of sarcastic retorts at his wife, whom he threatens to send home to her father if she doesn't "keep her spying eyes" away from Menaechmus. He confides to the audience that he has stolen the dress from his wife to give to his mistress, Erotium.

Menaechmus knocks at her door; she greets him adoringly. While her cook prepares a meal for Menaechmus and the mooching parasite, the men go downtown for a drink. Meanwhile, the Sicilian twin and his slave, Messenio, approach from the port; this year, we learn, is the sixth year that they have been searching for the missing twin. Messenio grouses about the city, which he says is

> . . . full of rakes and swillers of booze; scads of swindlers and spongers live here, and everybody knows their women are the most seductive in the whole world. That's why the place is called Epidamnus; scarcely anybody can come here without getting damned.

Cylindrus, Erotium's cook, returns from shopping and greets Menaechmus II, much to his amazement. Then Erotium comes out, also mistaking the Sicilian twin for her lover. She twitters:

> Honey boy, why are you standing out here? You know that my home is always yours whenever you appear. All you ordered is prepared, the doors are opened wide, and your dinner is cooked. Come on in and take your place any time you like.

Because his purse is thinning from years of searching for his brother, the Sicilian twin plays along with the mix-up and agrees to stay for dinner.

The confusion becomes more convoluted when Erotium sends the Sicilian twin on an errand to the embroiderer's and when Erotium's slave girl sends him to the jeweler's with a bracelet. No sooner has he left the stage than Menaechmus appears, delivering a lengthy diatribe about the sorry state of the lawcourts. His wife, confirming her suspicions that Menaechmus is stealing her clothes and her jewelry and giving them to his mistress, sets up a howl. Brush, confused by an encounter with the Sicilian twin only moments before, joins the complainers.

Cowed by his wife's harangue, Menaechmus promises to return the stolen dress, but Erotium, who sent the dress downtown with the Sicilian twin, is unable to produce it. As a result, Menaechmus finds himself despised by his wife and by his lover. Dejected and homeless, he mourns, "Now I am the most shut out of men!"

The Sicilian twin returns and locks horns with Menaechmus' fiery-tempered wife, who spies her father approaching. The old man tries to remain neutral, but a family squabble ensues. The Sicilian twin threatens to "yoke my wild ungovernable horses and climb into my chariot, to trample down this stinking old toothless lion!" He mockingly gallops forward then falls, pretending to have a seizure. As the old man rushes to fetch a doctor, the Sicilian twin hurries back to the ship.

The real Menaechmus arrives on stage and encounters his father-in-law and a doctor, who wants to treat Menaechmus' malady. Menaechmus is ready to pull out his hair with frustration when Messenio enters, just in time to stop some onlookers from subduing Menaechmus and carting him off to an asylum. After an intense melee, Menaechmus mutters to himself, "A lot of strange things have certainly been happening to me today. . . . Heavens knows what it all means."

At the height of the confusion, the twins meet and fill in the missing information. They hold a joyous reunion and agree to return to Syracuse together. Messenio, who has obtained his freedom, begs to be made auctioneer for Menaechmus' property. He ends the play by braying to the crowd, "There's going to be an extraordinary auction here a week from today. . . . [and] the wife goes too if any one takes a fancy to her."

৵৶

CAPTIVI (THE CAPTIVES)

The most serious of Plautus' twenty extant plays, _The Captives_ sets out to break the mold of the typical Roman comedy. The argument, or summarizing statement, rendered in acrostic verse (with old-style Roman spelling), sums up the plot:

Captured in fight was one of Hegio's sons,
Another sold by a slave when four years old.
Prisoners from Elis now the father buys,
To give them in exchange for him who's ta'en;
Enrolled amongst them is the son he'd lost.
In hope of freedom he's changed with his master
Vestments and name; the old man is deceived.
Eager he brings the prisoner and the slave;
In him the slave points out the long-lost son.

The prologue is spoken alternately by Philocrates and Tyndarus, an Elean captive soldier and his slave, who are chained in front of Hegio's house in Aetolia. Tyndarus adds a reassuring note:

Our play is not in a hackneyed style like all the rest. There are no unrepeatable, scurrilous verses; no oath-breaking pimp appears today, no unprincipled prostitute, no swaggering soldier. Don't be alarmed because I said there was a war in the neighborhood. All battles will be waged offstage.

On that note, the captives exit.

Ergasilus, a parasite, appears. He agonizes over his scanty diet since the master's son, Philopolemus, was captured in Elis. If the master, Hegio, does not soon arrange an exchange of prisoners, the parasite will have to find another easy mark from whom to cadge meals. When Hegio appears to instruct the overseer, Ergasilus offers his condolences. Hegio invites him to share a humble dinner.

The overseer brings the captives back onstage. Philocrates asks for and receives permission to speak in private with Tyndarus. He reminds his servant that they must be on their guard since they have exchanged clothes and identities. When Hegio returns, he draws Philocrates aside, thinking him a slave, and tries to make a deal to free Philopolemus. Tyndarus, speaking as though he were the injured party, sniffs self-righteously, "There is a god who hears and sees all our actions; and as you treat me here, he'll see your son is likewise treated there."

Hegio strikes a bargain, sets the captives free to make the exchange, and congratulates himself on his clever trade. Tyndarus exults that he has raised himself from slave to master. Ergasilus returns and, still whining about his growling stomach, provides an interlude.

Hegio brings in Aristophontes, a friend of Philocrates. Tyndarus panics, fearing that Aristophontes will give away his secret. To counter that possibility, Tyndarus takes Hegio aside and explains that, at the moment, Aristophontes is raving mad and may "bite your nose off with his teeth." Ignoring Tyndarus' words, Hegio listens to Aristophontes' evidence and is convinced that he has been duped.

Tyndarus is soon rebound in chains, but he brags that through clever deception he has freed his master from slavery. Hegio threatens to kill Tyndarus for his lies, but sends him instead to work the quarries. Beset by self-pity, Hegio grieves for his sons—the one taken by the Eleans and a four-year-old, kidnapped long ago by a slave.

Ergasilus returns and knocks at Hegio's door. Hegio resists the tiresome sponger, but finally greets him. Ergasilus insists that he has good news from the port—the arrival of Hegio's son, along with Philocrates and Stalagmus, the Sicilian slave who stole Hegio's other son. As Hegio rushes down to the docks, Ergasilus hurries inside to raid the pantry.

Hegio returns arm-in-arm with Philopolemus and pours out profuse thanks to Philocrates, who arranged for his son's release. When Hegio questions Stalagmus, he learns that the slave sold his other son to Philocrates' father. Quick calculation proves that the long-lost son is Tyndarus. After a joyful reunion with his second son, Hegio orders chains for Stalagmus, who speaks the epilogue: "Few comedies of this sort you will find, where those already good may learn to be even better."

_____AULULARIA (THE POT OF GOLD)_____

A critical and popular success, Plautus' *Aulularia*, or *The Pot of Gold*, centers on the character of Euclio, a pinchpenny who finds it difficult to adjust to the discovery of a pot of gold coins. Set outside the houses of Euclio and Megadorus in Athens near the temple of Faith, the play opens with the words of the *lar familiaris*, or household god. Because of Euclio's father's greed, his grandfather buried the family fortune and entrusted the secret to the household god. Now, in the third generation, the god awaits a sign of a resurgence of family piety. When he discovers that Phaedria, Euclio's daughter, prays daily at the household altar, the god reveals the hiding place of the treasure and attempts to maneuver Euclio into accepting Lyconides as a son-in-law.

Euclio rushes from his house in Act I and berates Staphyla, his housekeeper, for coveting his new-found wealth. While Euclio thinks up ways to secure the absolute safety of his pot of gold, Eunomia, an Athenian matron, exits from the house of her brother, Megadorus; she is deep in conversation about the joys of marriage. Megadorus deplores his sister's meddling, but at length reveals the woman whom he would consider marrying—Euclio's daughter, Phaedria.

Keeping a pretense of poverty, Euclio greets his neighbor, who indicates an interest in marriage to Phaedria. Euclio is wary that Megadorus might be a potential fortune-hunter, and so he hurries indoors to reassure himself that his money is still there. On his return, Euclio rejects Megadorus' offer by reason that there is a "danger of climbing from one class into another, and being an ass, to try to be an ox." At length, however, Euclio agrees to Megadorus' marriage proposal for Phaedria.

In Act II, Euclio begins preparations for the wedding. Still suspicious of Staphyla, whom he accuses of having "blabbed to all our neighbors and gone chitter-chattering to all the town," he rushes off, leaving Staphyla to ponder the quandary of Phaedria, her pregnant mistress. Stobilus, who is Megadorus' slave, enters with two cooks, Congrio and Anthrax, and provides an interlude of humorous repartee.

Euclio returns from town terribly frustrated because he was unable to part with a farthing at the meat market, even to honor his daughter's wedding. Hearing the hubbub of preparations, he again races inside to secure his pot of gold and chases Congrio outside with a stick. Before Euclio will allow the hired help to continue their tasks, he hides his pot of gold under his cloak. His mood brightens when he overhears Megadorus singing the praises of a humble, unspoiled wife, but he sinks back into gloom when he construes Megadorus' offer of a cask of wine as a method of getting him drunk so that he can steal Euclio's money.

After Euclio departs to say his prayers in the temple of Faith, Lyconides' slave enters to spy on the wedding preparations. As Euclio exits the temple, peering over his shoulder at the new hiding place of his treasure, the slave overhears his secret and enters the temple to see the treasure firsthand. A raven foretells bad luck, and Euclio hurries back to the scene, dragging the culprit from the temple. He badgers the innocent slave and once more ascertains the security of his hiding place. When Euclio drags his treasure out of the temple and departs to bury it in Silvanus' grove, the slave, surly and spoiling for revenge, follows him.

Lyconides, Megadorus' nephew, enters with Eunomia, his aunt. Hearing Phaedria screaming for help, Lyconides realizes that she is in labor with his child. Eunomia perceives the young people's situation and agrees to intercede with Megadorus.

Lyconides' slave returns with the stolen pot of gold and searches for a hiding place. Euclio, this time truly panic-stricken, begs the audience to help him find the thief:

> What hope of life to one who's lost so much, so much that
> I have guarded? I denied myself all pleasure; others now will
> rejoice at my expense, my loss. I cannot bear it!

Lyconides hears the wailing histrionics and assumes that Euclio has learned of his (Lyconides') intimacy with Phaedria. Thus, he takes the direct approach and confesses, "'Twas wine and love that made me." When he realizes that he and Euclio are talking of two different matters, Lyconides declares that Megadorus has renounced his engagement to Phaedria. Euclio concludes that Megadorus knows of the theft and rejects a penniless girl. Lyconides begs that he be allowed to right his wrongs and marry Phaedria. Euclio wails, "Ah me! I am quite ruined! Evils come one on top of others, clinging fast. I'll go within and see if this is so."

Lyconides' slave divulges his crime, and Lyconides orders him to return the money. [The remainder of the play is missing. Lyconides probably returns the money to Euclio and wins Phaedria's hand. And no doubt, Euclio rewards the newlyweds with the treasured pot of gold.]

AMPHITRYON

Plautus' _Amphitryon,_ one of his most successful plays and the only surviving Roman comedy based on mythology, begins with two prefaces, both of which were written by other people and appended to the play at least a century later. The first preface states that Jupiter, disguised as Amphitryon, seduced Amphitryon's wife, Alcmena, while her husband was away at war. The second, written in acrostic verse, tells the same story and concludes with a happy ending – the settlement of the squabble between husband and wife and the birth of twin sons.

The play opens in Thebes on a street before Amphitryon's house. Mercury, disguised as Sosia, Amphitryon's slave, speaks the prologue, which explains how Amphitryon, a Theban general, went off to fight the Teloboans, leaving behind Alcmena, his pregnant wife. In Amphitryon's absence, Jupiter, who "is in these same matters somewhat free, and when the fancy takes him, loves with all his strength," is smitten with love for Alcmena. As Mercury puts it, the god "borrowed her" and left her pregnant with a second child. Both Jupiter and Mercury fool the household with their disguises, but two details of their costumes remind the audience that they are imposters – the feather in Mercury's cap and the tassel under Jupiter's hat.

As Act I begins, Sosia, bearing a lantern, returns from the harbor, complaining of his labors. When Mercury eavesdrops on the soliloquy, he learns that Amphitryon has been victorious in battle and is returning home to his wife. Mercury provokes a fight with Sosia and promises to make him "eat my fists." Sosia, fearful of the stronger man, declares, "I do not eat at night; and I have dined; pray give your supper to those who starve." The cowardly Sosia, confronted with the fake Sosia, gives in to anything Mercury wishes to say and hurries away to the harbor to report the incident to his master.

Jupiter, disguised as Amphitryon, and Alcmena exit from the house. Jupiter bids goodbye to his petulant lover, who is due to give birth at any moment, and pretends to return to his troops in the field, taking his servant with him. Meantime, the real Amphitryon and Sosia enter, wrangling over Sosia's confused tale of a second Sosia at Amphitryon's house. Sosia whimpers, "the greatest trouble that befalls an honest servant when he speaks the truth is, sure, to find that truth rammed down his throat and disbelieved."

Amphitryon overhears his wife, who pines for his quick return. Alcmena, so recently parted from the imposter husband, is confused by his arrival. Sosia, catching sight of Alcmena's big belly, mutters, "I see Alcmena has already dined." As husband and wife pursue their misunderstanding, Sosia notes to his master, "I thought that she would have a boy; I was mistaken. . . . 'Tis folly she produces."

Alcmena displays the golden cup that is Amphitryon's war trophy. Amphitryon, dumbfounded that she already possesses it, tells Sosia to look for the cup in their baggage. When Sosia is unable to locate it, Amphitryon asks how Alcmena received it before he arrived home to give it to her. Her explanation leads to the key issue—she spent the previous night in bed with Amphitryon. He cries out in anguish, "O God! She's as good as killed me."

Threatening divorce from his adulterous wife, Amphitryon sends for Naucrates, a fellow soldier and Alcmena's kinsman, to prove his identity and whereabouts. Jupiter reappears to help Alcmena, but he only confuses her further. He soothes her ruffled feelings and suggests that they invite Blepharo, the pilot of the ship, to dinner.

Meanwhile, Mercury, appearing on the roof, tries to get Amphitryon drunk. [There is a gap in the text. Apparently, Mercury dumps a pail of water on Amphitryon. Blepharo arrives for dinner and is totally befuddled by the two Amphitryons.] Bromia, the chambermaid, appears to explain the action inside the master's house; on the night of the uproar, she says, Alcmena went into labor. Jupiter, who spoke through clashes of thunder and lightning, promised to aid her.

Bromia consoles her troubled master with news of the birth: after her painless labor, Alcmena was delivered of two sons. One, large and strong, refused to let Bromia tie him in his crib. Then two fierce snakes appeared in the rain barrel and menaced the twin baby boys.

The stronger twin strangled them, one in each hand. At this point, the heavenly voice spoke again and acknowledged that he, Jupiter, was Alcmena's lover and that he had fathered one of her sons. Cowed by Jupiter's presence, Amphitryon accepts the situation. Jupiter then appears above and promises immortal fame to his son (Hercules).

THE ROMAN REPUBLIC

- Ennius
- Roman Drama
- Terence

ENNIUS

- The *Annales*

ENNIUS

LIFE AND BACKGROUND

Known as the father of Roman literature after Cicero referred to him as "Father Ennius," Quintus Ennius (239–169 B.C.) was born in the Roman outback — the "heel of the boot" of Italy in Rudiae, Calabria, near modern-day Lecce, a geographical section heavily populated by Greek settlers. Bilingual from childhood, he spoke Greek and Latin in addition to Oscan, which he acquired from his long residence in Campania, outside Naples. In 204 B.C., because of Ennius' gift for languages, his eclectic tastes, and his appreciation of the three cultures that formed Rome, Marcus Porcius Cato, a military official who became consul, urged Ennius to leave his post as centurion with the Roman army in Sardinia and come to Rome.

There, in the ferment of intellectual exchange, he established a new life for himself as a Greek teacher and scholar, translator of Greek drama, critic, and writer. Living in modest circumstances, he seems to have been wholly absorbed in his work. He gave his tragedies, comedies, satires, and epigrams a distinctive Greek quality and introduced the Greek hexameter into Latin poetry. A lesser achievement was his invention of Latin shorthand, or *notae*. Because of the purity of his work, he obtained patronage under Marcus Fulvius Nobilior, general, politician, and renowned Grecophile.

While under the influence of Nobilior, Ennius journeyed to Aetolia, in the central portion of Greece, north of Corinth, and served as the recorder of his patron's military achievements. His payment, which he obtained in 184 B.C., through Nobilior's son, was ample — Roman citizenship and a piece of land at Potentia, east of Salerno at the southern tip of the Apennines.

Although Ennius lived marginally on his meager pension and suffered from gout, Cicero (in his essay *De Senectute*) proclaimed him a model of patient submission to old age. Before his death, Ennius undertook the education of his sister's son, Marcus Pacuvius, who attained a certain amount of fame in his time as a tragedian.

Ennius' literary output, particularly his essays, was enormous and broad, reaching from works of philosophy to cookbooks, from works on religion to a commentary on spelling. His most noted work is the *Annales.* In addition to the *Annales,* however, Ennius also wrote a collection of poems which he called *Saturae,* or *Hodge-Podge,* and at least twenty tragedies, all but one of which were adaptations of Greek dramas. He modeled his work after the tragedies of Euripides, particularly the plots dealing with the Trojan War. Ennius' major contribution to the Roman stage was *The Rape of the Sabines.* Unfortunately, not enough of the play remains to make feasible any critical comment.

THE *ANNALES*

The *Annales,* an eighteen-book epic history of Rome, is based on Homer's models, blending the chronological data of a chronicle with passages of fervid detail. Ennius appears to have made the poem his life's work, publishing it in six three-book installments and adding to it well into his old age.

Although Ennius' subject matter covers the timespan from the arrival of Aeneas in Italy until two years before the poet's death, Ennius focuses primarily on the Second Punic War. Because of Ennius' incredible grasp of the sweep of history, his *Annales* was popular for many centuries, although his lack of craftsmanship and depth make it a poor second to Virgil's *Aeneid.* A century later, however, the great patriot Cicero memorized great portions of the *Annales* because, until Virgil wrote the *Aeneid,* the *Annales* was Rome's national epic.

The *Annales* opens with some of Rome's favorite legends—the birth of Romulus and Remus, the establishment of Rome, the accomplishments of the early kings, and the wars fought with neighboring states. In his description of the naming of the city, Ennius writes:

Remus prayed for a sign; all by himself he watched for

welcome birds. But Romulus the Fair stood on the Aventine and watched for the winged breed. They vied for the name of their city: "Remora" or "Roma"?

The people, awestruck by the event that is unfolding before them, wait to see which twin the omens will designate as the rightful king. True to Roman superstition, a "white bird of good omen" appears on the left at sunset and, with its downward flight, assures Romulus that he will have "dais, throne, and crown."

In alliterative and onomatopoetic verse, Ennius' *Annales* feature other memorable heroes of Rome's early days: the resounding noise of Pyrrhus as he chops down great oaks, holly, ash, fir, and pine to make a postwar funeral pyre on which to burn fallen warriors; an epitaph honoring Scipio Africanus, whom "no man can repay for his noble deeds"; and a paean to Quintus Fabius Maximus, the wily military strategist whom Ennius christens "The Delayer" and lauds for his "radiant glory."

Ennius has a gift for dramatic situations. For example, he emphasizes the alarm of Hecuba, queen of Troy, whose grim nightmares spur Priam to consult Apollo's oracle. As her vision indicates, the couple learn that they will bear a son who will be "the ruin of Troy, the destruction of Pergamum." Hecuba, in a frenzy because of the oracle's "prophetic utterances," hurries to Cassandra, her clairvoyant daughter, for confirmation of the news.

Cassandra, too, grieves that their doom is sealed by a "firebrand consumed by blood and fire!" She foresees "a great fleet of seagoing vessels rapidly constructed, its sails filling with winds that direct death-dealing forces to the shores of Troy." Enrapt with terror, Cassandra cries out, "Alas, look! . . . O light of Troy, Hector, brother dear to my heart, your torn remains dragged before our very eyes." Her last words predict a "horse heavy with armed men in one great effort will burn Pergamum to the ground."

ROMAN DRAMA

- **Roman Theater**

- **Costumes**

- **Acting**

ROMAN DRAMA

Like much of Roman culture, its drama from earliest times was borrowed from the literature of other peoples. According to Livy, the first stage productions in Rome were mimetic dances imported from Etruria in 364 B.C. in an effort to "disarm the wrath of the gods" during a serious bout of plague. These *ludi scenici,* or theatrical games, along with the *fabulae Atellanae,* adapted from the satiric, prank-filled rustic farces popular in Atella, Campania, and the *saturae,* or plotless medleys, variety shows, and revues satisfied the need for amateur entertainment for two centuries before spawning professional troupes in the first century.

Early Roman comedy found endless possibilities in a set of stock characters or stereotypes, such as the braggart soldier; Maccus, the bumbling bumpkin; Bucco, the conniving parasite; Pappus, the doddering old crank; Manducus, the glutton; and Dossennus, the hunchback clown. These stock figures probably found their way into the *commedia dell'arte* of the Italian Renaissance under the names of Arlecchino, the wily servant; Pantalone, the senile old fool; Pulcinella, the rustic; Dottore, the wise philosopher; Miles Gloriosus, the swaggering captain of the guards; Pasquella, the old woman; Columbina, the eavesdropping chambermaid; and the cooing lovebirds—the sweet young thing and her good-hearted, ingenuous boyfriend.

In 240 B.C., the year after the First Punic War, Lucius Livius Andronicus, a Greek slave and actor from Tarentum, composed the first plays in Latin, to the delight of his audiences. Andronicus introduced a uniquely Roman innovation—lip-syncing. Because his voice failed when he tried to sing and dance simultaneously, he employed an actor, or cantor, offstage to speak for him while he danced and pantomimed onstage. Andronicus' use of Greek models presaged a mindset among later writers that *fabulae togatae,* or Roman subject matter, was naturally inferior.

In 235 B.C., Gnaeus Naevius, a native of Campania, began writing and producing his thirty comedies and six tragedies, including *The*

Rape of the Sabine Women, a distinctly Roman subject. His opinion-ated satire earned him a prison sentence after he insulted the power-ful Metellus family. A generation later, Quintus Ennius composed two comedies and over twenty verse tragedies that merged the Greco-Roman-Oscan influences of his home territory, Rudiae, or modern-day Lecce in Calabria, the heel of Italy's boot. He was succeeded by his nephew, Pacuvius, also a tragic poet, who specialized in contrived, original plots.

When Plautus began his successful career near the end of the second century, his plays carried distinctive Greek trappings, par-ticularly the Greek cloak, or *pallium,* and probably masks, although the importance of Greek masks to Roman theater is a matter of schol-arly debate. Plautus naturalized the so-called New (Greek) Comedy (the plays of Menander and Apollodorus, in particular) and eliminated the choral interludes in favor of song-and-dance routines characteristic of minstrel shows or vaudeville, which made up nearly a third of the production and appealed to the less discriminating tastes of his day.

The subject matter of Plautine comedy was distinctly Greek with good reason: the strait-laced, censorious Roman of Plautus' day was a far cry from the worldly, licentious citizen of late republican Rome. To assail fastidious sensibilities with wild young men, smart-mouthed slaves, wily parasites, and smirking prostitutes would have offended the audience. Public censors would have reacted by closing the show. Public laws forbade his lampooning officials. The only way Plautus could introduce the titillating situations of Greek comedy was to main-tain Greek names and settings.

When Terence began writing near the middle of the second cen-tury, he too preserved and enhanced Greek models, but his object was witty, complicated plots as opposed to the pratfalls and shenani-gans of Plautus' less polished efforts. Terence was supposedly dis-covered by Caecilius Statius, a Milanese comic playwright, while reading aloud from his *Andria.* Because of the success of his sensitive, probing style, he was never without patronage. The elevated tone and sophisticated plots of Terence's plays remained popular in Europe throughout the Medieval and Renaissance eras.

This zenith of comedic expression was followed by a rapid nadir as Roman militarism led to a demand for spectacle. The festivals, athletic contests, military triumphs, mock sea battles, and politically motivated extravaganzas that colored the republican era were eclipsed by even gaudier, more bestial displays during the Empire. Until the hand of the Catholic Church halted their vulgar, sadistic excesses, Roman entertainments reached the limits of bad taste and outright savagery during the rule of Caligula and Nero, when no expense was spared to appease the unruly Roman mob.

Tragedy, never a major influence in Roman drama, lacked the religious thrust that brought greatness to the Greek stage, for Romans throughout history put little trust in the supernatural. The pioneer dramatist Lucius Accius (170–*ca.* 85 B.C.), a native of Pesaro near modern-day San Marino, wrote forty-five adaptations of Greek tragedies, none of which have survived. His work is known for violence and melodrama.

In the first century A.D., the works of Seneca, Rome's single contribution to the canon of tragedy, continued the Roman practice of borrowing from ancient sources. These closet dramas, filled with overly dramatic, bombastic speeches, were obviously intended for recitation by a *rhetor,* or declaimer, with choral accompaniment. They were filled with spine-chilling details of horror, sadism, and mayhem from Greek mythology and directly influenced the Renaissance "tragedy of blood," as illustrated by Shakespeare's *Titus Andronicus* and *Hamlet,* Kyd's *Spanish Tragedy,* and Webster's *Duchess of Malfi* and *The White Devil.*

By the end of Hadrian's reign in 138 A.D., the establishment of Christianity drove the professional troupes underground. As troubadours, jongleurs, and vagabond players, this disenfranchised, classless society was quickly reduced to the outskirts of respectability. Throughout the Middle Ages, they wandered about, seeking temporary patronage, or, when all else failed, food and shelter for the night in exchange for a hastily arranged performance.

ROMAN THEATER

Early Roman drama had no permanent home. Instead, amateurs set up an improvised raised platform, or *proscenium,* in an open space. At times, they nailed together a rickety backdrop, or *scena,* to serve as a sounding board. As theater became more sophisticated, a stock set was painted onto the backdrop reminiscent of Greek staging and featuring two or three doorways facing an altar and a single street. The audience came to expect entrances from the right to indicate city traffic and from the left, arrivals from rustic or foreign settings.

The inflexibility of such a system is obvious. Characters had to interact out-of-doors. Contrived entrances and exits had to be explained through dialogue. Any interior action had to be reported secondhand. To offset these handicaps, actors were forced to overact their intrigues by elaborate gestures, mugging, and mime. The lack of an expository prologue forced the audience to be attentive to every nuance in order to follow the flow of the drama.

During the ascetic days of early Rome, the senate proclaimed that no Roman citizen could be an actor. Consequently, acting companies and often their managers were composed of slaves or foreigners. During his off-hours, an actor, who bore the stigma of questionable moral repute, was persona non grata in respectable society, a situation that was perpetuated into the Middle Ages, a time when actors could not be buried in hallowed ground. This stigma surrounding actors survives in modern times, when movie magazines and gossip columns titillate their readers with exaggerated claims of actors' immoral escapades.

Financing for dramatic productions generally came from one of two sources. At holiday time, the government decreed public games and amusements at the taxpayers' expense. More frequently, a single benefactor, often a candidate for public office, would display his wealth or curry favor by underwriting a performance. The impetus for a day of entertainment could come from almost any situation, from a military victory to the funeral of a local notable.

The general audience of early Roman drama had limited experience and education, and, consequently, they appreciated theater on a superficial level; they paid no admittance and, at first, had to sit on the ground. Senators occupied seats of honor on the front row of the semicircle that faced the stage. As social stratification rose in importance, more rigid seating arrangements took on significance for aristocrats who wished to distance themselves from the lower classes. In the era of the Empire, the emperor and his entourage occupied box seats, where they competed with the actors onstage for the audience's attention by outrageous, unpredictable behavior.

Eventually, temporary seating in the form of backless wooden benches was provided, but it was not until the time of Pompey in the first century B.C. that Rome could boast a permanent theater. The Romans also introduced reserved seating and tokens marked with symbols or numbers that corresponded to marks on the seats. The audience was heavily infiltrated by claques, who were paid by the donor to applaud vigorously. Near the front of the stage sat security guards armed with truncheons to insure order.

Because of the diminished importance of a chorus, the Roman stage adapted the acting space of the traditional Greek theater, omitting entrance ramps and the full-circle orchestra. Stage areas increased to accommodate a growing number of musicians. As the popularity of pantomime increased during the Empire, the flute was augmented by panpipes, harp, cymbals, drums, lyre, and horns. Productions became more lavish, emphasizing complicated libretti and elaborate costuming over dialogue and sentiment. Dancers became the star performers, eclipsing actors and singers. Some enhanced the impact of their movements by attaching *scabilla*, or taps, to their shoes.

Roman theatrical architecture was a curious mixture. Alongside the magnificent ovals of the Colosseum and the Circus Maximus, where races, games of strength, and beast fights dominated all other uses, the first Roman theater was an austere stone edifice disguised as a temple. Named the Theater of Pompey and built in 55 B.C., it was dedicated to Venus Victrix in keeping with the Roman preoccupation with military might. Two more theaters, donated by Cornelius Balbus and Augustus Caesar, were completed in 13 B.C. during the early days of the Empire. The second of these, named the Theater of Marcellus in honor of Augustus' nephew, still stands.

Even though the temporary stages and most of the permanent theaters have succumbed to wars, vandals, earthquakes, and the ravages of time, an engineer of the Augustan Age, Marcus Vitruvius Pollio, preserved architectural details in the fifth volume of his ten-volume technical manual, *De Architectura*. His work explains how the basic layout of the Roman theater modified Greek design by joining the seating to the *scena*. The external wall, decorated with niches filled with statues, supported a network of doorways, called *vomitoria.*

The paved orchestra, semicircular in shape, held seats for prominent patrons. The stage, elevated about five feet above the audience, extended a hundred feet in length and twenty feet in depth. The *scena,* from its primitive beginnings, developed into an elaborate wall and was decorated with columns, bas-relief, and statuary. A permanent roof, augmented by removable awnings, protected the acting area and enhanced acoustics. Onstage, the Romans utilized the Greek painted scenery, or *periaktoi,* and added touches of their own, including fountains, trapdoors, fake trees and mountains, and balconies. An elaborate curtain, held to the portico by ropes, was dropped onto the apron of the stage at the beginning of the performance. Daylight performances eliminated the need for artificial lighting, although torches and lamps could be employed for occasional evening presentations.

As the Roman Empire spread throughout the Mediterranean world, more than one hundred and twenty theaters of similar design appeared in far-flung places, as far away as Syria, France, Portugal, England, Spain, and North Africa. Where Greek theaters were still in use, the Romans adapted each of them to their standards by halving the orchestra and enclosing the whole structure with a high wall.

COSTUMES

Costuming, like other aspects of Roman theater, followed Greek tradition. While masks may not have been a permanent fixture of dramatic productions, it is clear that models made of terra-cotta were used by Roscius (*ca.* 126–62 B.C.), Rome's most prominent actor, to hide an undesirable squint. The facial features of masks, posed in an exaggerated expression, emphasized the stereotyped nature of each character and enabled a single actor to assume multiple roles.

Costumes, too, followed the Greek models — long gowns and elevated *cothurnus* boots (much like today's hunting boots) for tragedy and short tunics with *buskins* (similar to today's high-topped running shoes) for comedy. Only men acted in tragic and comic roles, but pantomimists could be either sex. Mimes and dancers preferred bare feet and flowing robes for their performances. To enhance facial expression, they used heavy makeup and wigs. With the decline of decorum came scanty, flimsy attire for dancers. Some danced nude.

_____ ACTING

Actors, who were plentiful during the heyday of the Empire, specialized in certain stock roles. For example, the well-known actor Demetrius preferred gods, ingenues, fathers, slaves, and matrons. Aesopus excelled in great tragic roles, especially Agamemnon, Atreus, and Andromache. Pylades danced tragic roles; Bathyllus, comic roles. Paris, Nero's favorite, played his mimetic roles so well that the emperor, himself an actor, grew jealous and had him executed. Cytheris, the famed dancer of Julius Caesar's time, served as Antony's traveling companion when he campaigned throughout Italy.

The star system was in operation in antiquity. Star-struck admirers courted favorite performers with lavish gifts. Both Roscius and Aesopus, darlings of Roman audiences, prospered in their profession and opened acting schools. Roscius, the most popular Roman actor, earned the equivalent of twenty thousand dollars annually and received the rank of knight from Sulla, the Roman general; however, most actors earned considerably less, some even working for no pay. Aristocratic men frequently chose female mimes as mistresses and showered them with attention.

TERENCE

- *Adelphi*
  (The Brothers)

LIFE AND BACKGROUND

Characteristically mentioned in the same breath with Plautus, his predecessor, Publius Terentius Afer, or Terence, the second of Rome's great comedy writers, made a career from the most unlikely of circumstances. He was born in slavery shortly after the Second Punic War in Carthage, Rome's great rival and archenemy, on the northern shores of Africa about 195 B.C. Terence was transported to Rome and sold to Publius Terentius Lucanus, a Roman senator, who treated him like a son and educated him in the patrician style.

After his manumission, Terence showed his appreciation in the fashion typical of freedmen – he took his master's name, appending the cognomen "Afer" to indicate the place of his birth. Because of his talent and refinement, Terence came to the attention of Gaius Laelius, the consul, and Scipio Aemilianus, an adopted son of Scipio Africanus, the greatest general and most prominent cult figure in Rome's early history. As a member of the exclusive Scipionic Circle, Terence prospered, developing his comedic style and profiting by association with the elite.

Around 161 B.C., Terence traveled to Greece and is thought to have translated all one hundred and eight of Menander's comedies. From his intense association with the New Comedy of Menander and Apollodorus came the six extant comedies for which Terence is known: *Andria,* or *The Girl from Andros* (167 B.C.), *Hecyra,* or *Her Husband's Mother* (165 B.C.), *Heautontimorumenos,* or *The Self-Tormentor* (163 B.C.), *The Eunuch* (161 B.C.), *Phormio* (161 B.C.), and *Adelphi,* or *The Brothers* (160 B.C.), Terence's last work, composed the year before he sailed back to Greece and died there of unknown causes.

Unlike the colloquial musical comedies of Plautus, which Julius Caesar characterized as having *vis comica,* or comic energy, Terence's work appealed to a more refined, less energetic taste. The cultivated patrician theatergoer admired his superb renderings, Ciceronian language, and moral outlook. He catered to polite society with subtle characterization, in contrast to the caricatures and stock figures of earlier comedy.

Terence's stylistic changes were meant to accommodate Greek comedy to Roman audiences. He discarded the prefatory prologue, thereby introducing a new strategy—suspense and a surprise ending. He enhanced dramatic irony with foreshadowing and snatches of realism, and he broadened the scope of his dramas by merging plots and situations from more than one Greek source. As a result of his adaptations, purists raised a howl of protest, which Terence rebutted in literary prologues, which have little bearing on the plays themselves. Consequently, modern translations often omit these prologues.

A direct comparison of the earlier comedies of Plautus with those of Terence reveals two playwrights with differing audiences in mind. The two bodies of work represent the two halves of Roman society— the haves and the have-nots. For Plautus, the ribald mirth of the early stage was a direct outgrowth of working class associations. Plautus, the millworker, set out to entertain uncultivated plebeians. Terence, a generation afterward, rose above humble beginnings and wrote to please and inspire the Roman aristocrats with a more delicate stagecraft, proverbial wisdom, and well-paced repartee.

৯৩

ADELPHI (THE BROTHERS)

An adaptation of Menander's work by the same title, Terence's *Adelphi* was produced in 160 B.C. at the funeral games in honor of Lucius Aemilius Paulus, Roman consul and military leader. The play, which illuminates the problems of parenthood and character-building, established the playwright's name as a master comedy writer. Among his many imitators are Beaumont and Fletcher, Molière, Steele, Garrick, Diderot, and Fielding.

Act I, set in the early morning in Athens before the houses of Micio and Sostrata, is preceded by a prologue, which discusses Terence's use of source material, but reveals little of the plot. Micio, the aged uncle of Aeschinus and Ctesipho, appears and paces about, worrying because Aeschinus, the nephew whom he adopted and raised as his own, did not come home the previous night. He explains his philosophy of child-rearing:

> I give, I overlook things, I don't think it necessary to exert
> my authority on every occasion. In short, I have accustomed
> my son not to conceal from me those little extravagances
> natural to youth, which others are at so much pains to hide
> from their parents.

Micio adds that his brother, Demea, is a much more severe parent who criticizes Micio's liberality, but Micio remains firm in his belief that openness between father and son produces an honest relationship.

Demea hurries in from the country, eager to be the bearer of bad news. Aeschinus, he blurts out, broke into a house, beat the master, and abducted his sweetheart. Demea adds maliciously that Ctesipho, in contrast to his brother, is "working away in the country thriftily and soberly." Micio, reasoning calmly, refuses to be shouted down and blames Demea for the crime. Demea departs in a huff.

In spite of his cool exterior, Micio reveals that he, too, worries about his son:

> What courtesan is there in all Athens whom he has not been
> in love with, or to whom he has not made a present. . . . I
> hoped that he had sown his wild oats and was glad of it; now,
> behold, he has begun afresh.

After Micio moves on toward the forum, Aeschinus arrives with a music girl, followed by her enraged pimp. There is a scuffle, but Aeschinus saves the girl and follows her into his father's house.

Ctesipho enters and exults that his "dear brother" has done him a good turn by rescuing his girl friend. He acknowledges that Aeschinus "has taken upon his own shoulders all the scandal, reproach, intrigue, and blame that belongs to me." The brothers part company, Ctesipho going in to comfort the girl, Aeschinus hurrying off to settle accounts with Sannio, the slave-dealer.

Sostrata and her slaves, in an uproar over an impending birth, deplore the news that Aeschinus has disgraced himself over a music girl. Gradually they reveal their interest in the matter – Aeschinus has pledged himself to Sostrata's daughter and now appears unfaithful.

The scene shifts to Demea, who is still fussing over Aeschinus' indiscretions. Playing along with the brothers' deception, Syrus, Aeschinus' slave, tries to appease the old man's ego by admiring the way he has brought up Ctesipho. Syrus attempts to maneuver Demea out of the way of the truth, but, before Demea departs, Hegio, an old friend, joins him to gossip about the scandal and to console him for the embarrassment that Aeschinus has brought on the family.

Hegio discloses a second scandal – that Aeschinus has impregnated Pamphila, who lives next door to Micio. As they talk, Pamphila cries out in the throes of labor. Demea hurries out to find Micio and tell all. Ctesipho, congratulating Syrus on keeping Demea out of the way, suddenly catches sight of his father. Syrus goes into a second contrived scenario, this time blaming Ctesipho for beating him for taking part in the abduction. Demea grows even prouder of his son. Syrus sends Demea on a meandering route to find Micio.

Hegio returns with Micio, to whom he has explained Pamphila's situation. As the old man investigates the birth of Aeschinus' illegitimate child in Sostrata's house, Aeschinus returns to the street to have a deep conversation with himself. At Sostrata's door, Aeschinus confronts his father. The moment of truth between parent and son leads to confusion and embarrassment for Aeschinus. Micio leads him on, making him believe that another man will marry Pamphila. Aeschinus attempts to plead the case of the unnamed father of Pamphila's infant.

When Aeschinus breaks down in tears, Micio is quick to say, "I have heard all, Aeschinus, and I know all; I love you, and so I take all the more interest in what you do." His admonition is light and ends with the words that Aeschinus wants to hear: ". . . she shall be your wife." Just as Micio predicted, good treatment brings out the best in Aeschinus, who is even more anxious to please his good-hearted and forgiving father.

Demea returns, exhausted by the diversion that Syrus concocted to keep him away. He berates Micio further for Aeschinus' supposed shortcomings. Demea clucks to himself:

> Oh, Jupiter, what a life! What morals! What folly! A bride
> without a dowry is to be brought home; there's a music girl
> in the house; an extravagant establishment; a youth given over
> to debauchery, an old dotard. Why, the goddess of Salvation
> could not save this household, even if she wanted to.

Demea's self-righteousness gets out of hand when Syrus totters back onstage under the influence of too much wine. A word from Dromo, Micio's slave, destroys Demea's inflated illusions about Ctesipho.

When Demea hears that Ctesipho is in Micio's house, Demea is aghast. Micio brings to a head the mounting disagreement, but maintains his gentle touch with diplomacy. Left to himself, Demea ponders:

> No man ever lived in so well-regulated a fashion but what circumstances, years, and experience must continually present something new to him and suggest something to him. You don't know what you once thought you knew, and you cast away what you once supposed to be of first importance.

Chastened by his experience, Demea, like Dickens' Scrooge, has a change of heart. In his enthusiasm for a family wedding, Demea presses Micio to marry Sostrata.

THE GOLDEN AGE

- Cicero
- Julius Caesar
- Lucretius
- Catullus
- Virgil
- Livy
- Tibullus
- Propertius
- Horace
- Ovid

CICERO

- **Essays, Letters, & Orations**

CICERO

Marcus Tullius Cicero, often referred to as Tully, was the Roman equivalent of the Renaissance man. A renowned orator, statesman, essayist, politician, attorney, and scholar, Cicero was both a producer and a product of the age, as well as a major voice during Rome's Golden Age. His ignoble death, a classic example of the old aristocracy quelling a rising outsider, suggests the great price exacted by power and influence.

Cicero was born in 106 B.C. in Arpinum in the Volscian hill country, sixty miles southeast of Rome. His father, a country aristocrat, desired more for his son and moved his family to Rome around 92 B.C. He spared no expense to hire the best tutors for Cicero, who excelled in literature and rhetoric, law, and philosophy. Unfortunately, but not surprisingly, Rome's political unrest between the Marian and the Sullan factions brought chaos to Cicero's life. His teacher, Scaevola, was murdered, as was his kinsman Marius Gratidianus.

An idealist and republican at heart, Cicero preferred neutrality, but was forced to side with the Sullan party. The choice was propitious, for in 82 B.C., Sulla was installed as dictator. Consequently, despite his personal distaste for Sulla's heavy-handed tactics, Cicero profited from his political affiliation, proving himself an able prosecutor at the murder trial of Sextus Roscius in 80 B.C. The following year, Cicero retired to Athens for his health and studied philosophy with Antiochus and Molo.

The upward spiral of Cicero's brilliant political career began in 76 B.C. He married Terentia, a wealthy Roman matron, was elected to the *quaestorship* in 75 B.C., and served his term in Sicily. After his brilliant prosecution of Gaius Verres, a wily scoundrel and demagogue, Cicero advanced to *aedile* in 69 B.C. and *praetor* in 66 B.C. To make the final leap to the consulship, Cicero, an outlander by birth, needed an alliance with Rome's old money. He strengthened his ties with

Pompey, a former army buddy, and by clever, somewhat unprincipled political maneuvering, won by a landslide vote.

Cicero closed ranks with conservatives to defeat agrarian reforms. When he discovered that Catiline was leading a conspiracy to foster uprisings, Cicero pounced with all his political might. His most famous speech, "Against Catiline," resulted in the collapse of the cabal, which Cicero exaggerated in order to magnify his contribution to the state. At the height of his success, Cicero, much like Winston Churchill, was uneasy when he realized where political victory could lead, for the tide of public opinion turned against him. No longer seen as man of the hour after Clodius Pulcher organized a faction against him, Cicero earned the reputation of executioner for championing the immediate deaths of five conspirators.

When Pompey pulled away from Cicero's political camp, allying himself with Julius Caesar and Crassus, Cicero's downward slide was inevitable. At the peak of his career, charged with executing Roman citizens without a trial, he was banished beyond a radius of four hundred miles of Rome and spent fifteen months in exile, first, in Thessalonica in Macedonia and then, in Epirus. In his absence, his wife suffered persecution; his house was demolished and a temple to Liberty erected on the site. His outlook improved in 57 B.C. when Pompey had him recalled. Yet, Cicero was unable to halt the growing power of the First Triumvirate and found his principles compromised when he was forced to sanction the Gallic campaign of Julius Caesar, Pompey's ally, in 56 B.C.

During this quarrelsome time in Roman political affairs, from 55 to 51 B.C., when the freedoms of the Republic were rapidly waning, Cicero diverted his energies to scholarship and produced some of his most incisive work. Recalled to active duty in 51 B.C., he served as governor of Cilicia in southeast Asia Minor. When civil war broke out between Caesar and Pompey in 50 B.C., Cicero, with some reservation, chose Pompey, the loser. An unwilling sycophant in an era of Caesar worship, Cicero was a broken man.

Isolation took its toll on his personal life. He divorced his wife after thirty years of marriage, quarreled with his brother, agonized over his wastrel son and namesake, and suffered the death of his beloved daughter, Tullia. As in earlier times, he found consolation in his studies.

When Caesar was assassinated in 44 B.C., Cicero, who had no part in the conspiracy, exulted and congratulated the assassins. His political zeal restored, he supported Brutus and Cassius and delivered four-teen strident, ill-advised *Philippics* against Antony. Unwittingly, Cicero played directly into the hands of Rome's most powerful duo. When Antony and Octavius conducted their purge, Cicero was high on their list of victims. In Formiae, outside Rome, he was stalked like an animal and murdered. His head and right hand were lopped off and put up for public display on the rostrum of the Forum.

—————— ESSAYS, LETTERS, & ORATIONS ——————

Overall, Cicero's literary output is marked by energetic language, punctilious spelling and diction, emotional involvement, and fanati-cal patriotism; in his final speeches, there is an intense focus that approaches monomania. Throughout his life, he corresponded with a variety of friends, associates, and family members, offering observa-tions about law and justice, admonitions concerning morality and right conduct, and encouragement to people like himself who were suffer-ing hard times.

To Appius Pulcher, the censor, he begins in the standard abbre-viated, unpunctuated salutation of a typical Roman business letter:

M T C S D Appio Pulchro ut spero censori
Marcus Tullius Cicero sends greetings to Appius Pulcher [who
    is still], I hope, Censor.

Having learned of Appius' acquittal of a charge of malfeasance against the Roman people, Cicero rejoices, ". . . far away as you were, I threw my arms around you in thought, and I really did kiss the letter . . ."

In a friendly exchange with Cicero in May, 45 B.C., Lucius Luc-ceius begins with a stereotypical opening line:

Si vales bene est ego valeo sicut soleo . . .
If you are well, it is good; I am well as usual . . .

Moving rapidly to personal observations on Cicero's withdrawal from city life, Lucius comments:

> . . . nothing can be more refreshing than such solitude, not only in these cheerless and lugubrious times [that is, Caesar's dictatorship, which Cicero deplored] but even in times of tranquility . . .

By return mail, Cicero reveals the perpetual unrest and dissatisfaction that marred his public and private life during his declining years: "Accordingly, I resort to literary work on which I spend all my time – not to get out of it a lasting cure, but some little forgetfulness of my sorrow."

That same year, Cicero speaks his grief a little more openly, noting in a lengthy letter to Aulus Manlius Torquatus, a respected judge who was exiled to Athens:

> Although the universal upheaval causes everyone to complain of his own lot as being worse than any other, and there is not a person who would not rather be anywhere else in the world than where he is, still I have no doubt that the worst form of misery at the present time for an honest citizen is to be at Rome.

Cicero encourages Torquatus to abandon despair and fear, but he cannot deny that Rome is, indeed, in dire straits. As Cicero puts it, "The present crisis . . . holds us all breathless with suspense." Having no illusions about his own tenuous welfare, he concludes that no situation can impede a person from accomplishing some good.

About a year and a half before his assassination, Cicero wrote one of his more famous treatises, "On Old Age," which he dedicated to Titus Pomponius Atticus, a fellow writer and lifelong friend. He describes the demanding schedule he has set himself – the composition of a history of Rome, a revision of his speeches, an overview of Roman law, and his continuing study of Greek literature. These tasks, he states, "are my intellectual gymnastics" which keep his mind in shape.

To quiet the fears of those who dread the uselessness that often accompanies advancing age, Cicero vigorously declares: ". . . my old age sits light upon me . . . and not only is not burdensome, but is even happy." With characteristic Roman practicality, he looks at the approach of death from both the positive and negative perspectives. If there is an afterlife, he is eager to join "the assembled hosts of souls divine and leave this world of strife and sin!" If, on the other hand, there is only nothingness beyond life, "it is desirable for a man to be blotted out at his proper time. For as Nature has marked the bounds of everything else, so she has marked the bounds of life."

An equally upbeat essay, Cicero's "On Friendship," written shortly after his "On Old Age," maintains a similar stance on life after death. Opposing the skeptics of his time, Cicero harks back to the optimism of his forbears who believed that

> . . . upon their departure from the body, a return to heaven lay open to [the dead], and that in proportion, as each soul was virtuous and just would the return be easy and direct.

Equally optimistic about life on earth, Cicero believes that people should search diligently for friends to love, "for if goodwill and affection are taken away, every joy is wrung from life."

In contrast to Cicero's introspective letters and essays are his *Philippics,* his brash outpourings condemning Antony. These were the documents which proved to be Cicero's undoing. From the same pen that once wrote hopeful letters to friends in distress comes the vitriol of political disenchantment. Dwelling at length on his personal grudge against the political reversal in Rome, Cicero blasts the status quo:

> To be a citizen dear to all, to deserve well of the state, to be praised, courted, loved, is glorious; but to be feared and an object of hatred is invidious, detestable, a proof of weakness and decay.

To this caustic public outburst, made on September 2, 44 B.C., Antony prepared a formal reply, withdrawing to Scipio's villa until September 19, to compose his rebuttal, which Cicero describes as being "spewed" rather than spoken.

Undaunted, Cicero prepared thirteen more volleys against the man on whom he projected the multiple ills of the dying Republic. In the *Second Philippic,* he accuses Antony of a disgraceful debauch of "drinking, gaming, vomiting." In the *Third,* he assures Antony that every loyal citizen would advocate Antony's destruction. The *Fifth Philippic* depicts Antony as a war-mongering savage—"passionate, insulting, arrogant, always grasping, always pillaging, always drunk."

By the time Cicero had vented his spleen, he was reduced to jingo-istic, flag-waving rhetoric which strayed from the real situation – the crumbling of a system of government. Wrapping himself in noble sentiments, Cicero called for the Senate to declare a fifty-day period of thanksgiving, an unprecedented event, and to honor the veterans of the civil war by paying "their due reward to them all." He demanded a monument cast "in the noblest possible shape" and consolation for the families of the fallen, the "staunch bulwarks of the state," to "wipe the tears from all their eyes." Cicero's final remark, mere wishful think-ing that the "state has been reestablished," proved, unfortunately, that he was whistling in the dark.

JULIUS CAESAR

- *De Bello Gallico*
  (The Gallic War)

JULIUS CAESAR

LIFE AND BACKGROUND

One of the world's renowned military and political strategists, Gaius Julius Caesar was born to an old, illustrious family which claimed to be able to trace its ancestry back to Iulus, Aeneas' son. By luck, Caesar possessed the right combination of talents and opportunities to skyrocket him to the greatest position of power in the known world.

According to his earliest biographer, Suetonius, Caesar was an imposing, energetic figure with a magnetic personality and a remarkably alert mind. He capitalized on his stature and good looks by fastidious grooming and striking dress. He was careful to hide indications of weakness, such as his premature baldness, migraine headaches, and epileptic seizures, and chose the surest path to power, leaving himself open to the designation of genius and/or opportunist, labels which succeeding generations have debated.

Caesar cultivated membership in the *populares,* or people's party, partly as a result of his kinship with its leader, Marius. Early in his career, Caesar was appointed a *flamen,* or priest, of Jupiter. He strengthened his political position by marrying Cornelia, daughter of Cinna (the consul, not the poet), but he was unprepared for the aggressive political moves on the part of Sulla, a powerful consul who defeated Marius' supporters, confiscated Caesar's property, and ordered him to divorce Cornelia.

Caesar refused to give up his wife and sought refuge in Asia Minor in 81 B.C., but returned to Rome upon the death of Sulla. There he climbed the traditional ladder to political success, impressing his seniors with his oratorical prowess, which he gained from study under Apollonius Molon at Rhodes. Caesar made steady political progress — from *quaestor* in 68 B.C. to *aedile* two years later. In 63 B.C. he was elected *pontifex maximus* (chief priest), and the following year, he became a *praetor,* or judge.

After a successful term as *propraetor,* or provincial governor, of Spain, Caesar's widespread popularity increased when he returned to Rome and joined a coalition with Pompey and Crassus – a triumvirate which made the most of Crassus' money, Pompey's military experience, and Caesar's popularity. From one success to another, his influence spiraled. He served as *consul* in 59 B.C., governed the northern provinces of Italy, and fought a series of Gallic wars from 58 to 51 B.C., during which time he chronicled the exploits of his skillfully organized military operation, thereby securing his place as the people's favorite.

A temporary weakening of Caesar's political troika occurred in 54 B.C. when Julia, Caesar's daughter and Pompey's wife, died. The coalition, shaky for other reasons as well, came further apart when Crassus was killed during the Parthian War. Envious factions furthered enmity between Caesar and Pompey, hoping to undermine their grasp on Rome's leadership. When the crisis reached its peak in 49 B.C., Caesar elected to cross the Rubicon River, south of Ravenna, the boundary between Cisalpine Gaul and Italy, thus bringing an illegal military force into Italy and initiating the civil war that had threatened for five years.

Employing his characteristic battle techniques of *blitzkrieg* ("lightning war") and "divide and conquer," Caesar soon controlled all of Italy, but Pompey quickly re-established himself in Spain and Greece. After months of trying to out-maneuver each other, the two powers climactically clashed at Pharsalus in northern Greece. Caesar defeated Pompey, who managed to escape to Egypt, where he was murdered by agents of Ptolemy XIII, Cleopatra's brother.

During the winter of 48–47 B.C., Caesar, dazzled by Cleopatra's skill and daring, supported the young Egyptian queen against Ptolemy and established her on the throne, at the same time ensuring Rome's ties with the greatest grain-producing nation in the Mediterranean. After tidying up an uprising in Asia Minor in five days, Caesar uttered his famous three-word summary of events: *"Veni, vidi, vici."* ("I came, I saw, I conquered.") He then completed his annihilation of Pompey's forces and returned victorious to Rome.

Caesar's attempts to reform Rome are legendary. In the short time before his assassination on March 15, 44 B.C., Caesar managed to create the Julian calendar, release Rome from staggering debts, reduce the welfare burden, improve roads, initiate a major building program, reward veterans, and extend citizenship to the outer provinces, thereby improving the tax base.

The conspirators that ended his spectacular rise to power feared that Caesar's many honors, including being named *imperator,* dictator for life, and father of the country, would lead to monarchy, with Caesar as king. Crumpled at the feet of Pompey's statue, Caesar died on the Senate floor of multiple stab wounds. The aftermath of Caesar's untimely death (which forms the plot of Shakespeare's tragedy, which is based on Plutarch's biography of Caesar) was ten years of bloody civil war, during which time many noble Romans, including Cicero, were either killed in battle or executed.

Caesar's third wife, Calpurnia, survived him. Despite his numerous affairs, the most flagrant producing a son, Caesarion, by Queen Cleopatra, Caesar left no legitimate male heirs. Octavius, however, Caesar's grandnephew and adopted son, successfully countered Brutus and Cassius, the leaders of the faction that murdered Caesar. Mark Antony, greatly weakened by Caesar's choice of Octavius as his successor, preferred death in Egypt with his lover, Cleopatra. Octavius, who was left as sole ruler, inaugurated the Roman Empire, proclaiming himself Augustus Caesar, its first emperor.

In his lifetime, Caesar dabbled in many types of writing, although he is more likely to have considered himself an orator rather than an author. He wrote two poems, "The Journey" and "Praises of Hercules"; a tragedy based on Oedipus' life; two grammar books; criticism, notably his "On Analogy"; a collection of aphorisms; pamphlets; letters; speeches, in particular, "Against Cato"; and military and social commentary.

The *De Bello Gallico (The Gallic War),* his most polished, representative prose, is a model of understatement. By contrast, the *De Bello Civile (The Civil War),* which lacks the candor and incisive quality of the former work, was published posthumously, obviously in an unfinished state. In addition to the foregoing works, a few extant lines in hexameter contain Caesar's negative reactions to Terence's plays. For unknown reasons, Augustus suppressed publication of his uncle's creative works, which exist today largely in fragments.

———CHRONOLOGY OF CAESAR'S LIFE———

100 B.C.   Born in Rome July 12.

87   Receives the *toga virilis,* which symbolized manhood and citizenship.

83   Marries Cornelia, Cinna's daughter.

82   Defies Sulla and refuses to divorce Cornelia.

81   Flees to Asia Minor. Fights against Mithridates at Cilicia.

80   Receives the civic crown of oak leaves for saving the life of a Roman citizen in battle at Mitylene.

78   Joins Servilius Isauricus' fleet, which wars against Cilician pirates. Returns to Rome after Sulla's death.

77   Conducts his first major legal trial, where he prosecutes Dolabella for extortion and corruption.

76   Studies oratory under Apollonius Molon at Rhodes. While traveling, he is captured by pirates and negotiates his release upon payment of twenty talents ($20,000). Hires a fleet and returns to the pirates' hideout, captures and hangs them.

74   Is made military tribune. Helps overthrow Sulla's constitution.

68   Is appointed *quaestor,* or public treasurer, in Spain.

67   Cornelia dies. Caesar marries Pompeia, Pompey's cousin and Sulla's granddaughter.

65   Is elected *curule aedile* in charge of public games and entertainment, which plunges him into serious personal debt.

63   Is named *pontifex maximus,* a ceremonial title indicating the head of the Roman state religion.

62   Is advanced to the post of *praetor,* or judge. Divorces Pompeia when Clodius, Pompeia's purported lover, enters Caesar's house under false pretenses and interrupts the secret ceremony of the Bona Dea, the Good Goddess.

61   *Propraetor,* or governor, in Spain.

60   First Triumvirate of Caesar, Pompey, and Crassus.

59   Is elected *consul,* one of two chief executives of Rome, with Marcus Bibulus. Marries Calpurnia. Pledges his daughter, Julia, to Pompey in marriage.

58   Attains the honor of *proconsul,* or governor, of Cisalpine and Transalpine Gaul and Illyricum.

58–50   Fights the Gallic Wars.

58   Defeats the Helvetians (Swiss). Defeats Ariovistus, a German chieftain.

57   Conquers the Belgians.

56   Conquers the Veneti in a naval campaign in northwestern Gaul.

55   Invades Germany and Britain.

54   Conducts the second invasion of Britain. Julia dies from loss of blood following a miscarriage.

53   Undertakes the second invasion of Germany. Triumvirate ends with the death of Crassus in battle in Parthia.

52   Vercingetorix and the Gauls surrender.

49   January 11, Caesar proclaims, *"Alea iacta est"* (The die is cast!) and crosses the Rubicon River with his army, initiating a civil war against Pompey.

48   Wins second consulship. Defeats Pompey at Pharsalus, Greece.

47   Defeats Ptolemy, king of Egypt. Establishes Cleopatra on the throne of Egypt and becomes her lover. Conquers Pharnaces in Pontus in Asia Minor and proclaims, *"Veni, vidi, vici"* (I came, I saw, I conquered).

46   Achieves third consulship. Defeats Metellus Scipio and Juba I, king of Numidia, at the Battle of Thapsus.

45   Defeats Pompey's sons in Spain at the Battle of Munda. Is named dictator for life. Establishes the Julian calendar.

44   Is attacked by assassins while presiding over the Roman senate on March 15, the Ides of March. According to Suetonius, Caesar cries out in Greek to Brutus, *"Kai su teknon?"* (You, too, my child?) Dies from 23 stab wounds.

A.D. 121   Suetonius publishes Caesar's biography.

___DE BELLO GALLICO (THE GALLIC WAR)___

Probably the most studied of military handbooks, Caesar's clear, straightforward account of the Gallic War is a masterpiece of battlefield reportage. While galloping over the roughest terrain, Caesar kept stenographers at his side and dictated events as they occurred. The swift publication of these exploits, phrased in a modest, third-person account, enhanced his rapport with working-class Romans. His energetic narration, detailing the pragmatism and strategy which enabled him to win the seven-year war against Gaul, has achieved an honored place not only in beginning Latin classes as a model of Latin prose, but more important, in the private libraries (and military tents) of subsequent generals and leaders as a monument to careful planning and bold, decisive maneuvers.

Writing about Caesar's notebooks, Cicero commends the fact that they are "sinewy, forthright, and charming, stripped of all finery as of a garment." Hirtius, Caesar's staff officer and editor, writes from an insider's viewpoint:

> . . . our admiration is higher than other men's; others know how well and meticulously he wrote, but we know how effortlessly and quickly he finished his writing.

Another opinion, however, is less favorable. Caesar's contemporary, Asinius Pollio – literary critic, consul, and founder of Rome's public library – accuses Caesar of accepting at face value the accounts of officers in the field. Also, he blames Caesar for distorting events to his credit.

BOOK I (58 B.C.)

Opening with his immortal words, "All of Gaul is divided into three parts," Caesar sets about his task with organization and dispatch, assembling legions and appropriate backup in record time. After establishing the geographical and social background of the Gauls, Caesar explains the causes and outcome of his war with the Helvetians (Swiss).

He projects himself as an impartial spokesman for Rome, although he turns to his advantage a particularly bloody episode:

> It was this canton which had marched forth, in the memory of our fathers, and killed the consul Lucius Cassius and [humiliated] his army. Whether by chance or by plan of the immortal gods, that portion of the Swiss who had inflicted so devastating a loss upon the Roman people was the first to pay the penalty.

A closer examination of fact reveals that these adversaries are a band of farmers and local tribesmen. Hardly the bloodthirsty enemy one might imagine in an ambush against the Roman army, they are merely settlers moving in a slow procession across Roman territory in order to reestablish themselves in less mountainous terrain.

Despite his occasional self-aggrandizement, Caesar is careful to include realistic glimpses of battlefield tactics, noting how easily good planning can sometimes fail. After sending a detail ahead to reconnoiter the enemy's location, Caesar settles in to await the dawn:

> At this moment, Considius rode up at a gallop and said that the hill which Labienus [Caesar's most trusted officer] was to occupy was in possession of the enemy; he had recognized the Gallic insignia and weapons.

Caesar admits that Considius panicked, wrecking a well-planned maneuver which might have rid the Roman army of an annoying menace to the rear.

Caesar concludes his campaign against the Swiss with true Roman efficiency. Using captured information, he estimates his kill, noting that of the 368,000 who emigrated from Helvetia, less than a third returned home. A model for later conquerors, Caesar conducts the post-war settlement with clemency and wisdom. In an early version of the Marshall Plan, he provides new homes for the losers so that Rome will not have to fight a future, repetitious battle with a disgruntled populace. Calling on his famed diplomacy, he bestows pardon where it will do the most good, and he binds foreign chieftains to Rome in a pact of mutual respect.

Caesar gives credit to his enemy—in particular, to Ariovistus, the German chieftain who hinders Caesar's progress by cutting off Roman supply lines. Caesar, however, bides his time until his troops can be deployed in the most favorable location. Then, striking at a time when German superstition forbids battle, Caesar's famed three-line battle formation outperforms the German phalanx. In typical Roman style, Caesar returns his victorious fighting forces to winter camp, having completed two successful campaigns in a single season.

BOOK II (57 B.C.)

During the winter, Caesar receives disturbing dispatches from Labienus that the Belgians, fearful of the Roman presence in Gaul, are initiating an offensive. After strengthening his forces with two newly conscripted legions, sending out spies to gather more information, and bolstering the grain supply, Caesar arrives in Belgian territory in record time and learns as much as possible from the Remi, his allies.

After establishing camp on the Axona (Aisne) River, he bides his time and observes Belgian military technique before committing his troops to a serious confrontation. When the Belgians besiege the town of Bibrax, the Remi send for help. Caesar, having made quarters at a favorable location, mobilizes six legions (around 30,000 troops), retaining two newly recruited legions as reserves. His initial engagements are successful.

Tribe after tribe falls to Caesar's divide-and-conquer method. Yet, the Nervii, the most warlike, remain at large and press toward an alliance with neighboring tribes in order to bolster their numbers. Attacking in hopes of plundering Caesar's supply train, the Nervii catch the Roman troops off guard in the most desperate battle of Caesar's entire Gallic campaign. In his terse, controlled prose, Caesar describes the harrowing experience:

> Caesar had everything to do at one time: to raise the stan-
> dard . . . ; to sound the trumpet; to recall the solders from
> the fortifications; to summon those who had proceeded some
> distance to seek materials for a rampart; to form a battleline;
> to encourage the men; and to give the signal. A great part of
> these arrangements was prevented by the shortness of time
> and the sudden approach and charge of the enemy. Under
> these difficulties, two things proved of advantage: the soldiers'
> skill and experience . . . and the fact that Caesar had forbidden
> his several lieutenants to depart from their respective legions
> before the camp was fortified.

Unable to group themselves into companies, the soldiers stand and
fight wherever they happen to be.

In a rare glimpse of Caesar in hand-to-hand combat, the passage
describes how he joins the fray:

> . . . he realized that matters were at a crisis, and that there
> was not any reserve which could be brought up; having,
> therefore, snatched a shield from one of the soldiers in the
> rear (for he himself had come without a shield), he advanced
> to the front of the line, and addressing the centurions by
> name, and encouraging the rest of the soldiers, he ordered
> them to carry forward the standards and to extend the com-
> panies, that they have more room to use their swords.

Under the command of Labienus, the tenth legion (Caesar's favorite)
turns the tide of battle. Soon the area is strewn with the carnage of
battle; the Nervii, terrified by the speed and efficiency of their adversary, ask for terms of surrender.

Throughout the Belgian campaign, Caesar continues to impress
the Gauls with his skill and control. Eventually, the Belgian tribes
are subdued, and Caesar prepares to withdraw for the winter, leaving
behind a substantial occupation force to prevent further outbreaks.
As he turns his attention toward winter quarters in northern Italy,
word of his victory reaches Rome. To commemorate Caesar's triumph,
the senate proclaims a signal honor, a fifteen-day holiday of thanksgiving.

BOOK III (56 B.C.)

To control the St. Bernard Pass through the Alps, thereby creating a sure passage into Gaul, Caesar sends Servius Galba ahead to open the route. The enemy, seizing the initiative and establishing themselves in strategic locations above the Roman camp, threaten Galba's camp. Calling his officers together, Galba discusses the seriousness of their situation and arrives at a consensus—the Romans must summon all their strength in a single swift response to the Gallic offensive. The plan works. Galba kills 10,000 enemy troops. The rest flee to their villages.

Caesar feels relatively secure in the third year of the war. However, before he can relax his grip on the situation, the Veneti, a northern seafaring tribe, launch an offensive, encouraging other tribes to follow suit. They pique Caesar's anger by imprisoning Roman officers. Although the lay of the land proves difficult, Caesar divides his force, sending ships and fighters in from the north and dispatching land troops from the south.

In the face of experienced enemy sailors and more maneuverable ships, Caesar's forces resort to a clever device:

> . . . sharp hooks inserted into and fastened upon poles, not unlike siege-hooks in shape. When the ropes which fastened the sail-yards to the masts were caught by them and pulled, and our vessels vigorously rowed forward, these were severed; and when they were cut away, all control of the ships was lost at a stroke.

The effectiveness of their method, along with improvement in the weather, is enough to tip the battle in the Romans' favor. Caesar speedily ends his war with the Veneti, dealing more harshly than usual with the tribe that dared imprison his officers. In retaliation, Caesar orders their senators executed and captured warriors sold into slavery.

BOOK IV (55 B.C.)

The fourth year of the Gallic War is the most grueling. Caesar comes out of winter quarters to face German hostilities. To discourage the warlike Germans from crossing the Rhine and terrorizing his Gallic allies, Caesar sets out earlier than usual to make war on the Germans. At the junction of the Meuse and Rhine Rivers, Caesar's legions slaughter the enemy. By a stroke of luck, not a single Roman dies as a result of the encounter and only a few are wounded.

Carrying the offensive into German territory, Caesar crosses the Rhine River by means of a bridge, which his corps of engineers constructs:

> He joined together at an interval of two feet, two piles, each a foot and a half thick, sharpened a little at the lower end and proportioned in length to the depth of the river. After he had, by means of rafts, lowered these into the river and fixed them at the bottom, and then driven them in with pile-drivers, not quite perpendicularly like a stake, but bending forward and sloping, so as to incline in the direction of the current. . . . Within ten days after the timber began to be collected, the whole work was completed, and the entire army led over.

Caesar immediately employs a "scorched earth" policy, burning villages and destroying grain fields. To protect their families, the German women and children hide in the woods while the men assemble a defensive line. Before they can strike, Caesar withdraws, cutting down the bridge behind him and leaving the Germans to reconsider carefully before threatening Roman allies.

Although little time remains to launch a second campaign, Caesar turns his attention toward Britain, which has assisted his Gallic enemy in past wars. He makes the usual preparations, sending scouts ahead to reconnoiter enemy readiness, mending diplomatic fences with tribes to the rear, and outfitting ships. Arriving at Dover on the opposite side of the British Channel, Caesar finds the Britons armed and ready on the cliffs above.

The landing proves treacherous to Roman soldiers who are more accustomed to ground tactics. Hampered by high waves and projectiles hurled from above, Caesar's men fail to live up to their reputation as the best of Rome's fighting force.

Suddenly, the standard-bearer of the tenth legion pushes forward, shouting encouragement to his comrades:

> "Jump, comrades, unless you wish to betray your eagle to the enemy. I, for my part, will have done my duty to my country and commanding officer." When he had shouted this, he leaped from the ship and proceeded to bear the eagle

toward the enemy. Then our men, encouraging each other not to disgrace themselves, all leaped from the ship. Those in the nearest vessels who saw them speedily followed their example.

A complete victory seems at hand, but unforeseen storms hinder the Romans' landing. The Britons take advantage of the difficulties, but Caesar's men eventually crush them.

BOOK V (54 B.C.)

Caesar corrects earlier mistakes during the winter months by building more suitable siege ships. Renewing the offensive of the past year, Caesar again risks the hazards of marine warfare, this time losing forty ships during a storm. Doing his utmost to repair and replace his diminished fleet, Caesar returns to war in the field. He faces a massed force under the command of Cassivellaunus.

At this point in the commentary, Caesar expounds upon the geography of Britain and the social customs. He notes that the Britons "account it wrong to eat of hare, fowl, and goose," keeping them only for "pastime or pleasure." Of the shaggy, skin-clad Britons, Caesar writes:

All the Britons, indeed, stain themselves with woad [an herb of the mustard family], which tints them blue. This coloration gives them a terrifying appearance in battle. They wear their hair long, and shave the whole of the body except the head and upper lip.

He notes with particular interest that communes of a dozen Briton men share wives and consider the father of the resulting children to be the man who first married the child's mother.

Swiftly returning to the military situation at hand, Caesar describes chariot warfare, which stymies the Romans at first. After a concerted effort, Caesar's men make advances against the Britons, relying on surprise and speed to overcome their advantage. Eventually, Caesar exhausts the enemy, accepts Cassivellaunus' surrender, and exacts an annual tribute from participating tribes. Eager to return to Gaul, Caesar again experiences difficulty in crossing the channel, this time having to resort to two expeditions before reassembling his men on the Continent.

A renewed hostility with the Gauls occupies Caesar with intense fighting. In Chapter 44, he lauds two former rivals, Titus Pullo and Lucius Vorenus, who display unusual courage and ingenuity during a pitched battle:

> Pullo's shield was pierced and a javelin fastened in his belt. This mishap turned his scabbard around and obstructed his right hand as he was trying to draw his sword, and the enemy crowded around him while he was helpless. His rival, Varenus, ran up to him and helped him in this emergency. Immediately, the whole host turned from Pullo to him, supposing the other to be pierced through by the javelin.

After Varenus recovers, the two comrades kill many of the enemy, earning for themselves an equal amount of glory.

Near the end of the campaign, Labienus creates the impression that his forces are inadequate against the attacking Gauls. He lures them on, at the same time building his cavalry with local conscripts. When the Gauls finally approach the Roman camp to hurl missiles and get no answer, they drift away, assuming that Labienus' cavalry has departed. At a signal from within, the Romans attack, driving the panicked Gauls into a rout. Labienus' men slaughter great numbers; the enemy chieftain is killed and beheaded.

BOOK VI (53 B.C.)

After building a new bridge across the Rhine, Caesar again prepares for war with the Germans. At this point, he halts his military reportage and describes the peculiarities of the Druids, the Gallic priests of sacrifice:

> They take charge of all divine matters, procure public and private sacrifices, and interpret religious matters. . . . Their chief belief is that the soul is immortal and migrates from one body to another after death, a doctrine which greatly inspires them to courage and a contempt of dying.

He describes a kind of feudal system by which the Gallic knights, attended by their slaves, defend the country in times of danger.

Because of the number and types of details that strike his fancy, Caesar is obviously fascinated with Druidism. He remarks that the Gauls are superstitious and that they appease their gods through public burning of live victims, who are encased in huge, hollow, twig-woven cocoons which are painted to look like human beings. Their chief god is Mercury. They believe themselves to be descendants of Pluto, whom they honor by reckoning the passage of time by nights rather than days.

In contrast to the highly superstitious Gauls, the Germans are less interested in religion. Instead, they focus on hunting and warfare, matters which dominate the lives of the males. The men, who remain virgins until the age of twenty, are praised for their chastity. They are hardy lads, washing themselves in cold river water and covering their nakedness with a minimal number of reindeer skins. They live communally, abandoning their land each year and moving on to another location. They take great pride in driving off their neighbors, yet bind themselves to strict codes of hospitality.

BOOK VII (52 B.C.)

Caesar's account of the seventh year of the Gallic War culminates in a combined effort of Gaul against Roman. Led by Vercingetorix, who refuses to acquiesce to the Roman occupational forces, the Gauls fight loyally to the finish, but they are finally defeated at the town of Alesia, a place naturally fortified by hills and two rivers. According to Caesar:

> Under the walls, on the side of the town facing east, lay all the enemy's encamped forces; these had fortified themselves with a ditch and a wall of stones heaped up eight feet high.

To counter the enemy advantage, Caesar is careful to draw up his own defensive position, staffing the twenty-three temporary defensive earthworks with round-the-clock observers.

In the final siege, as Labienus finds himself in peril from the advancing enemy, Caesar rides to the rescue:

> His arrival was soon seen by the bright [red] of his cloak, which he used to wear in battle, and the troops of cavalry and cohorts which he had ordered to follow him, being observed from the higher ground, the fight began. They set up a shout on both sides, which was returned from the rampart and all the fortifications around.

By nightfall, the tide turns in favor of the Romans, who ride down the fleeing enemy and slaughter great numbers.

Caesar concludes the business of surrender, taking prisoners, dispensing mercy where he thinks fit, and binding as many tribes as possible into submission to the Roman occupation of Gaul. He then dispatches his men to a well-earned winter respite and sends word of his campaign to Rome. The senate, in gratitude for Caesar's hard-fought victory, declares a twenty-day public thanksgiving.

LUCRETIUS

- ***De Rerum Natura***
  (On the Nature of Things)

LIFE AND BACKGROUND

Titus Lucretius Carus (ca. 96–ca. 55 B.C.), Rome's chief exponent of Epicurean philosophy, wrote only one work, *De Rerum Natura,* a long, intensely didactic poem in hexameter verse. Upon this single, unfinished six-volume work rests most of the world's knowledge about Lucretius and his beliefs. Devoted to revealing the secrets of the natural world, Lucretius studied the phenomena of the universe with the aim of explaining its beginnings and eventual demise. His enthusiasm for scientific inquiry exceeds any in the preceding generations, including Democritus.

Lucretius' secondary purpose in writing *De Rerum Natura* was to fashion an expose of Roman contemporary life in order to expound a new relationship between human beings and the divine. Lucretius believed that his writings could free his countrymen from fear of death and enslavement to petty, anthropomorphic gods. Morally outraged by the decadence, opulence, and vulgarity of Rome's dying republic, he railed against the frivolous life which was wasting itself in ostentation and luxury. He believed that Romans surrounded themselves with possessions and trumped-up honors in order to stave off insecurity, which Lucretius maintained was an outgrowth of the fear of death. Oddly enough, although he insisted on a realistic outlook, he closeted himself in a scholar's world, ignoring the great civil wars that raged about him.

A key factor in Lucretius' doctrine is his distaste for the supernatural, including gods, mythology, creeds, cults, rites – in short, all forms of religion, all suggestions of ignorance. In place of traditional beliefs, he proposed natural laws, based on the observation of phenomena. Lucretius insisted that the earth is mortal and has no central plan, form, or function. He believed that the earth, like all living matter, would perish. Hoping to free Romans from mundane struggles and make them focus their attention on the simple, contemplative life, the poet offered in place of the frenetic pace of his generation a godlike tranquility and inner satisfaction.

To Lucretius, the most worthwhile study was physics, particularly the branch containing the laws that explain the makeup and inter-relation of the universe. Some of his zoological and anthropological theories prefigure Darwin's laws, notably his concept that organisms adapt and that domestication is necessary for the survival of a species. Because he differed so markedly with his contemporaries, his work was virtually unnoticed in his lifetime. Only later, when his physical principles proved feasible, did succeeding generations grant him stature for his genius.

Since little is known about Lucretius' personal life, we assume that because of his illustrious family name, he was born an aristocrat, although some evidence suggests that he may have been the son of a freedman. He devoted his life to his master, Epicurus, the fourth-century Greek philosopher who established the principles of material-istic hedonism. A modest, unassuming man, Lucretius appears to have surrounded himself with equally unimpressive associates and disci-ples, all of whom dedicated themselves to the ascetic philosophy of Epicureanism.

In a spurious account written in the fourth century, St. Jerome notes in his *Chronicle* that Lucretius was victimized by a jealous woman and driven insane by a love potion; during periods of sanity, he worked on his long poem, but he finally succumbed to madness and committed suicide. The likelihood that so sensitive and high-strung a man could kill himself is not unthinkable. However, the no-tion that he was driven into psychosis by a love potion is pure fic-tion, possibly the spiteful work of an anti-atheist.

De Rerum Natura, dedicated to Gaius Memmius, a second-rate politician and noted patron of the arts who achieved the rank of *praetor* in 58 B.C., sets out to instruct one of Lucretius' respected pupils in the doctrine of Epicureanism. Marcus Cicero, who is thought to have edited Lucretius' work, says of the poem in a letter to his brother Quin-tus: "Lucretius' poetry is exactly as you describe it: it is filled with flashes of genius, but at the same time, it shows great technical skill."

DE RERUM NATURA
———— *(ON THE NATURE OF THINGS)* ————

Despite Lucretius' disdain for mythology, he follows the pattern of his predecessors and invokes Venus, the "all-fostering mother of Aeneas' clan," as his muse. He enshrouds himself in his task, begging the goddess to:

> . . . give eternal beauty to my words;
> Grant me that while I write,
> Fierce war on land and sea may sleep and rest . . .
> Pour out sweet whispered words, O Goddess famed,
> And beg the quiet of peace for Roman folk.

In a graceful turn of phrase, the poet suggests that Venus, lover of Mars, should use her wiles to subdue the fierce war-god's violence by distracting him with caresses.

Early in **Book 1,** Lucretius makes clear that human beings waste their humanity by paying homage to religion, which crushes them to the earth and holds them in cruel slavery. He heralds a champion, a Greek who "longed to be the first to crack the cramping bonds of nature." Although he does not call Epicurus by name, the poet indicates that this hero set out on "mental voyages" and brought back the "news of nature's laws" to all.

Lucretius sets forth his atomic theory and explains that creation is the result of atoms moving about in the void of space. Like a wise teacher, he comforts the weary minds of his audience with soothing words:

> Come hear the rest, come lend your ears
> To more prophetic strain.
> I know how difficult my topic is.
> I tread the trackless heights,
> Not trodden earlier by foot of man.

Before concluding Book I, he explains his method. Just as doctors coat the edge of the glass with honey to entice children to drink their medicine, so too must the poet use the charms of verse to "hold your mind to theme both high and hard, until you'd mastered nature's shape and form."

Book 2 finds Lucretius happily seated in his "ivory tower, whose battlements are thought and high philosophy, the wisdom of the wise."

He offers to his reader, whom he envisions as "tortured by sickness and by fever racked," an answer to the mysteries of life that keep him "trembling in the dark." To introduce his atomic theory, Lucretius reasons:

> . . . we see that things grow small
> And all things, like a river, flow away
> In time's long lapse; and yet
> The sum of things remains the same.

Although he believes that atomic particles are homogeneous, he advances a second supposition – that atoms swerve in their movements, thereby creating the universe and allowing human beings free will.

Book 3, the most quoted section of the *De Rerum Natura,* contains Lucretius' greatest praise of Epicurus. Comparing his master's words to nectar, he says:

> As bees in flowery meadow suck each flower,
> So we your golden words [suck] repeatedly;
> We feed on them and find them golden,
> Worthy of eternal life.

At this point, the poet firmly grasps his main theme, decrying the human fear of death, which is most evident during stressful times, when people make a multitude of sacrifices to the gods.

Buoyed by his optimism, Lucretius rejects traditional notions and declares that

> Death then is nothing, affects us not at all,
> Since the soul is held to be of mortal stuff . . .
> So, when we're dead,
> When soul and body out of which we're formed,
> One entity,
> Are torn apart in death,
> Nothing can touch our sense at all
> Or move our consciousness . . .

Describing the malaise that drives people from home to the outdoors and back again in pursuit of contentment, Lucretius summarizes that great malady that assaults his generation: "Every man is striving to avoid himself."

Book 4 refutes the common notion that love is the answer to human ills. Physical passion, contends Lucretius, is just another form of slavery:

> He who shuns love does not lose love's reward.
> He picks a pleasure less alloyed with pain.
> For surely pleasure's purer when you're fancy free.

The poet blames love for goading human beings into greater fits of anguish while denying the victims the release they seek. Locked in perpetual struggle, lovers neglect work, home, and fortune as they waste their time and money purchasing "linens, dainties for the feast, games, frequent toasts, perfumes, garlands, and wreaths."

Book 5, after a brief return to praise for Epicurus, sets out to describe creation. Referring to his earlier concept of atomic particles, Lucretius explains:

> I must show the cosmos
> Likewise made of mortal stuff,
> And how the meeting of material particles
> Created each and sky and sea and
> Stars and moon and sun.
> And then what living creatures
> Came to be on earth . . .

After a lengthy account of man's evolution from a primitive lifestyle to the current status, Lucretius concludes that human beings created divinities out of their desire to escape fears. He insists that crawling before a stone altar is not holiness. Rather, people should devote themselves to "contemplate with mind serene the whole," a task that will bring them inner peace and contentment.

In stark contrast to the calm of the preceding book, **Book 6** deals with the horrors of natural phenomena—lightning, volcanoes, and earthquakes—and with disease, in particular, the plague at Athens which Thucydides describes. Steeped in gory detail, Lucretius seems bent on terrifying the reader:

> The breath poured noisome odors from their mouths,
> Smells like the stench of rotting flesh,
> When thrown outdoors.
> And straightway all the strength of mind
> And all the body's energy

Grew faint and dim,
As if the victim, even now,
Were at the gate of death.

Piling detail upon horrid detail, Lucretius describes all manner of physical torment – phlegm, ringing ears, cramping muscles, stiffened limbs, and the slow decay of bowels, ulcerated and wracked with flux. Even the birds and dogs that pecked and sniffed the heaps of corpses died from contamination with the awful disease. In justification of his morbid verse, Lucretius reveals his purpose – to show that propitiation of the gods is fruitless in times of pestilence.

CATULLUS

- *Poems*

CATULLUS

LIFE AND BACKGROUND

Rome's most enigmatic love poet, Gaius Valerius Catullus (*ca.* 87–*ca.* 54 B.C.), lived fast and hard and died at an early age; he was simply ill-equipped to survive among the glitzy, dissolute crowd whom he called friends.

A native of Verona, in northern Italy between Milan and Venice, he probably gained access to the homes of the rich and famous because of his father's ties with Julius Caesar, who used their villa as a way station on his journeys to and from Gaul. In his early twenties, Catullus left his mountain home and came to the big city, although he often returned to the Italian lake district, where he kept a villa at Sirmio, on Lake Garda, and a second residence in the Sabine hills near Tibur, twenty-five miles east of Rome.

In Rome, he joined the frivolous bohemian set known collectively as "the new poets." His gift for poetry, however, was more than a burst of flashy, erotic poems, for even Ovid referred to him in his *Amores* as *doctus* (learned), possibly in appreciation of his knowledge of Greek poetry and his ability to imitate the Alexandrine school. Buoyed by his acceptance among Rome's sophisticates and, no doubt, supplemented by his wealthy father, Catullus had no difficulty establishing himself with adequate patronage and quickly ingratiated himself into the most fashionable circles.

Reveling in Rome's amoral *la dolce vita,* Catullus became passionately involved with a married woman ten years his senior, whom he refers to as Lesbia in 30 of his 116 extant poems, some of which survive in fragments. Her name, probably taken from Sappho, the Lesbian poet, fits the metrical pattern of the name of a real Roman matron, Clodia Metelli, wife of her haughty cousin, the consul Quintus Metellus Celer, and elder sister of Clodius Pulcher.

Like her brother, who ran afoul of both Julius Caesar and Cicero with his adolescent shenanigans, Clodia was a powerful, passionate woman who fed her ego on a series of adoring young men. Members of a ruthless, aristocratic family, Clodia and Clodius were spoiled, materialistic heirs to an extremely wealthy family, accustomed to getting what they wanted and caring not a whit about whom they hurt in the process. Upon the sudden death of Clodia's husband in 59 B.C., Cicero referred to Clodia as a "two-bit Clytemnestra" and initiated widespread suspicion that Clodia poisoned her husband.

Catullus' alliance with this unscrupulous, faithless femme fatale was intensely painful, causing him untold grief and humiliation as she dallied with an ever-widening circle of new lovers, five of whom Catullus names in his verses. Many of his vitriolic poems were launched at these rivals; one poem is even addressed to Clodius, who, Catullus insinuates, was his sister's lover. The possibility is not unthinkable, given Clodia's reputation.

Yet, Catullus' moments of happiness with Clodia seemingly more than repaid the sleepless nights and self-doubts that plagued him throughout their relationship. He apparently realized Clodia's shallow self-interest and facile manipulations much earlier, but he was unable to dissociate himself from the allure of so lovely and intelligent a woman.

About 57 B.C., Catullus accepted a post with the staff of Memmius, a provincial governor, and he journeyed to Bithynia, in the Asian portion of modern Turkey, on the southern shore of the Black Sea, a place which must have seemed like the end of the earth to one who had previously thrown himself into the glitter, sport, and amusement of Roman high society.

Possibly as an escape from his ill-fated love, Catullus found contentment in the distant outpost, where he wrote two of his most famous works. The first, *"Ave atque vale"* ("Hail and Farewell"), pays tribute to his dead brother, who was buried near Troy. The second, "Attis," is a long narrative detailing the misadventures of a Greek youth caught up in the cult of Cybele, the Great Mother; it is remarkable for its broken rhythms and frenetic energy.

Upon his return to Rome in 56 B.C., Catullus again involved himself in scandal during the trial of Marcus Caelius Rufus, one of his rivals, whom Clodia accused of trying to poison her. Cicero, by means of clever disputation, gained acquittal for the accused and, at the same time, ruined Clodia's already tarnished reputation. In

Cicero's honor, Catullus wrote a paean to him, "Most Eloquent of Romulus' Grandsons."

Perhaps to take his mind off of his abortive love affair with Clodia, Catullus showed passing interest in a teenage boy, Juventius, who eventually gravitated to the beds of two of Catullus' friends, Aurelius and Furius. As a result, Catullus wrote some of his most biting verses; in rapid sequence, he hurls vicious, vengeful, and graphic recriminations at his former friends, in much the same way that he did when he had to face the fact that Clodia was sleeping with other men. For the fresh-faced and supple Juventius, however, Catullus reserves only a meager, but regretful chastisement.

When Catullus was about thirty, he wrote a series of trenchant, scathing epigrams aimed at Julius Caesar and his rapacious coterie, including Caesar's chief engineer, Mamurra, seedy toady to whom Catullus appends the snide nickname "Mentula" – roughly, "Pricko." It appears, however, that Catullus and Caesar eventually settled their differences, most likely at Caesar's instigation, at Catullus' villa in Verona and that Catullus was subsequently invited to Caesar's house for dinner.

Catullus continued to write all sorts of personal attacks, usually for political reasons, but he finally called a halt to these petty poison-pen poems, as well as to his erotic verses, and created a lovely, small-scale epic, "The Marriage of Peleus and Thetis."

Although he died young, Catullus had a great influence on writers in his own time, as well as writers in later years – particularly such English poets as Edmund Spenser, Ben Jonson, Robert Herrick, John Keats, and Alfred, Lord Tennyson. He lacked the philosophical depth of Lucretius and the polish and control of the leading Augustan poets (Virgil, Horace, and Ovid), yet Catullus was noted and widely imitated for his flexible verse forms, which he adopted from the Hellenic poets of Alexandria. As the nineteenth-century writer Macauley said in his simple, but obviously admiring summary, "No Latin writer is so Greek." Equally famed for his metrical experimentation, childlike sincerity, needling colloquialisms, and spontaneous, mercurial explosions of emotion, Catullus' work was revived by nineteenth-century romantics, who raised him to new heights.

POEMS

Catullus' poems run the gamut of emotion from bitter rage to loving tenderness, from love of home to sneering put-down; he bares his innermost feelings with no qualms. The litany of verse that chronicles his love affair with Clodia Metelli contains his most intense poetry. On seeing Lesbia (Clodia) in the company of her husband, Catullus paraphrases Sappho's famous lines:

> He seems equal to the gods,
> If it isn't a sin to say so, even more,
> Who sits beside you, hears your sweet voice tinkling with
>   laughter,
> And repeatedly gazes into your eyes . . .

Caught up in whirling passions, the poet details the downward rush of flame that suffuses his limbs, echoes in his ears, and dims his vision.

This all-consuming love affair, however, has its ebb and flow. During the good times, obviously intent on possessing Lesbia, Catullus orders her to forget the crabbed rumormongers and to concentrate on their kisses:

> So kiss me, give me a thousand kisses,
> Another thousand, hundreds more,
> Then hundred thousands by the score
> Until we lose count . . .

But when they are quarreling, he gives himself good advice: "Leave off playing the fool." Certain that he can live without her, he makes a solemn vow to harden his heart and abstain from love.

A significant pair of poems that captures the less tempestuous moments with Lesbia are the so-called sparrow poems. The first celebrates Lesbia's love for the little bird, which she teases as it hops across her thighs; the second poem, filled with hyperbole, mourns the death of the small pet:

> Now it journeys down the shadowy path
> From which none ever comes back;
> O damn you, evil shades of Hell,
> Which gobble up all beautiful things . . .

Carrying his dirge to extremes of sorrow, Catullus worries that the "poor little eyes of [his] sweetheart are red and swollen with weeping."

At odds with himself over his fascination with the faithless Lesbia, Catullus declares that she often says that she would rather have him in bed than Jupiter. But, he sighs in retrospect, "What a woman says to her hot-blooded lover should be written on the wind and the rushing waters," a line that Keats paraphrased in his famous epitaph. Catullus summarizes his on-again, off-again love affair in a famous couplet:

> I hate and I love.
> Perhaps you wonder why I do it.
> I don't know, but it's happening,
> And I am tormented.

This ambivalence, more than any other stimulus, is responsible for the tension and energy that permeate Catullus' poetry.

Other moods color the poems that Catullus produced after he left Rome for a one-year stay in Bithynia. The most moving of those poems, his *"Ave atque vale,"* honors his brother's death. The poet explains how he traveled long distances in order to bestow the traditional "gifts to the dead." He laments that his brother did not deserve to die so young. Confronted with a silent tomb, Catullus can only weep, make his dutiful offering according to family custom, and bid "hello and goodbye."

In a jollier vein, Catullus sings a traditional tune – a marriage hymn, which details the standard trappings of a wedding; Catullus gives us fascinating details about the mock kidnapping of the bride, her crown of fresh-picked flowers, her saffron-colored slippers, and the solemn vows before the altar of "Hymen, god of marriage." In the background are the jostling, joking well-wishers, singing "sweet nuptial melodies" and bearing "the torch of marriage," which lights the way to the couple's home. Concluding the song of matrimony as the bride and groom enter, he says, perhaps wistfully:

> Shut the door, maidens
> We have sported enough.
> Happy couple, live well . . .

VIRGIL

- **Virgil and the *Aeneid***

- **The *Aeneid***

- ***Eclogues*, or *Bucolics***

- ***Georgics***

VIRGIL

LIFE AND BACKGROUND

Born in the small northern village of Andes, between Mantua and the Po River, on October 15, 70 B.C., Publius Vergilius Maro grew into a young man who was tall and lanky, dark-eyed, somewhat unpolished in appearance and behavior, and bashful with strangers and in public gatherings. He had two brothers — Silo, who died in childhood, and Flaccus, who lived to young manhood. Virgil's father, an industrious potter and cattle farmer, married his landlord's daughter, worked at beekeeping, and invested in the lumber industry. An ambitious man, he strove to provide his son with an aristocratic education to prepare him for a law career. Virgil showed early promise of greatness, but despite his rise to fame among the rich and influential, he absorbed enough of the outdoors in northern Italy to remain a lifelong nature enthusiast and preferred uncomplicated country living to the clamor of life as a celebrity in Rome.

When he completed his studies at Cremona and Milan, he went to Rome about 53 B.C. to study law and rhetoric in Epidius' academy, where he may have met Octavian (later, Caesar Augustus), seven years his junior. Around 48 or 47 B.C., during Caesar's war with Pompey, Virgil appears to have served in the military, an experience which he mentions with a shudder in the *Catalepton (Trifles)*, a collection of minor poems sometimes attributed to him.

From Rome, Virgil went to Naples in 47 B.C. to study philosophy under Siro. As a result of their friendship, Virgil probably modeled the character of Silenus in the *Eclogues* after his teacher. About this time, Virgil joined a circle of Epicurean thinkers outside Naples, in Campania, at a retreat known as "The Garden," under the direction of Siro. After his teacher's death in 42 B.C., Virgil inherited his villa, the most treasured of his residences, where he lived with his mother and surviving brother, Flaccus. It is possible that Virgil, a peace-loving man, was retreating from the turmoil that followed Julius Caesar's

assassination, Cicero's execution, and the ten-year miasma that preceded the establishment of the Empire.

While Virgil lived in Naples, his father's land was confiscated and
given to veterans of the Battle of Philippi in 42 B.C. The poet was
deeply despondent over his father's eviction from his farm—even more
upset than he was by the post-assassination bloodbath or the political
jockeying of the interregnum period. In his *Eclogues,* he was inspired
to write with poignant grace of the farmer's love of land. Virgil probably never returned to his birthplace, but, instead, traveled throughout
much of the Italian peninsula and Sicily, although he eventually obtained another retreat in Cisalpine Gaul through friends.

A quiet, unassuming man who suffered from chronic illness,
possibly tuberculosis, Virgil gave up his early plans to practice law
after pleading only one court case and devoted himself to philosophy
and literature. Most of his life was spent in the quiet countryside of
Campania, the province containing Naples, Pompeii, and Hercu-
laneum. In addition, he kept a house on the Esquiline Hill in Rome,
given to him by Maecenas, and he associated with patricians, states-
men, and literati, including Augustus and Horace. His style was greatly
influenced by Lucretius' *De Rerum Natura* and by the poetry of
Catullus, one of the "new poets" who experimented in epigram, elegy,
and the short epic.

Although much light verse in the *Appendix Vergiliana,* including
the *Culex (The Gnat), Catalepton (Trifles), Aetna (Mount Etna),* and *Ciris
(The Ciris Bird),* is attributed to Virgil's youthful period, scholarly opinion concerning its authenticity has wavered in both directions during
the twentieth century. The current rationale for its rejection makes
sense. Virgil was a slow, methodical writer. According to Suetonius,
his biographer, he dictated his verses each morning and spent the remainder of the day reducing them to a distilled perfection. Consequently, he wrote nothing hastily or frivolously; he had published only
one volume of verse by the age of thirty-three.

Virgil's first major work was composed between 42 and 37 B.C.
A ten-book pastoral poem known variously as the *Bucolics (Rural
Poems),* or the *Eclogues (Selections),* it was modeled on the *Idylls* of
Theocritus, a fourth-century Sicilian Greek. Virgil's emphasis is on
flowing rhythms and an idealized setting in northern Italy, but also
includes many realistic details—in particular, Virgil is concerned with
the political confiscation of the rural estates in his homeland. From

the beginning, it is clear that Virgil intended this poem to be read aloud, as was the Roman custom; from all reports, he enjoyed reading it to friends and fellow writers.

The most famous section, Eclogue 4, contains a mystical prophecy about a Golden Age of peace and goodwill, ushered in by the birth of a divine child. Critics have made definite connections between Virgil's fictional characters and real people, and they have suggested, for example, that Daphnis, the shepherd, is an allegorical name for Julius Caesar and that the divine birth refers to Pollio's son (to whom the work is dedicated); they have also conjectured that the divine birth refers to Mark Antony, or possibly to Virgil's friend Octavian, who became Augustus, Rome's first emperor. Other critics see the fourth eclogue as a reference to Christ.

During the next stage of Virgil's career, from 37 to 30 B.C., he devoted his time to the *Georgics,* a technical and philosophical manual on farming, interspersed with winsome, poetic digressions. For information and style, Virgil relied heavily on earlier writings, particularly the Greeks – Aristotle, Theocritus, and Hesiod – and certain Roman writers – Marcus Porcius Cato, Marcus Terentius Varro, and Lucretius. The four-book poem deals with planting, caring for orchards and vineyards, stock management, and beekeeping, but it emphasizes the inherent values of Roman life – particularly the work ethic. Later on, Virgil's major motifs in this literary work – hard work and piety – became essential themes of the *Aeneid.* For these reasons, the *Georgics* is considered a near-perfect example of Roman poetry.

Virgil is best known for his last work, the *Aeneid,* an epic which he wrote from 30 to 19 B.C. in twelve books of hexameter verse, modeled on Homer's epics, and dedicated to Augustus and his illustrious ancestry. Virgil is thought to have deviated from rustic themes to historical themes after witnessing Julius Caesar's grand triumph, the spectacular thanksgiving parade which marked Pompey's defeat in Egypt. To link his work to Homer's heroic poetry, Virgil selected a Trojan hero, Aeneas (son of King Priam and Queen Hecuba), as his central character. Virgil's skill in integrating history, prophecy, and stylistic details from many sources resulted in a cohesive, readable work, despite its also being a political tribute to Augustus, the empire builder.

All of Rome, particularly the royal family, followed the progress of the *Aeneid.* Augustus; his sister, Octavia (Mark Antony's wife); and

Augustus' minister, Maecenas, listened to Virgil read aloud from rough drafts. As he refined his work during his latter years, the poet led a comfortable, worry-free life, devoting himself to historical research and enjoying the luxuries that his father's bequest and the emperor's patronage provided. Unfortunately, however, in Megara, on the first leg of a three-year fact-finding mission to Greece and Asia on September 21, 19 B.C., Virgil became ill with fever. Augustus accompanied his old friend to Brundisium, where he died before his epic could be revised and polished to his satisfaction.

To prevent its being read in rough form, the poet left instructions in his will that the *Aeneid* be destroyed. Augustus, however, interceded and assigned two of Virgil's poet friends, Varius Rufus and Plotius Tucca, to edit the manuscript for publication, but he cautioned them not to make additions. The work was completed near the end of 18 B.C. It achieved immediate acceptance throughout the Mediterranean world as the definitive Roman epic. On his deathbed, Virgil immortalized himself with a short, suitable epitaph which his friends inscribed above his grave near his home outside Naples; it ends with this line: "I sang of pastures, farms, and rulers," a touching summary of Virgil's three great works, which chronicle the history of Rome – from shepherds to farmers to soldiers.

Virgil's influence as one of the great epic writers of world literature is found among the major poets – Dante, Chaucer, Spenser, Milton, Dryden, Tennyson, and Eliot. While much ancient literature was suppressed when Christianity spread across the civilized world, Virgil, known as the "virtuous pagan," retained his preeminence, partially because of his messianic prediction of a miraculous birth. The *Aeneid* served as a textbook in European schools and was revered for a time as a magic work, capable of foretelling the future.

Virgil's surname, which evolved from the original "Vergilius," may have been deliberately altered to reflect the word *virga,* "magician's wand," or to echo the word *virgo,* the Roman translation of his Greek nickname, "Parthenias," or "maiden," referring to his shy, modest nature. Ironically, the world came to revere Virgil as the "Roman Homer," despite his rejection of Rome's citified ways and public adulation. Although Virgil was famous the last twenty years of his life, he preferred his suburban home and a small circle of intimates, especially Maecenas, Horace, and Augustus. His timid voice, which quavered with diffidence in conversation, spoke clearly and sonorously in verse as he revealed Rome's illustrious history to the civilized world.

_____ **VIRGIL AND THE *AENEID*** _____

The *Aeneid* is not a personal epic about Aeneas; instead, it is a national epic, a glorification and exaltation of Rome and a saga about the destiny of the Roman people. The poem is not really concerned with the life and adventures of its hero, Aeneas, but with the part he played in founding the Roman state and with the way in which Aeneas embodies the most important Roman personal qualities and attributes, particularly the Roman sense of duty and responsibility.

As a thinker, Virgil has a spiritualized, idealistic, and aspiring concept of Rome, a city which he views as majestic and sacred, ordained by destiny and Providence to rule the world. For Virgil, all human affairs are controlled by superhuman forces, and, thus, the gods must have ordained that Rome attain the greatness of which he sings. He saw a new Golden Age of human life emerging during the reign of Augustus, a Golden Age which he had already praised in his fourth "messianic" eclogue. As a result, the *Aeneid* is designed to exalt Rome, to show the hand played by the divine in its establishment, and to glorify its virtues and finest features by their personification in Aeneas, an epic hero who is meant to represent the archetypal Roman.

The Roman public quickly accepted the *Aeneid* as their national epic despite certain minor faults caused by the unfinished state of the poem at Virgil's death. Throughout the remaining centuries of the Empire, readers studied, admired, and imitated the *Aeneid;* it served as a standard textbook in all the schools. Later, influential Roman writers and critics, from Horace and Petronius onward, considered Virgil the nation's greatest poet.

As Christianity spread throughout the civilized world, most pagan Greek and Roman literature dropped by the wayside, admired by only a few antiquarians and religious nonconformists. Virgil's work, however, maintained its major position. This was due partly to the fact that, as mentioned above, Virgil predicted in his fourth eclogue that a child would be born, during whose lifetime a new Golden Age would be conferred upon humanity. It now seems likely that Virgil intended to compliment Augustus Caesar, but many Christians of the period read this as a prophecy of the birth of Christ. In their study of Virgil's works, early Christians discovered some similarities between his thought and that of the Hebrew prophet Isaiah. It was decided that Virgil was one of those few virtuous pagans who had been rewarded with a foreknowledge of the messianic age.

From the time that such conclusions were drawn, Virgil's poetry gained an air of religious sanctity. His works were safely preserved during the barbarian incursions which caused the downfall of the Empire; they were revered almost equally with the Bible and other Christian writings.

By the Middle Ages, Virgil's legend had gained fantastic proportions. Among literary people, he was extolled as the greatest of poets, and his works were the most important models for new authors. For instance, Dante, in his *Divine Comedy*, praised Virgil as the master from whom he derived all his skill and art, and, in Dante's epic, Virgil serves as the poet's guide through Hell and Purgatory.

In the Renaissance, the works of other Greek and Roman authors were rediscovered and studied, but the *Aeneid* retained its preeminence. Chaucer regarded Virgil as the perfect teacher, a writer whom all poets should respect and emulate.

In the years that have followed, the *Aeneid* has continued to hold a central place in European literature. Virgil's epic has an almost universal appeal; every age has rediscovered Virgil's insights into the nature of man and his relation to the universe.

LIST OF CHARACTERS _____

HUMAN BEINGS

Acestes

A chieftain of Trojan ancestry who rules a kingdom in the western portion of Sicily. He offers friendly assistance to Aeneas on the two occasions that the Trojan expedition lands within his domain.

Achaemenides

A Greek sailor from Ulysses' crew; he meets the Trojans near Mount Etna and warns them of the dangerous Cyclopes in the vicinity.

Achates

Aeneas' armor-bearer. He is a devoted follower of his chieftain throughout the *Aeneid.*

Aeneas

Son of Anchises and Venus, a prince of Troy, and leader of the expedition to Italy. Virgil has personified in him all those qualities which he believed had built the Roman Empire and made it great.

Amata

The wife of King Latinus and mother of Lavinia. She is a patron of Turnus and favors his marriage to her daughter. Falsely believing Turnus to be dead, she kills herself during the Trojan assault on Laurentum.

Anchises

Aeneas' father. He accompanies his son on the expedition to Italy and is a frequent source of advice and moral support.

Andromache

The widow of Hector, the most important Trojan chieftain. She is now married to Helenus, a Trojan soothsayer who is one of Hector's brothers. Along with other Trojan exiles, Andromache and Helenus have settled near Actium.

Anna

Dido's sister and confidante, who acts as her adviser and messenger during the queen's romance with Aeneas.

Ascanius (also known as **Iulus**)

The son of Aeneas and Creusa; he is the founder of the family from which the Caesars claimed descent.

Camilla

An Amazon-like Italian warrior-maiden who leads a contingent of troops to aid Turnus.

Creusa

Aeneas' first wife and Ascanius' mother. She dies during the sack of Troy.

Dardanus

The mythical founder of the city of Troy who, legend said, emigrated to Asia Minor from Italy. The Trojans were frequently called Dardanians after his name.

Dido

Sychaeus' widow and queen of Carthage. She is an honorable and proud woman of great sensitivity and powerful passions. The romance between Dido and Aeneas crystallizes the conflicts between duty and self-interest that Aeneas must resolve before reaching Italy.

Diomedes

A Greek hero of the Trojan War; he is now the ruler of several Greek colonies in southeastern Italy.

Drances

A Latin nobleman who leads the embassy to Aeneas and speaks out for peace and against Turnus at the Latin council.

Euryalus

A young Trojan warrior who bravely sacrifices himself in an attempt to carry a message to Aeneas during the Latin attack on the Trojan camp.

Evander

The king of Pallanteum; Pallas' father. He is a wise old man and a benevolent ruler; his subjects and the neighboring peoples revere him.

Helenus

Andromache's husband, ruler of a group of Trojan exiles living near Actium. He warns Aeneas of the dangers along the sea route to Italy and advises him to consult the Sybil of Cumae.

Laocoön

A Trojan priest of Neptune who warns his people that the wooden horse left by the Greeks is a dangerous trap. They refuse to listen to him; he and his sons are killed by a large sea serpent.

Latinus

The Latins' king, Amata's husband, and Lavinia's father. He is friendly toward Aeneas because of certain oracles concerning the landing of a stranger in Latium, but he is unable to prevent his people from attacking the Trojans.

Lausus

Mezentius' son, a brave and noble young warrior who sacrifices his life in an effort to rescue his wounded father.

Lavinia

Latinus and Amata's daughter. She is the most sought-after maiden in Latium and has been betrothed to Turnus. Because of certain prophecies, however, her father offers her to Aeneas. This betrothal is the initial cause of the war between the Trojans and Latins. It is indicated in the poem that she and Aeneas do eventually marry, and that Lavinia becomes the mother of his second son, Silvius.

Mezentius

The tryannical king of Etruria; Lausus' father. He is a great warrior and Turnus' ally.

Nisus

A veteran Trojan soldier who is killed in an attempt to carry a message to Aeneas.

Pallas

Evander's son, a brave and gallant young man who becomes one of Aeneas' close friends.

Palinurus

He serves as the helmsman on Aeneas' flagship.

Priam

The aged king of Troy, whom Pyrrhus kills.

Pyrrhus (Neoptolemus)

Achilles' son; he receives Andromache as a war prize.

Sinon

A Greek spy disguised as a deserter; he convinces the Trojans that the enormous wooden horse is an offering to Minerva.

Sychaeus

Prince of Tyre; Dido's husband. After his death, Dido sails to Carthage, prior to the events narrated in the *Aeneid*.

Tarchon

The leader of Aeneas' Etruscan allies.

Teucer

An ancestor of the Trojan royal family; according to legend, he originally came from Crete.

Turnus

Prince of the Rutulians. Because he is betrothed to Lavinia, he becomes Aeneas' chief opponent in Italy.

GODS AND SUPERNATURAL BEINGS

Aeolus

The king of the winds. Juno bribes him to create the storm which scatters the Trojan fleet.

Celaeno

The leader of the Harpies, a band of cruel flying monsters with the bodies of birds and the heads of women; they attack the Trojans.

Charon

The old boatman who ferries dead souls across the River Styx to Hades.

Cupid (Greek: Eros)

The god of love; Venus' son. He is usually portrayed as a young boy. Following his mother's orders, Cupid disguises himself as Ascanius and causes Dido to fall in love with Aeneas.

Cymodoce

The leader of the sea-nymphs whom Jupiter creates from the sacred wood of the Trojan ships.

Deiphobe

The Sybil of Cumae, an old woman with the gift of prophecy who advises Aeneas and guides him to Hades.

Diana (Greek: Artemis)

Goddess of hunting and patron of maidens. Her favorite among the Italians is the female warrior Camilla, whose death she avenges.

Harpies

See Celaeno.

Janus

A native Italian divinity who is usually portrayed with two faces; the doors of his temple must be opened so that the Latin declaration of war can be legalized.

Juno (Greek: Hera)

Jupiter's wife; queen of the gods. Juno is bitterly hostile to the Trojans and Aeneas throughout the *Aeneid.*

Jupiter (also known as Jove; Greek: Zeus)

King of the gods. The other deities, such as Venus and Juno, often interfere in human affairs, but the effects of their interference can usually be explained on purely natural grounds.

Juturna

An Italian forest nymph; Turnus' sister.

Mercury (Greek: Hermes)

The messenger of the gods and the guide for dead souls bound for Hades. It is Mercury who reminds Aeneas that he must leave Dido.

Minerva (Greek: Athena)

Goddess of wisdom, domestic arts, cities, and defensive warfare. The wooden horse which the Greeks use to trick the Trojans is supposed to be an offering to her.

Neptune (Greek: Poseidon)

The god of the sea. He is an old friend of the Trojans and makes their final voyage to Italy a safe one.

Polyphemus

A Cyclops; the one-eyed giant who leads a group of his comrade Cyclopes in an attack on Aeneas and his band when the Trojan ships anchor near Mount Etna.

Venus (Greek: Aphrodite)

Goddess of love; Cupid and Aeneas' mother; Vulcan's wife. Throughout the *Aeneid,* Venus intercedes in mortal affairs in order to aid her son and protect him from Juno's wrath.

Vulcan (Greek: Hephaestus)

God of fire and metal-working; Venus' husband. He has a workshop beneath Mount Etna, an active volcano, where he is assisted by the Cyclopes.

_____ THE *AENEID* _____

BOOK 1

Emulating stylistic details of Homer's *Iliad,* Virgil opens Book I of the *Aeneid* with a sweeping description of Aeneas – a Trojan prince, a valiant warrior, and a national hero of Rome:

> I sing of arms and the man who came of old, a fated wanderer, from the coasts of Troy to Italy and the shores of Lavinium; hard-driven on land and on the deep by the violence of heaven, by reason of cruel Juno's unforgetful anger, and woeful losses in war until he could found a city and carry his gods into Latium; from whom is the Latin race, the lords of Alba, and high-walled Rome.

The poet appeals to the Muse to explain the reasons for Aeneas' struggle so that he might write a clear explanation of the events that led to the establishment of Rome.

He begins by explaining that Juno was scheming against Aeneas because he was destined to found a city that would eventually outstrip her favorite city, Carthage, which is south of Rome, across the sea and on the northern shore of Africa. Other factors, however, in addition to Aeneas' destiny, aroused her wrath, particularly the events of the Trojan War:

> . . . nor had the springs of her anger nor that bitter pain yet gone out of mind: deep stored in her soul lies the judgment of Paris, the insult of her slighted beauty. . . . fired by these also, she drove all over the ocean the Trojan remnant left by the Greek host and merciless Achilles, and held them afar from Latium; and many a year were they wandering, driven by fate around all the seas.

Thus, Virgil links the legends of Homeric lore to the story of Aeneas, who suffers from the spite of a goddess embittered by catastrophic events for which he is blameless.

Like Homer, Virgil begins *in medias res,* in the middle of the story. After long, frustrating years on the Mediterranean, Aeneas and his faithful companion, Achates, find themselves shipwrecked on a foreign shore, following a great storm which Juno persuaded Aeolus to raise. Mindful of his followers' trials since leaving their homeland, Aeneas assuages their sorrowing hearts with a speech:

> O comrades, for not ere now are we ignorant of ill. We have been tried by heavier fortunes, and to these also God will appoint an end. . . . Recall your courage, put sorrow and fear away. This too sometime shall we remember with delight. . . . Keep heart, and endure till prosperous fortune comes.

Led by Aeneas' mother, Venus, who disguises herself as a huntress, Aeneas and Achates reconnoiter and learn that they are near Carthage, a colony still being built, which is ruled by Dido, a widowed queen.

Virgil employs a Homeric simile to describe the colonists as they build Carthage:

> . . . even as bees when summer is fresh over the flowery country ply their task beneath the sun when they lead forth their nation's grown brood, or when they press the liquid honey and strain their cells with nectarous sweets, or relieve the loaded incomers, or in banded array drive the idle herd of drones far from their folds; the hive is aswarm, and the odorous honey smells of thyme.

The two castaways, Aeneas and Achates, whom Venus enshrouds in a cloud of invisibility, are suddenly stricken with melancholy when they notice that the wall paintings on Dido's temple depict scenes from the Trojan War.

Later (much like Odysseus' entrance into Alcinous' palace, in the *Odyssey*), Aeneas' captains from his lost ships are ushered in and receive hospitality from the beautiful queen. At this point, the spell is broken and Aeneas becomes visible to Dido and her subjects:

> Aeneas stood discovered in a sheen of brilliant light, like a god in face and shoulders; for his mother's self had shed on her son, the grace of clustered locks, the radiant light of youth, and the luster of joyous eyes; as when ivory takes beauty under the artist's hand, or when silver or white stone from Paros is inlaid with gold.

Aeneas introduces himself to the astonished queen, and she invites the famed hero to a royal banquet in the Trojans' honor.

When Aeneas sends to the ship for suitable gifts and for his son, Iulus (Ascanius), so that he can introduce the boy to Queen Dido, Venus tricks Aeneas and disguises Cupid as Iulus. Employing his ready arrows, Cupid inflicts Dido with a "living love in the long-since-unstirred spirit and disaccustomed heart." To hold Aeneas as long as possible at her table, Dido asks him to recount the story of Troy's destruction and his wanderings in the intervening seven years.

BOOK 2

Aeneas hesitates before complying with the queen's wishes. To explain his reluctance to revive old memories, he says: ". . . though my spirit shudders at the remembrance and recoils in pain, I will try." A hush falls over the guests as he recounts the holocaust that ended the Trojan War. An eyewitness to the arrival of the treacherous wooden horse, a gift to the goddess Minerva, Aeneas recalls how the sole dissenter, Laocoön, Neptune's priest, along with his two sons, was punished for hurling a spear into the side of the enormous wooden horse:

> . . . over the placid depths (I shudder as I recall) two snakes in enormous coils pressed down the sea and advanced to-gether to the shore; . . . and now twice clasping his waist, twice encircling his neck with their scaly bodies, they towered head and neck above him.

Despite Laocoön's horrible death by strangulation, the people of Troy, instead of rejecting the Trojan Horse as Laocoön recommended, insist that the giant horse be dragged into the city so that they can placate Minerva.

Aeneas receives a warning in a dream from Hector's ghost that a band of Greeks, now hiding within the horse, are about to destroy the city. The ghost gives explicit instructions:

> Ah, fly, goddess-born . . . and rescue yourself from these flames. The foe holds our walls; from her high ridges Troy is toppling down. . . . Troy commends to you her holy ob-jects and household gods; take them to accompany your fate; seek for them a city, which, after all the seas have known your wanderings, you shall at last establish in might.

Unable to save King Priam from Achilles' vengeful son, Pyrrhus (Neoptolemus), or to avert a catastrophe in Troy, Aeneas plunges into the fray.

He suddenly discerns Helen, whom he blames for their misery, cowering near Vesta's altar, and anger overcomes judgment as Aeneas "rises in wrath to avenge [his] dying land and take repayment for her crimes." Before he can complete the act, however, his mother, Venus, appears and stays his hand, reminding him that the Greeks are not to blame; instead, "the gods [are to blame, who] . . . in anger overturn this magnificence and make Troy topple down." To comfort him, she promises to stay close to him during his long voyage.

Aeneas returns home to gird himself for battle, but his wife, Creusa, begs him to defend his family, particularly his little son, Iulus, and his aged father, Anchises: "If you go to die, let us too hurry with you to the end. But if you know any hope to place in arms, be this household your first defense." After receiving an omen from Jupiter in the form of a peal of thunder and a shooting star, Aeneas lifts Anchises to his shoulders, and, leading Iulus by the hand, creeps fearfully through the backstreets on his way out of the city.

In the confusion, Aeneas loses sight of his wife, Creusa, who dies in the chaotic streets; yet she returns to her grieving husband as a spirit, and urging Aeneas to follow divine guidance which will lead him to Italy, she soothes his despair and exhorts him to greatness:

> What help is there in this mad passion of grief, my sweet husband? Not without divine influence does this come to pass—nor may it be, nor does the high lord of Olympus allow, that you should carry Creusa hence in your company. Long shall be your exile, and weary spaces of sea must you plow; yet you shall come to the land Hesperia. . . . There prosperity awaits you, and a kingdom, and a king's daughter for your wife.

Aeneas, reaching for the vanishing shape, mourns her going. Toward daybreak, however, he turns his attention toward the living, a "people gathered for exile, a pitiable crowd," who huddle at the base of Mount Ida. With renewed courage, he sets out with the sacred objects and household gods of Troy toward the safety of the mountains.

BOOK 3

Aeneas and his followers settle in the Phrygian mountains, build a fleet, and set sail the following summer, according to the advice of Anchises. Many are the frustrations of Troy's survivors as they discard several likely locations for a new Troy. They travel from Thrace to the islands of Delos and Crete before the Trojan gods appear to Aeneas in a vision and clarify their destination:

> Prepare a mighty town for a mighty people; do not draw back from the long, wearisome chase. You must change your

dwelling. Nor to these shores did the god at Delos counsel
you, or Apollo bid you find rest in Crete. There is a region
which the Greeks call Hesperia—an ancient land, mighty in
arms. . . . This is our true dwelling place . . .

As they sail up the western coast of Greece, Aeneas and his band
stay briefly on the island of Strophades, near Sparta. There, the
Harpies, fantastic creatures that are half-bird, half-woman, tear food
from the sailors' hands and defile it. Because he fights them off, Aeneas
is cursed by Celaeno, their leader.

Journeying on to Chaonia, near modern-day Actium, Aeneas encounters Andromache, Hector's widow, and Helenus, Andromache's
new husband (a noted Trojan prophet). Overjoyed to meet fellow
countrymen and survivors of the Trojan War, Aeneas learns that
Pyrrhus passed his captive war-bride on to Helenus, who inherited
Chaonia after Pyrrhus' death.

Deprived of news from home, Andromache presses Aeneas with
myriad questions:

How did the winds, how did the fates give passage? Whose
divinity landed you all unwitting on our coasts? What of the
boy Ascanius? . . . does his uncle Hector kindle anything in
him of ancient valor and the pride of manhood?

The happy group enters the gates of the town, admiring how the
king has modeled it after Troy, even naming the brook Xanthus after
a stream in their homeland.

Before journeying on, Aeneas asks Helenus to consult the gods
and advise him on the perils that lie ahead. Helenus, following a con-
sultation with Apollo, announces that there will be long days of
"trackless tracks," but there will be some definite signs to follow:

. . . a great sow shall be discovered lying under an ilexwood
tree on the riverbank, with her newborn litter of thirty . . .
her white brood about her teats. That shall be the place of
the city; there will be the appointed rest from your toils.

Helenus comforts Aeneas concerning the difficulties that lie ahead
and urges him to be faithful to his destiny and to call upon Apollo
in times of distress. He warns Aeneas to try to please Juno by strict
observance of her rites. Pleased with Aeneas' goal to reestablish the

glory of fallen Troy, he urges, ". . . go your way and exalt Troy to heaven by your deeds."

Relying upon Helenus' advice as well as that of Achaemenides, a marooned shipmate of Ulysses, Aeneas escapes the treachery of Scylla and Charybdis, as well as the Cyclopes. The exiled Trojans travel toward Sicily, only a short distance from Italy, and quickly spread their sails to avoid the smoldering volcanoes in the distance. Fate, however, strikes Aeneas unexpectedly: Anchises dies and is mourned as the "solace of my every care and change . . . my sire." At this point, Aeneas pauses in his narration, leaving his audience wordless with emotion.

BOOK 4

Dido, "pierced sore with passion," suffers the pangs of love for her handsome, eloquent visitor. For comfort and advice, she turns to her sister, Anna:

> Were my mind not planted, fixed and immovable, to ally myself to none in wedlock since my first love of old played me false in death, were I not sick to the heart of bridal torch and chamber, to this temptation alone I might haply yield. Anna, I will confess it . . . he only has touched my heart and shaken my soul from its balance.

Anna realizes that Aeneas is no ordinary man and that marriage between him and Dido would "exalt the Punic state." Her advice is practical: make Aeneas welcome, delay his departure until seasonal storms destroy his fleet, and keep him in Carthage for the remainder of the rainy season.

Although devout in his piety toward Troy's gods, Aeneas is distracted from his goal by his liaison with Dido. Juno, who allies herself with Venus in mutual connivance, fans the fires of love to promote a union of the two great powers. She tempts Venus with the prospect of ruling the kingdom of Carthage in an "equal lordship." At the instigation of the two goddesses, Aeneas and Dido take shelter in a cave during a storm:

> Primeval Earth and Juno the bridesmaid give the sign; fires flash out high in air, witnessing the union, and Nymphs cry

aloud on the mountain-top. That day opened the gate of death
and the springs of ill. For now Dido heeds not of eye or
tongue, nor sets her heart on love in secret: she calls it marriage, and with this word shrouds her blame.

Aeneas is now a key element in Dido's plans for her new city. They
live together openly as though they were man and wife.

To return Aeneas' attention to his sacred duty, Jupiter summons
his faithful messenger, Mercury:

Up and away, O son! Call the breezes and slide down them
on your wings. . . . Carry down my words through the fleet
air. Not such a one did his mother most beautiful vouch him
to us, nor for this twice rescue him from Grecian arms; but
he was to rule an Italy teeming with empire and loud with
war, to transmit the line of Teucer's royal blood, and lay all
the world beneath his law.

Mercury arrives at the place where Aeneas is "founding towers and
ordering new dwellings." His message delivered, he vanishes into the
air, leaving Aeneas dumbfounded, but burning with zeal to continue
his original mission.

At first, Aeneas tries to conceal his plans to abandon his lover,
but Dido hears rumors, rages through the city, and confronts Aeneas
with his treachery:

Do you fly from me? Me, who by these tears and your own
hand beseech you, since naught else, alas! Have I kept mine
own – by our union and the marriage rites begun; if I have
done you any grace, or anything of mine was once sweet to
you, – pity our sinking house, and if there yet be room for
prayers, put off this purpose of yours.

Aeneas, on the advice of Jupiter, hardens his heart and reminds Dido
that his first duty is to Troy and his band of followers.

Dido sends Anna to delay Aeneas from his intended voyage, but
to no avail. Dido, wracked by ominous dreams, spews out her anguish
with vile spells and incantations against her lover. She orders that
a great pyre be built from Aeneas' abandoned weapons, personal be-
longings, and an image of Aeneas himself. Decking the room in funeral
garlands, she falls into distraction and realizes that madness controls
her thinking.

At Mercury's prompting, Aeneas sails away from Africa. When dawn breaks, Dido discovers that he is gone and curses him and his offspring:

> Then do you, O [Carthaginians], pursue his seed with your hatred for all ages to come. . . . Let no kindness nor truce be between the nations. Arise, some avenger, out of our dust, to follow the [Trojan] settlers with firebrand and steel . . . shore to shore, wave to water, sword to sword; let their battles go down to their children's children.

Frenzied with frustration and anger, Dido climbs atop the pyre and stabs herself with her lover's sword. Juno sees her soul struggling for release and sends Iris to clip a lock of hair, thereby ending her torment.

BOOK 5

Aeneas and his crew spy the flames of Dido's pyre and, knowing "what women can do in madness," assume the worst. A storm diverts their attention from the queen's fate, however, and soon they are back in King Acestes' kingdom, from which they departed a year earlier. Acestes, whose mother was Trojan, welcomes them back and "comforts their weariness with his friendly store."

During their sojourn in Sicily, Aeneas makes a formal speech announcing his plans to honor Anchises with appropriate funeral games, which reflect another Homeric motif:

> . . . first for swift ships; then whosoever excels in the foot-race, and whosoever confident in strength, comes forward as champion in shot of light arrows, or adventures to join battle with gloves of rawhide; let all be here, and let merit look for the prize and palm.

An omen blesses Aeneas' libation when a snake, in seven coils, slithers out of the temple, tastes the offerings of wine, blood, and milk, and returns harmlessly to its lair.

Stirred by Iris, Juno's messenger, a group of female dissenters among the Trojan party, caught up in mourning for Anchises, falls into a manic state. Beroe, an aged matron, laments their homelessness:

> Ah, wretched we. . . . The seventh summer now rolls on

since Troy's overthrow, while we pass measuring out by so
many stars the harborless rocks over every water and land,
pursuing all the while over the vast sea an Italy that flies
[from] us . . .

Pyrgo, nursemaid to Priam's royal children, realizes that a divine
power has possession of Beroe, but is unable to stop the overwrought
mourners from violence. They gather branches and build a raging fire
on the sacred altars which quickly spreads to the fleet. Ascanius
notices their "strange madness" and calls the Trojans' attention to the
conflagration. The men halt their participation in the games and hurry
to extinguish the flames. The women, repentant of their frenzy, slink
into the woods in shame. Aeneas loses four ships before Jupiter sends
a rainstorm to douse the blaze.

Embittered by his loss, Aeneas reveals signs of stress in his dismay
and teeters on the brink of abandoning his noble mission. Nautes,
an old Trojan noted for his oratory, comforts his leader with a sensible
suggestion: "Choose the old men stricken in years, and the matrons
sick of the sea, and all who are weak and fearful of peril in your company." Anchises appears to Aeneas that same night and urges him to
take Nautes' advice and renew his expedition with only the hardiest
members of his band.

Aeneas rededicates himself to the task and proclaims a nine-day
feast in honor of Venus. The goddess, fearful that her son will again
run afoul of Juno's anger, begs Neptune to intercede:

It is not enough that her accursed hatred has devoured the
Phrygian city from among the people and dragged the remnant of Troy through every punishment; still she pursues the
bones and ashes of her victims. . . . Let the remnant, I beseech you, give their sails to your safekeeping across the
seas . . .

The sea god promises that the last stretch of Aeneas' voyage will be
uneventful, but that one life must be sacrificed in payment.

Relieved of his most pressing concern, Aeneas rejoices, giving little
thought to Jupiter's last words. The Trojan men prepare their fleet,
hoist their sails, and, meeting with auspicious weather, speed on their
way. During the night, the god of sleep overcomes the helmsman,
Palinurus; he falls overboard and cries in vain for his companions.
No one comes to his rescue, but Aeneas awakens as the ship sails

too close to the Sirens' rocks and realizes that the pilot has drowned. He himself takes the helm as the remaining ships of his fleet cross the Tyrrhenian Sea to Latium.

BOOK 6

Weeping for Palinurus, Aeneas finally arrives in Italy, near Cumae, where he immediately locates the Sybil's cave in the side of a cliff. The raging prophetess, her hair streaming in wild disarray, greets Aeneas by name. His companions shiver with dread as Aeneas confesses his need, begging her to commit her answer to words rather than write them on leaves (as is her usual fashion) lest the wind scatter them.

Maddened by Apollo's godly presence within her human frame, the Sybil utters a divine message, which echoes from the hundred portals of her dwelling:

> O you for whom the great perils of the sea are at last over, though heavier [perils] yet by land await you; the [Trojans] shall come to the realm of Lavinium. . . . relieve your heart of this care; but they shall not have joy of their coming. Wars, grim wars I discern, and the Tiber afoam with streams of blood.

Aeneas, undaunted by the terrifying supernatural spell which grips the prophetess, begs her to divulge the secret path to the underworld, where he must travel in order to seek advice from his father's spirit.

Following the directions of the Cumaean Sybil, who tries to dissuade Aeneas from so fearful a journey, Aeneas and his faithful companion, Achates, search throughout the forest for a golden bough, the magic wand which will enable Aeneas to enter Hades safely. Two doves, sent by Aeneas' mother, guide him to the ilex grove, where the golden bough grows. Aeneas completes the complicated rites that the Sybil has outlined and, led by the prophetess herself, he enters a chasm in the earth and follows the gloomy pathway. At the River Styx,

> Charon, the dread ferryman, guards these flowing streams, ragged and awful, his chin covered with untrimmed masses of hoary hair, and his eyes a steady flame; from his shoulders

hangs a soiled raiment. Himself he plies the pole and trims
the sails of his vessel, the steel-blue galley with its freight of
dead . . .

On the opposite shore, the forbidden reaches are filled with the souls
of old friends and acquaintances, including Palinurus, many warriors
who died in the Trojan War, and Queen Dido, who turns her back
on her former lover.

Beyond the grim parts of Hades lies Elysium, or the Fields of the
Blessed, where departed spirits enjoy earthly sunlight and starlight,
exercise on the green, dance, sing, and make music. Anchises, catching
sight of his son, hurries forward, his hands outstretched. Tearfully
he cries out:

Have you come at last? And has your love, child of my desire,
conquered the difficult road? . . . What lands, what space of
seas have you traversed to reach me, through what surge of
perils, O my son!

Although Aeneas is unable to embrace his father's disembodied form,
they sit in a sheltered spot and observe the movements of the other
spirits.

Aeneas observes the process by which former beings drink from
the River Lethe, forget the past, and assume new identities. Anchises
points out those who will one day lead Rome to greatness—Silvius,
Romulus, Numa, Tarquinius, Brutus, Cato, the Gracchi, Scipio, Julius
Caesar, and his nephew, Augustus Caesar, "a god's son, who shall again
establish the ages of gold in Latium over the fields that once were
the realm of Saturn . . ."

Aeneas asks about one outstandingly beautiful spirit around
whose head flutters a dark cloud. Anchises sadly replies that it is
Marcellus, who is promised an ill fate:

O my son, ask not of the great sorrow of your people. Him
shall fate but show briefly to earth, and suffer not to stay
further. . . . Alas his goodness, alas his antique honor and
right hand invincible in war! . . . Ah poor boy! if you can
break the grim bar of fate, you shall be Marcellus.

On his way back to the surface of earth, Aeneas is again eager to
launch his expedition and complete the task he undertook on the night
that Troy fell. Anchises ushers his son to the twin gates of Sleep,

where Aeneas exits by the ivory gate and returns to his ship and his comrades.

BOOK 7

Skirting the shores of Circe's realm, where Odysseus met his greatest hindrance, Aeneas goes ashore at the Tiber River in Latium and sets up camp. At this point, Virgil interrupts his narration to re-invoke Erato, the muse of lyric poetry, to help him relate the history of ancient Latium. The poet notes that old Latinus, a descendant of Saturn, rules the kingdom and searches for an appropriate husband for his daughter, Lavinia. Omens and prophecies warn Latinus that a stranger will come, bringing a conquering army. A wonderful vision reveals that Lavinia will know glory, fame, and fortune, but that Latium must endure a great war.

Disturbed by the seriousness of these portents, Latinus sacrifices a hundred sheep in payment for information from the oracle. The reply is immediate and unambiguous:

> Seek not, O my child, to unite your daughter in Latin es-
> pousals, nor trust her to the bridal chambers ready to your
> hand; foreigners shall come to be your sons, whose blood shall
> raise our name to heaven, and the children of whose race
> shall see where the circling sun looks on either ocean, all the
> rolling world swayed beneath their feet.

When Latinus returns home with an answer to his quandary, he hears a rumor that Trojan ships are already beached on the river bank.

At Jupiter's command, Aeneas spreads a feast under a tree, where a favorable omen blesses his arrival. Aeneas is overjoyed that he has at last found the promised site of the new Troy. He dispatches his companions to explore the countryside and learn what people live in the nearby town. Before he sets out from the spot, he performs the ritual offering to Jupiter and makes obeisance to Earth, as well as to its nymphs, its rivers, and to Night. Jupiter acknowledges Aeneas' piety with a three-fold thunderclap. Elated by the heavenly blessing, the Trojans renew their feasting, adorning their chalices with cere-monial garlands.

After sending a hundred messengers to the local authority, Aeneas outlines the first Trojan settlement in Italy with a shallow trench. While he works, his envoys are successful in establishing good relations with King Latinus, who welcomes them to his stately palace. Having settled himself on the ancestral throne, Latinus asks formal questions of his visitors:

> What seek you? What is the cause or whereof the need that has borne you over all these blue waterways to the Ausonian shore? Whether wandering in your course, or tempest-driven ... you have entered the river and lie in harbor; shun not our welcome ...

Ilioneus, Aeneas' chosen spokesman, replies that their arrival is not an accident but by the design of Jupiter, founder of Troy's royal line. Latinus realizes that the Trojans' leader is the foreign son-in-law prophesied by the oracle and offers Princess Lavinia as a wife for Aeneas.

Juno, foiled in her attempts to forestall the founding of Rome, unleashes Allecto, a belligerent spirit that stirs up rancor between Latinus and Queen Amata:

> At her the goddess flings a snake out of her dusky tresses, and slips it into her bosom to her very inmost heart, that she may embroil all her house under its maddening magic. Sliding between her raiment and smooth breasts, it coils without touch, and instils its viperous breath unseen ...

Amata reminds her husband that Lavinia is promised to Turnus, his kinsman and a fellow member of the royal line. Because Latinus is unmoved by her words, Amata flings herself into a Bacchic orgy, calling the women of Latium to follow her example.

Allecto stirs up enmity between the local chiefs and the interlopers; then, in a symbolic gesture, Juno swings open the doors of the temple of Janus, a sign that war has been declared. Led by Turnus, Lavinia's former suitor, the Latin faction joins forces with several neighboring tribes, among them such warriors as Mezentius and Camilla, both known for their military prowess.

BOOK 8

Local opposition continues to grow against the Trojans after Turnus girds himself for war, thereby setting an example. Aeneas is distressed by the mounting hostility until he receives advice from the god of the Tiber River in a dream:

An Arcadian people sprung of Pallas, following in their king
Evander's company beneath his banners, have chosen a place
in these coasts and have set a city on the hills. . . . These wage
perpetual war with the Latin race; take these to your camp
as allies and join with them in league.

As Aeneas sets out in a skiff the next morning, his rowers pass
the milk-white sow that Helenus prophesied. Buoyed by the good
omen, Aeneas' party continues up the Tiber to Evander's realm, where
Evander receives them warmly and prepares a feast in their honor.

Evander, like Aeneas, a pious man, meticulously follows the pre-
scribed ceremonies honoring the ancient gods. He concludes the rite
with a general call to worship:

Wherefore arise, O men, and . . . enwreathe your hair with
leafy sprays and stretch forth the cups in your hands; call
on our common god and pour wine in good cheer.

He narrates the noble history of his kingdom, taking great pride in
its accomplishments. Evander, although poor, is eager to join Aeneas
in conflict against the Latins, who have usurped his place and cast
him from his rightful inheritance.

After the two warriors reach an agreement, Venus, like Thetis
in the *Iliad,* worries that Aeneas will come to harm, and so she takes
immediate action to protect him. With tears, poignant words, and
alluring embrace, she wheedles a new suit of armor from her com-
pliant husband, Vulcan, who hurries to a volcanic island near Sicily.
There, beneath Mount Etna in the vaulted cave that houses his forge,
he halts the Cyclopes from their appointed tasks and sets them to work
making armor for Aeneas. Turning the molten material with their
tongs, they pound rhythmically on the giant anvil with mighty strokes:

Brass and ore of gold flow in streams, and wounding steel
is molten in the vast furnace. They shape a mighty shield,
to receive singly all the weapons of the Latins and weld it
sevenfold, circle on circle.

Repeated flashes of lightning in the clear sky interrupt Evander and
Aeneas' conversation. Looking heavenward, where the new armor
appears, Aeneas recognizes his mother's summons, and he reassures
Evander that Venus has given the sign of victory for their endeavor.

The cavalry then parades through open gates, Aeneas and "trusty

Achates" in the vanguard. With a clatter, they advance on their horses
to the camp, where Venus, beneath a sheltering oak tree, formally
presents the armor. Aeneas is gladdened by the "magnificence of the
goddess' gift," which he turns over, piece by piece, in his hands:

> . . . the helmet, dread with plumes and spouting flame, the
> death-dealing sword, the stiff corslet of brass . . . then the
> smooth greaves of electrum and refined gold, the spear, and
> the shield's ineffable design.

Reminiscent of Achilles' new armor in the *Iliad,* the shield is richly
decorated with scenes depicting the "story of Italy and the triumphs
of the Romans . . ." Beginning with Romulus and Remus, frolicking
beside the she-wolf that suckled them, the tableau covers the glory
of "Ascanius' future seed and their wars fought one after one."

Many scenes depict great men of Virgil's generation, such as Julius
Caesar, triumphantly entering Rome; Augustus Caesar, leading his
fleet at the Battle of Actium; Mark Antony, joining forces with Cleopatra; and General Agrippa, terrible to behold in his full armor.
Admiring the magnificence of his new shield, Aeneas shoulders it and
rejoices in the future greatness of his offspring.

BOOK 9

Juno dispatches Iris with a message for Turnus. Iris informs him
that Aeneas has left his comrades in camp and is marching toward
Evander's city, collecting troops of Lydian farmers along the way. Iris
spurs Turnus to action: "Why hesitate? Now! Now is the time to call
for a chariot and horses. Break through all hindrances and seize the
bewildered camp."

Turnus recognizes the divine messenger and promises immediate
action. The Trojans, who are working outside the enclosure, spy the
dust of Turnus' army and hasten inside the safety of their walls as
Aeneas instructed them. With a challenge to his own men, Turnus,
at the head of twenty select horsemen, hurls a threatening javelin and
leads the initial assault.

Turnus then rides furiously around the walls in search of an
entrance:

> And as a wolf prowling about some crowded sheepfold, when,
> beaten sore of winds and rains, he howls at the pens by mid-

night; safe beneath their mothers the lambs keep bleating on;
he, savage and insatiate, rages in anger against the flock he
cannot reach, tired by a long-gathering madness for food and
a throat unslaked with blood . . .

Enraged with frustration, Turnus calls for torches and leads his men
against the Trojans.

Soon the sky is filled with clouds of glowing ash, but Jupiter,
according to an ancient covenant, protects the ships from destruction. He changes them into sea maidens, and, dolphinlike, they dive
into the water and swim away. At this point, Turnus realizes that the
Trojans have no hope of flight, having lost their only method of escape.
Boasting of his own destiny, he rallies his men and plots a new charge
against the Trojan camp.

During the night, Nisus, a seasoned veteran of about thirty, and
his comrade, Euryalus, a handsome, raw recruit, guard the Trojan
gates. Nisus discusses his dream of performing great deeds, and
Euryalus immediately volunteers to go with him and carry a message
to Aeneas. At a late-night council, the Trojan captains consider the
daring patriotism of the two close friends. Iulus exhorts them to "recall
my father; give him back to sight; all sorrow disappears in his re-
covery." Promising war trophies, including Turnus' horse and armor,
twelve captured women, land, and gold, Iulus vows lifelong gratitude
if they succeed in reaching Aeneas.

Although Nisus and Euryalus evade the enemy's lookouts in the
shadow of night and slay unsuspecting guards in their path, the two
messengers meet up with a cavalry patrol, which catches sight of
Euryalus' glimmering helmet, which he captured from a fallen enemy
soldier. The two Trojans are surrounded.

Euryalus is captured, but Nisus manages to escape. He returns to
assist his young companion, but before Nisus can stop the slaughter,
Euryalus falls dead, Volcens' sword thrust through his ribs. Nisus,
true to a comrade, dispatches the killer with a vengeance, but is fatally
wounded himself and falls on his comrade's corpse, a victim of multiple stab wounds.

Making the most of the late-night foray, Turnus marshals his
leaders and, bearing the heads of Euryalus and Nisus on raised spear-
heads, he mounts a parade around the Trojan camp. The grisly sight
unnerves the Trojan spectators. Like the victims' wives and mothers

in the *Iliad,* Euryalus' mother collapses and shrieks her grief, bewailing the loss of her brave young son.

Turnus leads a renewed assault on the Trojan camp, but it is unsuccessful, and all the Latins except Turnus are killed. At one point, cornered within the Trojan fortification,

> . . . even Turnus draws lingeringly backward, with unhastened steps, and soul boiling in anger. Nay, twice even did he then charge amid the enemy, twice drove them in flying rout along the walls.

Jupiter sends Iris, the messenger goddess, with orders for Turnus to withdraw, but pushed to the limit of his strength, he fights valiantly. Finally, in a desperate measure, he leaps fully armed into the Tiber and swims to safety, where his comrades greet him with shouts of victory.

BOOK 10

Meanwhile, the gods hold a council on Mount Olympus, another Homeric touch. Jupiter begins the session:

> I forbade Italy to join battle with the [Trojans]; why this quarrel in the face of my injunction? . . . The due time of battle will arrive, call it not forth, when furious Carthage shall one day sunder the Alps to hurl ruin full on the towers of Rome . . . now let them be and cheerfully join in the treaty we ordain.

Venus, quick to speak in behalf of her son and his followers, details the desperate situation in which the Trojans find themselves. Leaderless, she emphasizes, they battle in trenches awash with blood. She begs for mercy, reminding Jupiter that the Trojans have endured enough warfare in the past.

Quick to retort with equal passion, Juno takes the opposing viewpoint, asserting her opinion that Aeneas deliberately provoked war in Italy. In answer to Venus' complaint about the miseries of the Trojan War, Juno alludes to the Trojan abduction of Helen, which launched the ten-year battle between Troy and Greece. Sneering at Venus' motherly concern, Juno reminds her that she pleads too late for Aeneas' safety.

Murmurs rise in behalf of both speakers. Jupiter, however, puts an end to the discussion:

Take then to heart and lay deep these words of mine . . . your
quarrel finds no term today; what fortune each wins, what
hope each follows, be he Trojan or [Latin], I will hold in even
poise . . . Jupiter is one and king over all; the fates will find
their way.

With an assenting nod from Pluto, his brother who rules the underworld, Jupiter rises from his throne and makes a royal exit, thereby
ending all further debate in the matter.

On the plain below, the bloody siege continues. Aeneas, sailing
his craft back to the Trojan fortress, encounters the nymphs which
were once Trojan ships. Their spokesperson, Cymodoce, informs him
of the dire situation which his comrades face and urges him to hurry
to their aid. Providing him with suitable escort, she pushes his boat
through the water.

The sight of Aeneas' officers, standing fully armed in formation
as they approach the encampment, cheers their beleaguered comrades:

> . . . looking back they see the ships steering for the beach,
> and all the sea as a single fleet sailing in. His helmet-spike
> blazes, flame pours from the cresting plumes, and the golden
> shield-boss spouts floods of fire . . .

They raise a shout and redouble their efforts against Turnus, who
mounts an attack against the Trojan fleet. Aeneas, piloting thirty ships
alongside his newfound ally, Tarchon, exhorts his men to row valiantly
to the beach. Tarchon's ship, however, strikes a shoal and breaks up.
His men run afoul of the entangling wreckage and drown in the
ebb tide.

With Aeneas' return, the war moves from siege to pitched battle.
Turnus, eager to punish Evander for joining forces with the Trojans,
attacks Pallas, Evander's son. Like a lion scouting a bull, he races
toward his prey, but Pallas wounds Turnus with his spear. Turnus'
answering blow pierces Pallas' shield and rips a gaping hole in the
boy's chest. Turnus stands over the cooling body and feeds his vengeful spirit with boasting words.

Aeneas, in turn, kills Mezentius' son, Lausus, piercing the golden
tunic that the boy's mother made for him and ripping open his chest.
In contrast to the vaunting Turnus, Aeneas suffers immediate regret
for killing the poor boy. Wishing that he could restore Lausus to his

parents, Aeneas lifts the young boy's body in his arms, soaking himself and the boy's well-combed hair with blood.

Mezentius, resting beside the Tiber and rinsing his wounds, calls for his son. His comrades bear the body to him on Lausus' armor. Mezentius cries aloud for his fallen son, bewailing the bitterness of war. Then he returns to the fray, seeking Aeneas alone to redress his grievance. Aeneas calls on Apollo, and with his spear ready, he meets Mezentius in single combat and kills both him and his horse. Before Mezentius dies, he, like Hector in the *Iliad,* begs for an honorable burial for himself and his son.

BOOK 11

Aeneas repays the gods for his victory, raising an oak limb on a ceremonial mound and arraying it with Mezentius' captured armament. He cheers his men with well-chosen words:

> The greatest deed is done, O men; be all fear gone for what
> remains . . . meanwhile let us commit to earth the unburied
> bodies of our comrades, since deep in Acheron this honor is
> left alone.

Overwhelmed with sorrow for young Pallas, Aeneas, like Homer's Achilles, concerns himself now with the rites of burial. He pledges to avenge the boy's death and dresses the body in purple and gold to make it more presentable for Evander. Drances, a Latin chieftain, requests a truce so that both sides may bury their dead. Aeneas agrees.

When Evander approaches his son's body, he throws himself on it, crying piteously. Evander regrets that he himself still lives, but he does not blame the Trojans for his son's untimely death. He turns to them with a single heartfelt mandate:

> . . . Turnus is the debt you see son and father claim: for your
> virtue and your fortune this scope alone is left. I ask not joy
> in life; I may not. Now must I carry my son deep into the
> underworld.

At dawn, Aeneas and Tarchon pile high the funeral pyres with their slain comrades. They stand transfixed by the flames and "cannot tear themselves away till dewy Night wheels on the star-spangled glittering sky." On the opposing side, the Latins do likewise.

Dissension spreads among the Latins. Led by Drances, they call for a duel between Turnus and Aeneas to end the carnage. Heavy with grief, Latinus emerges from retirement and exhorts his people to make peace:

> We wage an ill-timed war, fellow-citizens, with a divine race, invincible and unbroken in battle, who brook not even when conquered to drop the sword . . . let us name fair terms of treaty and invite [the Trojans] as allies to our realm; let them settle, if they desire it so, and found a city.

Echoing Latinus' sentiments, Drances, ever jealous of Turnus' popularity, suggests that Turnus face Aeneas in single combat.

Turnus, in an impassioned speech to his allies, makes a heated reply to his rival:

> Are we going to meet them? Why linger? Will your bravery ever be in that windy tongue and those timorous feet? . . . If I only am claimed by the [Trojans] for combat, if that is your pleasure, and I am the barrier to the public good, victory does not so hate and shun my hands that I should renounce any enterprise for so great a hope. I will meet him in courage, though he outmatches great Achilles and wears arms forged by Vulcan's hands.

The assembly is halted abruptly when a messenger warns that the Trojans are mounting a new attack. Boys and women ring the walls as Turnus takes charge of the harried Latins.

Turnus meets Camilla at the city gates. She pledges that her cavalry will engage Aeneas' cavalry. Grateful for her courage, Turnus proclaims her a captain and plots to cut off the advancing Trojan force by blocking the gorge on the highroad. The plan fails after Tarchon's forces defeat Camilla's cavalry. Climactically, Arruns sends his weapon deep into Camilla's breast; in vain, she tugs at it and, with her dying words, sends Acca, her comrade in arms, to find Turnus so that he can replace her.

After Camilla's death, the nymph Opis, aggrieved at her loss and promising everlasting fame, avenges her. Seeking out Camilla's killer, Opis chooses "Diana's weapons" as an appropriate end:

> [She] slid out a fleet arrow from her gilded quiver, and stretched it level on the bow. At once and in a moment,

Arruns heard the whistle of the dart and resounding air, as the steel sank in his body.

His comrades, pressed by the advancing enemy, leave him forgotten in the dust as Opis flies back to heaven. The Latins retreat in confusion, and Turnus, mindful of his perilous position, awaits the dawn when he will meet Aeneas in single combat.

BOOK 12

Buoyed by passions of war, Turnus faces his men with renewed courage. He issues a challenge to his adversary and announces that the winner of their duel will receive the hand of Lavinia. Latinus warns him that he is being foolhardy and suggests that he consider other unmarried maidens of high birth as potential brides. Latinus blames himself for initiating the conflict between Turnus and Aeneas when he broke earlier vows and offered Lavinia to Aeneas as a bride.

Queen Amata, realizing the danger that stalks Turnus, clings to him and pleads with him to avoid conflict with the Trojans. Turnus asks her not to weep for him and sends his final terms to Aeneas. Incensed with the challenge that faces him, Turnus readies himself for battle, brandishing his spear and cursing his adversary.

Aeneas, too, arms himself with the equipment that his mother commissioned from Vulcan and rejoices that this last encounter will end the war. With a few last-minute instructions to his comrades and a word of farewell for Iulus, he approaches the site of the duel. On each side, brightly clad warriors await the contest. Women and old men crowd the battlements, the gateway, and the rooftops so that they can watch Aeneas fight Turnus.

Unable to accept the fated outcome, Juno watches from Mount Alban. Then she hurries to Juturna, Turnus' sister, and plants an ill-conceived idea in her mind. Warning that she has no power to save Turnus from his destiny, Juno exhorts Juturna to "hasten and snatch thy brother, if it may be, from his death . . ." Then, leaving Turnus' fearful sister to execute her command, Juno departs.

As Latinus and Aeneas ride forth in pomp as representatives of their respective realms, all eyes watch the colorful display. Approaching the sacred altar, Iulus assists in the sacrifice. At sunrise, Aeneas draws his sword and pledges that if he loses, Iulus will withdraw from Latium; but if Aeneas triumphs over Turnus, Italians and Trojans shall rule jointly over the land as one nation and live under equal law. Latinus completes the compact with a solemn vow.

Following Juno's command, Juturna sows seeds of discord, spreading a rumor that should the Trojans win the contest, they would leave the Latins no honor. She also causes an omen to appear: an eagle, Jupiter's sacred bird, suddenly swoops down on a swan. It drops its prey, however, when the other birds join forces and attack. At Juturna's urging, one of the Latins breaks the truce by casting a spear toward the Trojan side. Hostilities resume between the opposing armies, and bloodshed on both sides soon reaches greater heights than ever before.

Aeneas, struck by a stray arrow, withdraws to the rear, leaving Turnus and his men to wreak havoc on the Trojan forces. Venus heals Aeneas' wound, and, in the absence of the local militia, Aeneas captures the undefended town of Laurentum. Queen Amata, alarmed by the turn of events, fears the worst and, fashioning a noose out of strips torn from her robe, hangs herself from an overhead beam.

Turnus orders Juturna to leave him to his fate, and once more, he challenges Aeneas to single combat. In fairness to the Trojans, Jupiter orders Juno to cease her interference in the contest, but he grants one concession to her – that the combined peoples of the new nation that results from this contest will not be known as "the Trojan nation."

The two heroes then face off before the assembled hosts. In vain, Turnus makes a final gesture of bravado and hurls a huge stone at Aeneas. Then, much like Achilles besting Hector in the *Iliad,* Aeneas defeats and slaughters Turnus:

> Carrying grim death with it, the spear flies in fashion of some dark whirlwind and opens the rim of the corslet and the utmost circles of the sevenfold shield. Right through the thigh it passes, hurtling on; under the blow, Turnus falls huge to the earth, his leg doubled under him.

Aeneas gazes on his wounded enemy and flies into a rage when he sees Turnus' sword-belt, which once belonged to Pallas, Evander's son. His fury renewed, Aeneas delivers the death blow, sending Turnus' spirit into the underworld.

For a more comprehensive, in-depth analysis of this work, consult Cliffs Notes on the *Aeneid.*

ECLOGUES, OR *BUCOLICS*

Virgil's *Eclogues* provide ten brief, idealized glimpses of rustic life. In **Eclogue 1,** two shepherds, Meliboeus and Tityrus, discuss their once-peaceful rural life, a way of life which has been changed by recent political upheavals. Meliboeus has been evicted from his farm, which is now enjoyed and managed by a veteran of the civil wars. Tityrus, however, has managed to retain his land, and he praises young Octavian for granting him retainership. In this poem, great joy and deep sorrow are evident – even in simple lives. Clearly, the depths and heights of emotion are not reserved for only the elite.

Eclogue 2 examines a different type of conflict – the shepherd Corydon's futile pursuit of a slave boy, "the fair Alexis, his master's darling." Corydon yearns for Alexis, but his overtures are not returned. Thus, he reaches a pragmatic conclusion: if the handsome Alexis continues to spurn him, he will console himself with work, and he will "find another Alexis." Now, he will put his mind to other things; he will seek simple tasks, such as weaving rushes or willow boughs.

Eclogue 3 begins by describing a genial teasing between two shepherds; then it focuses on a full-blown argument between the two young men concerning their respective singing abilities. This, in turn, leads to a singing contest. Their songs are about the gods, love's joys, and love's puzzlements, as individual men and women experience them.

In contrast, **Eclogue 4** is the most enigmatic of Virgil's eclogues. It looks not at individuals per se, but at the nation itself; it also looks forward to a new era – an age of national peace, heralded by the birth of a boy, "in whom the iron race shall begin to cease, and the golden to arise over all the world . . ." When this era begins, the snake shall die, "the plain shall grow golden with soft corn spikes, the reddening grape will trail from the wild briar, and hard oaks shall drip the dew of honey."

In **Eclogue 5,** two shepherds, Menalcas and Mopsus, enjoy the shade, reciting pastoral poems about the death of Daphnis, a "forester, known from here even to the heavens, keeper of a fair flock . . ." In tribute to the idealized, rustic Daphnis, Melancas sings: ". . . while bees shall feed on thyme and grasshoppers on dew, ever shall your honor, your name and praise endure." Clearly, the portrait of Daphnis is that of an ideal man at peace with himself and with his place (albeit humble) in the universe.

Eclogue 6 is filled with many images of fauns and divine beings of standard pastoral lore. Two shepherds discover Silenus, an aging satyr-attendant of Dionysus, "asleep in a cavern, his veins swollen as ever with the wine of yesterday." They force him to sing. Most critics believe that in the character of Silenus, Virgil was describing his teacher, Siro.

In **Eclogue 7,** the shepherds Corydon and Thyrsis engage in a singing contest, lauding the pasture greenery, as well as the myrtle, hazel, ash and bay trees, the poplars and the firs, and the "mossed springs and grass, softer than sleep, and green arbutus that covers you with thin shade . . ."

Eclogue 8, subtitled "The Sorceress," focuses on yet another singing contest. Here, we have typical nuptial verses: "Scatter nuts, O bridegroom; for you, the Evening Star leaves Oeta forlorn." The sorceress mentioned in the subtitle lures the handsome Daphnis home, away from the city and back to the country by means of a magic image formed of wax and clay, potent herbs, and a ritual involving ashes flung over the shoulder.

Eclogue 9 deals with the seizure of farmland in Mantua. Two rural fellows, Lycidas and Moeris, dedicate their verses to the poet Varus, and they sing in order to lighten their worries.

Eclogue 10 is sung in honor of the poet Gallus; Virgil rounds out the volume with ebullient optimism: *"Omnia vincit Amor!"* (Love conquers all.) In other words, "Let us yield to Love!" A shepherdly benediction concludes the verse: "Go home full-fed; the Evening Star comes. Go, my she-goats."

GEORGICS

Book 1 opens with paeans and prayers to Jove, Ceres, Liber, Dryads, Fauns, and other supernatural beings whom Virgil credits with governing nature. The poet describes the joys of farming, and as he contemplates his cornfield, he recalls:

In early spring, when chilly moisture trickles from the hoar hills and the crumbling clod thaws in the west wind, even then would I have the bull begin to groan over the deep-driven plow and the blade glitter with polish of the furrow. That field at last replies to the greedy farmer's prayers, which has twice felt the sun, twice the frost, and bursts his granaries with overflowing harvests.

Then breaking off from his lyrical contemplation, Virgil turns his attention to wise husbandry, or thrifty farm management. Noting the importance of the wind, the sky, and the soil conditions for successful farming, he organizes proper farm management by the seasons – beginning with winter, when the "rich floor of the earth" should be turned with the plow.

Virgil makes practical suggestions, particularly about the use of cover crops such as peas, vetch, and lupin; crop rotation; soil enhancement with manure and wood ash; and the burning of fallow fields. He comments that this is hard work, but that hard work was ordained by Jove:

He it was who gave the black snake his venom, taught the wolves to prey, and the sea to be tossed, who shook the honey from the leaves and took fire away, and stopped the brooks that ran wandering with wine: that so practice and pondering might slowly forge out many an art, might seek the corn-blade in the furrow and strike hidden fire from the veins of flint.

Hard work is part of the divine plan for man, Virgil says. Thus, he exhorts the farmer to harden himself to backbreaking labor – to "harass the weeds with ceaseless mattock and frighten off the birds with clamor . . ." Such devotion and commitment to hard work will produce a proud harvest. Throughout this work, Virgil stresses the dignity of hard work and the maxim that "work conquers all."

Laced among the broader themes of farm management are timely hints that may save the farmer effort and costly mistakes. Watch out, he warns, for mice and moles in the granary, toads in crevices, and vermin that live underground. Watch out, too, he says, for signs and omens in nature: the productivity of corn, for example, can be accurately predicted by the status of the walnut tree. Most important, he advises, planting should be done according to heavenly signs: ". . .

the setting Bear-warden will send you no uncertain sign: begin, and carry your sowing on to the mid-frost." Virgil also urges prudent time management. When bad weather keeps a farmer indoors, he should turn his hand to small tasks, such as the care and sharpening of his equipment, marking his stock, and stamping grain bags.

Virgil cautions the farmer to make the most of each day by paying close attention to the weather:

> If indeed you will regard the hastening sun and the moon's ordered sequences, never will an hour of the morrow deceive you, nor will you be taken in the wiles of a cloudless night.

He affirms his belief in forecasting according to signs and weather lore, and he offers historic evidence. The sun, he maintains, is always true; he insists that the sun took pity on Julius Caesar after his assassination by eclipsing itself, veiling itself in "dim rusty red." Moved by his long, horror-filled list of cosmic clashings, Virgil breaks off to pray that God will "forbid not at least that this our youthful prince [Augustus Caesar] may succor a ruined world!"

Book 2 turns from grain crops to the management of vineyards, woodlands, and olive groves. First, Virgil sings an invocation to Bacchus (god of wine), whom he thanks for sowing trees along the plains and rivers. He mentions his favorite varieties of trees – willow, poplar, oak, chestnut, elm, cherry, and bay. These trees, he contends, are a gift of Nature: ". . . in these wear their green all the tribes of forest and underwood and sacred grove." He forces himself to end his paean with a reminder: "The earth is in hand: I will not keep thee here in mazes and long-drawn preludes of fabulous song."

He then turns to the proper care of trees, which require grafting, transplanting, training, and suckering. He lists different varieties of trees by name, noting which bear best in light or heavy soils. He says that olive trees thrive in "stubborn soils and ungracious hills"; corn, however, does well only in black, crumbly loam. To test soil for poor consistency, he advises: ". . . when tossed from hand to hand, it never crumbles, but grows sticky like pitch on the fingers in the handling." To prevent cold from harming tender cuttings, he suggests turning the northerly fields first before transplanting slips. Flat land, he says, may be thickly planted, but knolls and slopes require wider spacing.

To improve yields, Virgil suggests working manure deeply into the furrows. Then, he says, add "porous stone or rough shells, for through them rains will trickle and thin vapor ascend, and the plants take courage . . ." Banking each stalk and supporting with peeled reeds helps new plants to climb. Later, after a successful harvest, farmers should

> . . . recite Bacchus' due honor in ancestral hymns, and bear cakes and platters, and led by the horn, the victim goat shall stand by the altar, and the fat flesh roast on spits of hazel-wood.

Such a rich life, says Virgil, is far better than the strife of war, which produces no bounty—only disappointment. The country life, he says, is a gift of Justice, who left the glades and valleys in her path when she walked the earth. It was also the lifestyle of Saturn when he lived on earth, long before war-trumpets were sounded.

Virgil dedicates **Book 3** to Pales, the herdsman's god, and he offers advice on the management of flocks. The first priority, he says, is finding good breeding stock:

> The best cow is ugly-shapen; her head coarse, her neck of the largest, with dewlaps hanging down from chin to leg; and to her length of flank there is no limit; large of limb and of foot, with shaggy ears under inward-curving horns.

He maintains that females breed best during the fourth and tenth years, after which they are unfit even as draft animals. Each year, a good husbandman should cull out the weak and the old; he should look for strong, young replacements to assure the health of the herd. Virgil urges objectivity in this matter: "Age is cold to love, and vainly drags on the ungrateful task . . ." To assure good breeding stock, Virgil says, a wise farmer should supply fresh river water and corn to the stallions, but starve the mares into leanness, so that they "thirstily swallow the seed and hide it deeper within."

Newborn animals should be graded as soon as possible. Breeders should be branded and introduced into the main herd, the best kept apart for the sacred altar. The rest should be turned to pasture and shaped "while yet ungrown, and set on the road of training while their minds are light in youth and their age flexible." To assure maximum benefit, "keep love and the stings of blind passion aloof . . . [and] banish the bull far into lonely pasturage, behind a mountain barrier and across broad streams, or keep him shut indoors by the rich farmyard." Love, the poet declares, is the same in dumb beasts as in human beings, a cause of driving, bizarre, and unruly behavior which is best avoided.

His canon on cattle complete, Virgil turns to sheep and goats, which present a special challenge to the farmer, for they require a diet of fodder, plus abundant straw and ferns in their pens to protect their tender hooves; in addition, they also need fresh, flowing water and shelter from the elements. The rewards of a well-managed flock are manifold—abundant milk and quality wool, both of which turn fat profits. The poet warns of pitfalls—burrs in the fleece, smelly pastures, poor breeding stock, and the scourge of black tongue.

To assure a good litter of dogs to help with tending the flocks, Virgil suggests fattening pups on whey and guarding against wolves and thieves. Special attention, he says, should be given to snakes, which lurk about the pens. To fend off snakes, the poet suggests:

> Snatch up sticks and stones, O shepherd, and as he [the snake] rises, threatening and puffing out his hissing throat, strike him down! And now he hides his head deep in fearful flight, while his coiling body and the last folds of his tail unwind, and he slowly trails the utmost curve of his rings.

Serpents thrive in moist places, Virgil says, and can be found near springs, ponds, and river banks, where they gorge on fish and frogs.

In closing his discussion about flock maintenance, Virgil warns of disease, notably mange, which strikes in icy winter weather. He offers a recipe for sheep dip, consisting of fresh water, olive dregs, sulphur, tar, wax ointment, hellebore, and asphalt. Excision of festering lesions is often necessary, but the best cure is prevention by singling out listless animals before they infect the herd. He concludes with a vivid, dire picture of livestock epidemics, fouling the air with a dreadful, all-pervasive stench and corrupting the fleece, the hides, and the meat.

Book 4 is devoted to beekeeping, which occupies a "tiny state." He notes, "Slight is the field of labor; but not slight the glory . . ." To assure a good bounty, the beekeeper must first establish a proper hive for the bees, one which is sheltered from the wind and from stray herd animals and lizards, which are notorious for raiding hives. There must also be clear springs nearby and mossy ponds. Likewise, there must be proper greenery, such as casia, thyme, and violets.

According to Virgil, bees are prone to fight. He describes their martial behavior in these mock heroic lines:

> So when they find the spring sky rainless and the field open, they sally forth from the gate; high in the air, the armies clash and the din swells; gathering, they cluster in a great ball and come tumbling down, thick as hailstones through the air, or the rain of acorns from the shaken ilex. The monarchs move splendid-winged amid the ranks, and mighty passions stir in their tiny breasts, stubborn to the last not to retreat, till weight of the conquerer forces these or those to turn backward in flying rout.

After the fray, one ruler will rise to omnipotence. The better breed will sparkle, "ablaze with spots of embossed gold," while the scruffier variety will appear rough, soiled, and sluggish.

Nearing the end of his volume, Virgil summarizes the joys of a well-tended farm, when honey is squeezed fresh from the comb, apples are stored for the winter, and well-pruned trees spread their shade. He narrates the mythic background of beekeeping and ends with a salute to husbandry from a subjective point of view:

> . . . I, Virgil, nurtured in sweet Parthenope [Naples], went in the flowery ways of lowly Quiet: I who once played with shepherd's songs, and in youth's hardihood sang thee, O Tityrus [the mythical, ideal shepherd], under the covert of spreading beech.

LIVY

- *Ab Urbe Condita*
  (From the City's Foundation)

LIVY

Although born in Patavium, modern-day Padua, in 59 B.C., Titus Livius devoted his energies to a comprehensive history of Rome, where he lived most of his life. Like Tacitus, Livy championed the republican cause and openly admired Brutus and Cassius, Caesar's killers, but he still maintained a close relationship with Augustus and his supporters. A master of prose, Livy crafted his life's work until his death.

In general, Livy attempted to reconstruct and preserve a history of Roman heritage from the time of Aeneas to the early days of the Empire, but his main purpose was didactic. Alarmed by the laxness of public morality, he wished to revive patriotism and restore Rome to its former civic virtue. His consummate overview of Rome, however, has provided the modern historian with insight into the moral decay that preceded the collapse of the Empire.

Livy's legendary single-mindedness kept him at his task from 29 B.C. to 25 B.C., when the first five books were completed. During this time, he did little else but write; he was limited in his interests, caring little for travel, extensive reading, public acclaim, or social life. Armed with integrity, a reverence for Ciceronian prose, and innate curiosity, he devoted himself to history, despite the fact that his commentary on the civil war era was withheld from publication until after Augustus' death.

Livy's shortcomings are numerous, including scant use of documentary evidence, weak research methods, and a barely average understanding of geography, politics, and military history. He disdains to hide his strong republican bias and boldly praises his country's victories while minimizing its defeats. Nor does he hesitate to embellish a meager plot for the sake of narrative effect.

Yet, his clever use of Rome's heroes, notably Scipio Africanus and Camillus, bolsters his narrative with moving, dramatic oratory and imaginative scenarios, all of which involve the reader in the ongoing tide of Roman affairs. Of the 142 books, 35 remain today, ample evidence of his abundant, splendid prose. Some of Rome's most stirring episodes – the rape of the Sabine women and Horatius at the bridge, for example – are vividly brought to life on the pages of his histories. For source material, Livy appears to have made good use of earlier histories and priestly records, which, like his history, are organized in single-year units.

Livy received his early education in Patavium and came to Rome probably after the Battle of Actium. At first, he taught rhetoric, dabbled in philosophy, and published a few monographs and a grammar book, which he dedicated to one of his two sons. He also had a daughter who married Lucius Magius, a grammar teacher. Escaping the political and social turmoil of the Augustan era into a less complicated lifestyle, he absorbed himself completely in his research, avoiding military service, public office, and the coteries of the literary elite.

Livy appears to have been a tranquil "family man" who responded to others with natural goodwill. Like his contemporaries, he breathed a sigh of relief when the senate restored law and order at the end of thirteen years of civil war, despite the plebeians' loss of personal freedom. He returned to his hometown and died there in 17 A.D. His tombstone, making no mention of greatness, reads simply: "Here lies Titus Livius and his sons, Titus Livius Priscus and Titus Livius Longus, and his wife, Cassia Prima."

Livy appears to have been lionized by his fellow Romans and to have received adulation from distant provinces. An industrious scholar, he published his books at frequent intervals and continued writing on his monumental history of Rome for more than forty years, averaging three and a half books a year. Of his work, he wrote: "I have attained enough personal fame and could lay my pen aside – but my very soul, restless within me, draws sustenance from work."

AB URBE CONDITA
────── (FROM THE CITY'S FOUNDATION) ──────

Livy's prefatory remarks offer convincing evidence that he knew the pitfalls of attempting a mammoth 700-year history of Rome. Yet he vowed to complete his work: ". . . it will be a satisfaction to have done myself as much as lies in me to commemorate the deeds of the foremost people of the world."

He also admits to personal reasons for wanting to write his history; he wishes, he says, to "avert my gaze from the troubles which our age has been witnessing for so many years." Thus, he absorbs himself, while diverting himself from too much contemplation of the Empire's shortcomings.

Livy follows the traditional genealogy, tracing Rome's founders to a celestial father, "none other than Mars." His cast of characters includes Aeneas and Ascanius, the "same whom the Julian family call Iulus and claim as the author of their name." His account of the birth and abandonment of the twin founders of Rome, Romulus and Remus, ends in a bloody contest between brothers and Romulus' proud words, "So perish whoever else shall leap over my walls!" Without commentary, Livy notes that the city grew from that violent act and continued to fight for its survival against envious neighbors.

Although Romulus ruthlessly grabs power, he realizes the importance of law and order to the developing city. Early in his administration, he ". . . called the people together and gave them the rules of law, since nothing else but law could unite them into a single body politic." To create an aura of authority, he devised the office of *lictor*, or palace guard, and surrounded himself with twelve bodyguards. To bolster the meager population, he established a sanctuary for "surrounding peoples, a miscellaneous rabble . . . eager for new conditions." To enhance his design, he appointed a hundred senators, who received the name *patres*, or fathers, from which came the class designation of "patrician."

Dwelling on the theme of "might makes right," Livy details the story of the Sabine women, whom Roman youths ravished. Desperate for women to bear future citizens for the city, the crafty Romans invited the curious Sabines to a spectacle and, after showing them around the city, made off with their wives and daughters. Livy notes that one maiden, seized and carried off by Thalassius, was of exceptional beauty. In memory of her being carried off, Livy says, Romans still cry out, "Thalassio!" at weddings just as the groom carries the bride across the threshold of her new home.

The orderly arrangement of legends continues, enumerating the accomplishments of the seven kings during Rome's early monarchy. Numa, the second king, famed for justice and piety, was followed by Tullus Hostilius, a bellicose monarch who extended Roman territory in all directions by means of constant warfare. During his reign, the famous battle between the Horatii and Curiatii, two sets of triplet-warriors, took place as an episode in Rome's war with the Albans, which resulted in a great victory for Rome.

Book I ends with Sextus Tarquinius' rape of Lucretia, an event which turned the Romans against Sextus' father, King Tarquinius Superbus, and brought about the end of the monarchy. A fascinating character in world literature, the distinguished Lucretia makes a poignant speech, characteristic of the noble, selfless Roman woman of the republican era:

> . . . what can be well with a woman when she has lost her honor? . . . my body only has been violated; my heart is guilt-less, as death shall be my witness. But pledge your right hands and your words that the adulterer shall not go unpunished.

She then reveals a knife which she hid in her garments, stabs herself in the heart, and dies before falling to the floor.

Junius Brutus, an illustrious ancestor of Marcus Brutus, a conspirator against Julius Caesar, draws out the gory knife from Lucretia's chest and brandishes it, shouting:

> . . . I swear, and I take you, gods, to witness, that I will pursue Lucius Tarquinius Superbus . . . with sword, with fire! – aye, with whatever violence I may; and that I will suffer neither them nor any other to be king in Rome!

Just as Mark Antony turns grief to anger in Shakespeare's *Julius Caesar*, Brutus leads a howling mob "to abrogate the king's authority and to exile Lucius Tarquinius Superbus . . ."

Book II opens with a general celebration of liberty, which Junius Brutus won for the people by driving the Tarquins out of Rome. These are grand days for the city, when the Republic is taking shape and examples of courage inspire strong patriotism in men and women.

Outstanding among the stalwart Romans are Horatius Cocles (One-Eye), who singlehandedly holds a bridge against the advancing Etruscans and escapes death by diving, fully armed, into the Tiber River and swimming to the opposite shore; Appius Claudius, father of the Appian Way; Menenius Agrippa, who halts rebellion by relating the parable of the war between the stomach and the other parts of the body; and Coriolanus, the turncoat general who leads the Volsci to the gates of Rome, only to be stopped by his noble mother.

Books III–X continue the parade of strong Romans, particularly Cincinnatus, who prefers the simple joys of farming to the honors of military dictatorship, and Titus Manlius, who springs into action against invaders when the sacred geese awaken him. Rome's continual battering from external forces provides Livy with ample evidence of Rome's resilience, particularly during the confrontation with Carthage, more popularly known as the First Punic War. (Note: Roman tongues had difficulty pronouncing *Phoenician,* so they simplified the sound to *Punician.*)

Livy laces his work with the traditional symbols of Roman history, the Vestal Virgins, the sacred hearth, bird auguries, the Tarpeian Rock, from which traitors are hurled, and the Seven Hills of Rome. In addition, he introduces the class struggles that plagued the periods of internal adjustment, an innovation that later writers imitated. Unfortunately, **Books XI–XX** are lost; in **Books XXI–XXX,** Livy details the Second Punic War, one of Rome's most desperate struggles.

In the preface to **Book XXXI,** Livy confesses that he has grown weary of his task. This period of history lacked the courageous, spunky individuals who spearheaded the fledgling Roman state during its rocky beginnings; nevertheless, Livy's narrative plods mechanically along, ending in **Book XLV** with the war against Antiochus and his eastern forces.

Yet, Livy's devotion to his initial theme never flags. Utilizing the example of moral decay that beset Rome in the remaining one hundred and fifty years, Livy dwells upon the loss of personal responsibility and uprightness which cheapened Rome's later accomplishments and tarnished its greatness.

TIBULLUS

- *Elegies*

TIBULLUS

Although little is known about Albius Tibullus (*ca.* 54–*ca.* 18 B.C.), he is reputed to have been the son of a wealthy man whose land was confiscated for political reasons, possibly after the Battle of Philippi in 42 B.C. Tibullus lived during the age of the great Roman poets, was a friend of both Horace and Ovid, and, in addition, he enjoyed the patronage and friendship of one of Augustus' most powerful associates, Marcus Valerius Messalla Corvinus, a man of learning and sensibility.

Tibullus undertook a military post during Messalla's campaign to Aquitania and attempted to push on toward Asia Minor, but illness forced him to remain on the island of Corfu until he recovered. Returning to his estate between Tivoli and Palestrina, in the hill country north of Rome, which was probably a gift of his patron, Tibullus completed his convalescence in comfort. Comments about Tibullus, made during his time, suggest that he was a tad effeminate and tended to be a bit of a hypochondriac.

The poet enjoyed a close association with Horace, who eulogized his kindness, beauty, delicacy, and good taste. The persona of Tibullus himself, as revealed in his poems, is similar – dreamy, languid, self-indulgent, often nostalgic, and usually deeply embroiled in love affairs, which are the soul of his verses. He refers to his lovers by pseudonymous names – Delia, Nemesis, and Marathus. Tradition identifies Delia as Plania, Nemesis is possibly Glycera, but no concrete information about the teenage boy Marathus exists. Overall, the most skillful portraiture in Tibullus' elegies is the picture of the poet himself, who was basically too egocentric to allot much emphasis to his lovers.

Although his poetry tends to repeat itself, Tibullus' skill with words has earned him the sobriquet "The Perfect Poet," mainly on the strength of four books of elegies, most of which deal with his emotional attitudes toward love, nature, pacifism, and the family.

Often compared to Catullus, one of his contemporaries, Tibullus comes out second best; he avoids Catullus' deep introspection, and instead, he concentrates on a rather insipid sentiment which attains neither the passion nor the emotional insights of Catullus. The last two books of elegies, although sometimes attributed to Tibullus and written in his characteristic style, were not written by him; they were composed by other poets of the Messallan circle, notably Lygdamus and Sulpicia, and were added by the editor after Tibullus' death.

───────────── *ELEGIES* ─────────────

Tibullus opens **Book 1** of his Elegies with a clear statement of his ideal:

> Let others heap up their treasure of yellow gold; let theirs
> be many acres of well-tilled ground; let them live in constant
> fighting and alarms . . . but let the humble fortune that is mine
> lead me along a quiet path of life, so my hearth but shine
> with an unfailing fire.

Like Horace, Tibullus finds contentment in his villa, where he devotes himself to the care of his vines and orchards. He seeks only a comfortable living from his acreage and scorns both great wealth and military glory.

The third elegy contrasts the speaker's ease at home with his fear of death in a foreign place. While traveling with Messalla, Tibullus falls ill and pleads:

> Keep off thy greedy hands, I pray, Black Death. Black Death,
> I pray thee keep them off. No mother have I here to gather
> the burned bones to her grieving bosom; no sister to lavish
> Assyrian perfumes on my ashes and weep with hair disheveled
> by my tomb.

In his terror of the unknown, Tibullus prepares for all contingencies, even providing an epitaph, should one be necessary:

> Here lies Tibullus, consumed by pitiless Death
> While following Messalla over land and sea.

Eager to end this harrowing ordeal, he envisions his return home, safe at last, where his beloved Delia will run to meet him, her hair in disarray and her feet bare.

Book 2 opens with a rare gem of verse, a tribute to the country festival. On the day that Bacchus and Ceres receive their annual honors, the plowman rests and no one spins yarn; everyone, washed fresh and dressed in the cleanest of clothes, joins the festive procession and approaches the altar. Tibullus lauds the advance of civilization, which has brought his countrymen from humble beginnings to noble heights; he is deeply grateful for the gods' blessings.

> Ah, wretched they upon whom our god bears mightily; and happy is he on whom Love in his graciousness breathes gently. Come to our festal cheer, holy lord. . . . Let each one call him for the herd aloud, but in a whisper for himself.

The fifth elegy continues this festival spirit of happy gratitude – this time in honor of Pales, divinity of shepherds. On the day that Pales is honored, Tibullus tells us,

> . . . the child takes hold of his father's ears to snatch the kiss; nor shall the grandsire find it irksome to watch by his little grandson's side, nor, for all his years, to lisp in prattle with the child.

The whole community, in devotion to the gods of plenty, spread their holiday meal on the grass beneath a great tree. Tibullus, too, cured of his malady, rejoices in the simple, rural pleasures of love and peace.

PROPERTIUS

- *Elegies*

PROPERTIES

LIFE AND BACKGROUND

Sextus Propertius' life (*ca.* 50–15 B.C.) parallels that of his contemporary and fellow elegist, Tibullus; however, the facts about his birth and background are sketchy. We know that he was born of a well-established family in Assisi, east of Lake Trasimene and north of Spoleto, in Umbria, about 50 B.C., and that his family's estate was confiscated during the political seizures following the Battle of Philippi in 42 B.C.

Propertius' father died when Propertius was young, and his mother brought him to Rome when he was ten. Well educated in the Roman style, he was encouraged to practice law, but he chose to indulge himself in romance and poetry. His first affair with Lycinna was shortlived, and not long after his mother's death, he met Cynthia, the love of his life and the focus of nineteen of his elegies.

Ranked among the great elegiac poets, Propertius filled his verses with loving tributes to Cynthia, a sophisticated and passionate older woman whose real name was Hostia. Her patronym is linked with a patrician lineage, although he refers to her as a freedwoman and, therefore, ineligible for marriage. Although their romance foundered at times, Propertius remained enamored of Cynthia throughout his life and immortalized her with vivid descriptions of her personal qualities.

Late in his career, Propertius eulogized Cornelia, an unidentified aristocratic matron, in a posthumous honorarium that has been called the "queen of elegies." In addition, Propertius, more than any other poet of his era, has much to say about the horrors of the Roman civil war, and he often expounds on his country's republican past with sensitivity and patriotic ardor. It was not until late in his life that his poetry began to show enthusiasm for the Empire.

For some time, Propertius kept to himself, partly because he did not share his colleagues' enthusiasm for Augustus' military triumphs over Mark Antony and Cleopatra. However, after he achieved some notoriety following the publication of his first book of elegies, he received the patronage of Maecenas, joined the circle of noted literati that included Virgil and Ovid, and lived on the Esquiline Hill, possibly with his patron.

Propertius formed a lasting friendship with Ovid, and it is quite possible that he prompted Ovid to write the *Heroides*. Likewise, he admired Virgil's *Aeneid*, which he appears to have read before its publication; in addition, he encouraged Virgil during its final stages. Concerning his relationship with Horace, another famous poet of his time, it is possible that because of Propertius' nervous, neurotic personality or because of the differences in their ages, he may have met with Horace's disfavor. However, he does echo Horace's poetry in his own verses.

Like Tibullus, Propertius was somewhat of an egotist because of his preoccupation with his own ideas and emotions. Noted for his meticulous care in dress, he gained a reputation for dandyism. He suffered from a delicate constitution, possibly from a debilitating childhood disease, and occasional bouts of depression late in his life. He had a morbid preoccupation with death and died shortly after Cynthia's death.

Propertius' poems are collected in four books, which appeared in 28, 26, 23, and 16 B.C. Unfortunately, there are lapses in all extant manuscripts, which were poorly edited and contain spurious interpolations and transpositions. Overall, his tone is tender, and his style achieves a shimmering quality through rich sound effects, unusual imagery, and lavish ornamentation. An Alexandrine at heart, he owes much to Callimachus, whom he emulated.

As he developed his poetic gift, Propertius turned away from purely erotic subject matter and gravitated toward national and patriotic themes, although there is evidence that it was Maecenas, or possibly Augustus, who persuaded him to adopt historical themes. Propertius set himself apart from the typical Latin poets by resorting to frequent rhyming and by employing obscure allusions. His work inspired the "Roman elegies" of Goethe, as well as the verses of Petrarch and Ezra Pound, who wrote "Homage to Sextus Propertius."

ELEGIES

Thoughts of Cynthia consume Propertius, coloring his elegies with the many tints of love's effect on him. In **Book 1,** the opening lines suggest that passion took him unaware:

Unscathed was I by Cupid's dart
Till Cynthia's eyes enslaved my heart;
Then staring down my brave conceit,
Love trampled me beneath his feet . . .
My goddess works me ceaseless spites,
And idle love leads to galling nights.
Beware my fate!

But wariness gives way to complete surrender in **Book 2,** where Propertius describes their lovemaking:

If she should grant me nights like this
A year would seem a life of bliss,
If many such she deigned to give,
I, in the seventh heaven, should live.

He concludes his praise of passion with a brief comment about the political tenor of the times. If Rome is about to suffer more internal conflict, he maintains, he and Cynthia would do well to enjoy the moment and "throw not the fruit of life away."

Toward the end of **Book 3,** Propertius agonizes beside Cynthia's bed as she suffers an unnamed illness. He is unable to imagine life without her, and he bargains with the gods to spare her:

Spare both! Not one alone, oh prithee!, spare!
I live, if she lives; if she sinks, I sink.
Wherefore I pledge myself in holy line
To write 'The might of Jove hath saved my girl.'

In **Book 4,** the poet faces his worst fears after Cynthia's death, as her spirit comes back to visit him:

'For now, let others have thee;
Ere long shalt be all mine:
We two shall lie together,
My bones shall cling to thine.'
She spoke: and in that instant,

Ere yet I was aware,
The shape my arms were clasping
Had vanished in thin air.

Even though Cynthia is dead, Propertius' love for her possesses him
utterly, pulling him down to an endless tryst in the underworld.

Propertius' greatest poem, an elegy on the death of Cornelia, contains similar strains of ghostly imagery and fascination with death.
On her journey from the upper reaches, paying Charon for her passage, Cornelia meets familiar characters of the Roman underworld—
Ixion, Tantalus, and Cerberus. With touching wistfulness, she says
to her family:

Perchance he shall see another bed,
And to my couch a second wife be led.
But be not vexed, dear children: praise the bride;
Soon by your love will she be pacified.
Nor praise too much your mother nor compare:
Words over-free a look of malice bear.

Content with her treatment on earth, Cornelia looks forward to the
peace of the afterlife.

HORACE

- *Sermonum (Satires)*

- *Epistles (Letters)*

- *Carmina (Odes)*

- *Ars Poetica (The Art of Poetry)*

- **Minor Poems**

_____ **LIFE AND BACKGROUND**

Edith Hamilton labels Horace as a man who "keenly enjoyed all life's simplest pleasures"—in short, Horace was "the complete man of the world, with tolerance for all and partisanship for none." A multi-talented, versatile, and unpretentious poet of the Augustan Age, Quintus Horatius Flaccus was born on December 8, 65 B.C., on a small farm in Venusia, Italy, halfway between Naples and Bari, near the southern end of the Apennine chain on the borders of Apulia and Lucania. Because Horace does not mention other family members, historians assume that he was an only child whose mother may have died when Horace was an infant.

Horace's father was a freedman (that is, a former slave), who earned his living as an auctioneer's clerk and tax collector; he scrimped and saved to provide for his freeborn son's academic and moral training, and later, Horace expressed deep gratitude to his father. In Rome, where Horace studied under Orbilius, a stern and exacting master, Horace's father served as his son's escort and protector, accompanying him to and from classes.

Because of Horace's carefully grounded, conservative early education, he developed a taste for the Greek classics and disdained most of the Roman poets. Not surprisingly, at the age of nineteen, Horace journeyed to Athens to study philosophy, and there he formed friendships with Romans of the privileged class, including Cicero's son and the influential Marcus Valerius Messalla.

The assassination of Julius Caesar in 44 B.C. altered Horace's life as well as that of the doomed Republic. Fired with Brutus' zeal for saving the Republic, Horace joined the republican army, rose to the rank of tribune, and two years later, he fought at Philippi in Macedonia, where Octavian and Antony's forces defeated Brutus and Cassius, the key conspirators against Julius Caesar. In one of his odes, Horace comments that he enjoyed the convivial side of military life, but that his memories are marred by a disorderly rout and the loss of his shield, which he cast aside in his haste to save himself from capture.

In 41 B.C., Horace, among the many who fought on the losing side, returned to Rome under Octavian's general amnesty. Although he was deeply disillusioned by the unsettled times, he eventually became a faithful supporter of the new order, even receiving a job offer to work as Augustus' private secretary.

After Horace's father died and his patrimony was confiscated as a result of his participation in the Civil War, Horace was virtually penniless, yet he managed to purchase a low-level political appointment as clerk of the treasury. To counter the tedium of his bureaucratic chores, he wrote satires and epodes in his spare time, and his early work reflects the chaotic upheaval that accompanied Rome's transformation from Republic to Empire. Eventually, his tinges of bitterness and self-pity faded with maturity as Horace faced the reality that the Roman Republic would never be resurrected.

Early in his development, Horace realized that poetry was his life. In one poem, he states his decision unequivocally:

> Everyone has his own way of enjoying himself. Mine is to put words into meter. No use talking about it. Whether peaceful old age awaits me or even now black-pinioned death flies round me, rich, poor, in Rome or, if chance so bids, in exile, whatever my life shall be, bright or dark, I will write.

A positive-minded, handsome young man, somewhat vain about his well-oiled black hair, he loved the pleasures of good food and, at times, kept company with Rome's spirited young men and women. Whatever his afterhours activities, however, two of Horace's colleagues – Virgil, in the early stages of his career, and Varius Rufus – helped him make the right connections in 39 B.C. by introducing him to Maecenas, Rome's chief literary patron and adviser to the emperor.

Although content with his humble, peasant perspective, Horace immediately fit in with the circle of noted writers and politicians, and a few years later, Maecenas gave him a small estate containing five farmhouses in the Sabine hills, twenty-five miles northeast of Rome, near modern Tivoli. Horace's farm, which became a focus of his writing, allowed him the leisure to develop his literary talents. Relaxed and happy in country surroundings, Horace, sometimes teased because of his short, chubby frame, was an unassuming man and a sympathetic adviser and friend to all.

Deeply satisfied with his good fortune, he settled into a conservative, contemplative lifestyle, from which evolved his highly polished poetry. In 35 B.C., he published his first book of ten *Sermonum,* or *Satires,* a series of rambling talks in verse form, and he completed another eight, along with seventeen *Epodes,* or *Refrains,* in 30 B.C. Then, turning his attention to the classic Greek style and meter of Alcaeus, Sappho, Simonides, and Pindar, Horace completed three books of *Carmina,* or *Odes,* in 23 B.C. and three years later, he published twenty epistolary poems to friends, entitled *Epistles,* or *Letters.*

After the death of Virgil, his friend and mentor and the leading poet in Rome, Horace hoped to turn his talents from lyrical to philosophical writing, but became, instead, the poet laureate of the Empire. He was commissioned by Augustus to compose the *Carmen Saeculare (Secular Hymn)* in 17 B.C. in honor of the revival of the Secular Games, held every *saeculum,* a period of 110 years. At the games, the official state hymn, a mixture of religious and patriotic sentiment, was sung in honor of Apollo and Diana by a select sampling of Rome's elite youth. After his completion of the stately verse, Horace received a second imperial commission to honor the victories of Drusus and Tiberius, Augustus' stepsons.

A steady flow of works followed: a fourth book of 103 odes, a second volume of twenty epistles, and the *Ars Poetica,* also known as the *Epistula ad Pisones,* around 20 B.C. This last endeavor, a notable book of dramatic criticism, is considered his most mature writing because of its sensible advice to young writers.

Clear classification of Horace's style has often eluded critics. Some consider him an imitator of the writers who flourished during the Golden Age of Greece; others call him a hedonist or an Epicurean, while a strong contingency of critics labels him a stoic and an Aristotelian. His unique blend of amusing wit, biting satire, moral reflection, common sense, provincial tastes, and trenchant cynicism suggests a complex, eclectic mind.

Horace developed his themes along philosophical and ethical lines, returning often to the single thought that *life is short and uncertain and should be enjoyed.* He emphasized that peace of mind should precede riches and ambition in human priorities. According to Horace, man should leave this life as he leaves a banquet table – contented. As did the great classic minds that preceded him, he fostered the ideal of the Golden Mean—"nothing in excess." He observed moderation in all aspects of his daily life, although at age forty, he suggested that some defect in health afflicted him, making him prematurely gray and sapping his energy. As a curative, his doctor, Antonius Musa, ordered him to spend the winter months on the sunny shores of southern Italy.

His individualism and his sincere devotion to decency has illuminated the paths of later writers. Although widely read and appreciated in his own day, his verse has also found proponents among a diverse group of spokesmen for the Christian era, including St. Jerome and Prudentius. In the Middle Ages, his ethical standards influenced Dante, and in the Renaissance, Petrarch championed his cause. Montaigne, the French essayist, reflects Horace's style, as do Ben Jonson, Andrew Marvell, Robert Herrick, Alexander Pope, Joseph Addison, Richard Steele, Samuel Johnson, Henry Fielding, John Gay, Lord Byron, and William Gladstone.

Horace was fifty-seven when he died unexpectedly on November 27, 8 B.C., a few months after Maecenas, who requested that Augustus be "as mindful of Horace as of himself." Ironically, when Horace had heard that Maecenas was ill, he wrote, "If you were to die of a sudden stroke, I too would die, for you are the other half of me. Your death would be death for us both."

Horace's ashes were buried in Rome on the Esquiline Hill, alongside those of Maecenas, and he was mourned by Rome's intellectual and social elite, who counted him as a friend and patriot. His reputation for literary perfectionism resulted in a legacy of self-discipline, which has passed down to subsequent generations of poets who followed his example. As Horace states with pride in the last work of the third book of his odes, his works comprise a monument "more lasting than bronze."

SERMONUM (SATIRES)

Examining various examples of discontent, Horace concludes that materialism causes discontent. He begins **Book I** with a direct question to his patron:

How comes it, Maecenas, that no man living is content with the lot which either his choice has given him, or chance has thrown in his way, but each has praise for those who follow other paths?

In answer to the person who believes that "one can never have enough," Horace states that such a fool deserves misery "since that is his whim." Unfortunately, he concludes, "seldom can we find one who says he has had a happy life, and who, when his time is sped, will quit life in contentment, like a guest who has had his fill."

The next two topics in Book I deal with similar concerns about human happiness – namely, intolerance and violations of the Golden Mean. Then, turning to other matters, Horace justifies the place of satire in the poetic arts and describes a grueling journey to Brundisium. Satire VI gives a close, personal glimpse of Horace:

Now to return to myself, 'son of a freedman father,' whom all carp at as 'son of a freedman father' . . . I count it a great honor that I pleased you, who discern between fair and foul, not by a father's fame, but by blamelessness of life and heart.

Horace expounds on his relationship with his father, a tax-collector, who "boldly took his boy off to Rome to be taught those studies that any knight or senator would have his own offspring taught." Horace expresses gratitude that his father kept him free from vice and shame. Content with himself as he is, Horace concludes that happiness comes from within and not from noble birth.

Book II opens with an imaginary verbal joust with a critic. In defense of his chosen profession, Horace declares that "both my dagger and pen shall never of my free will assail any man alive but shall protect me, like a sword laid up in its sheath." Satire II defends the poet's simple lifestyle. As an explanation of his unassuming tastes, he states:

The chiefest pleasure lies not in the costly savor, but in yourself. So earn your sauce with hard exercise. The man who is bloated and pale with excess will find no comfort in oysters, trout, or foreign grouse.

Satire IV develops this idea more fully with examples of the best foods — oblong white eggs, cabbages grown in well-drained soil, hens soaked in wine, and "mushrooms from the meadows." Likewise, he prefers the health-giving qualities of mulberries, mussels, pork, venison, and well-mixed sauces. He concludes the piece with recommendations for the best apples and grapes.

Satire VI, containing the tale of "The City Mouse and the Country Mouse," is Horace's most famous, incorporating a fable to illustrate the virtues of country living. As the fable opens, the country mouse is unsuccessfully entertaining an old friend — a finicky city mouse, who is somewhat of a gourmet and man-about-town and simply cannot abide the straw mattress nor the dried peas, oats, and raisin concoctions that he is served.

Finally, the city mouse confronts his friend and ridicules the boring, frugal rural life; he praises the ultimate happiness that can be found in sophisticated city life, and he urges the country mouse to "be happy." No one, he says, lives for very long, and during the short, uncertain span of years that we have, we should do our best to be happy. And, since happiness is certainly not inherent in country living, it's best to live in the city, where happiness is guaranteed. Thus, the country mouse packs his bags and travels to the city, anxious to discover the glories of city life.

In the grand manor where the city mouse lives, the rustic mouse is treated as though he were royalty; the city mouse cooks up a multitude of rich, exotic foods and scurries back and forth, waiting on the country mouse's every whim. The country mouse, lying "stretched out on purple covers," thoroughly enjoys having all sorts of delicacies brought to him; he is almost ready to believe that here, at last, he has found happiness.

Suddenly, however, a frightening disruption sends both mice fleeing for their lives. When both mice are safe from the banging doors and the huge, barking dogs that terrorized the elegant dinner, the country mouse decides to return to his humble country home, happy to be "secure from alarms" and pleasantly comfortable again, pleased with his simple supper of dried beans.

EPISTLES (LETTERS)

Written in the same witty, conversational style as his *Satires,* Horace's letters focus on human frailties, philosophical principles, and the ins and outs of the poet's daily affairs. The epistolary form is comfortable to Horace, who uses it to express literary criticism and social problems as easily as he describes more intimate matters. The *Epistles* are the product of his mature years and reveal keen judgment and the subtle refinements of a man who has weathered many storms, both personally and professionally.

In the opening letter of **Book I** of the *Epistles,* foregoing lyric poetry in favor of letter-writing, Horace freely gives advice to his patron, Maecenas:

> The slave to envy, anger, sloth, wine, lewdness—no one is so savage that he cannot be tamed, if only he would lend to treatment a patient ear. To flee vice is the beginning of virtue, and to have got rid of folly is the beginning of wisdom.

He notes with some alarm that Roman morality reminds him of the story of the fox and the sick lion. In that fable, the fox chooses not to follow the lion because all footprints lead toward his den, "and none lead back." Likewise, the Romans waste their virtue in pursuit of such vices as greed, speculation, and other forms of corruption.

Horace's epistle to Julius Florus, a young man of letters, in contrast to the forbidding tone of the first letter, inquires about other writers, the literary climate of Rome, and the recipient's career. Likewise, Horace's letter to Tibullus is affable and laced with tidbits of wisdom: "Amid hopes and cares, amid fears and passions, believe that every day that has dawned is your last. Welcome will come to you another hour unhoped for."

In another example of social niceties, the poet invites Torquatus, a descendent of the Roman hero Manlius Torquatus, to a dinner on the evening of September 22. To Numicius, Horace evinces an ebullient mood:

> If he who dines well, lives well, then—'tis daybreak, let's be off. . . . Let us fish, let us hunt. . . . While gorged with undigested food, let us bathe, forgetful of what is or is not seemly . . . without love and jests there is no joy, live amid love and jests. Live long, farewell. If you know something better than

these precepts, pass it on, my good fellow. If not, join me
in following these.

In contrast, other verses indicate that Horace occasionally suffered
bouts of petulance or depression. The quarrelsome, heavy-lidded tone
in some of his poems is startling to readers who are accustomed to
finding him in a more cheerful, upbeat mood.

In a spritely, capricious letter to Vinius Asina, Horace gives instructions to the messenger boy who is carrying a book of Horace's
poetry to court:

Put forth your strength over hills, streams, and fens; when
once you have achieved your purpose and reached your journey's end, you are to keep your burden so placed as not, for
instance, to carry the little packet of books under your arm-
pit, even as a bumpkin carries a lamb . . .

An equally auspicious sentiment that permeates Horace's letters is his
delight in country living. As he comments to his newly appointed
bailiff, people often covet what others have, but one should realize
what a treasure the pleasant countryside is.

Horace provides a fitting epilogue to his first book of letters. The
personified book, we learn, loves company and hates to be sealed in
its case. The poet predicts, "You will be loved in Rome till your youth
leaves you . . ." He hopes that the book will serve as an autobiography,
telling people that Horace was a freedman's son—poor, but ambitious,
one who "spread his wings too wide for his nest . . ." He concludes
with his age; he was forty-four in December, 21 B.C.

Book II opens with a lengthy formal letter to Augustus Caesar,
whom Horace praises for "guarding our Italian state with arms, grac-
ing her with morals, and reforming her with laws." Noting that the
emperor prefers the words of Virgil and Varius to Horace's own verses,
Horace confesses that his own talents are indeed too meager to describe Rome's great history. Yet, he is satisfied with his accomplishments, and he hopes that his verses will never be over-praised and
then discarded, to be used as waste paper in the grocer's stall, wrapped
about "frankincense and perfumes and pepper and everything else
that is wrapped in sheets of useless paper."

The second epistle in Book II contains a kernel of biographical
fact that gives us a clearer picture of Horace's experience at Philippi
and his decision to become a poet. To Florus, he writes:

But troublous times tore me from that pleasant spot, and the tide of civil strife flung me, a novice in war, amid weapons that were to be no match for the strong arms of Caesar Augustus.

When Brutus' army suffered defeat, Horace returned to Rome, "brought low with wings clipped and beggared of paternal home and estate; bare-faced poverty drove me to writing verses."

CARMINA (ODES)

Horace's most famous work, his four books of *Odes,* reveals the poet's most sincere beliefs through closely worked, highly distilled verses that defy translation. Beginning in **Book I** with a dedication to Maecenas, his patron, Horace justifies his choice of profession by comparing himself to the farmer, sailor, traveling salesman, soldier, and hunter. He rejoices that "me the cool grove and the lightly tripping bands of the nymphs and satyrs withdraw from the vulgar throng . . ."

A memorable stanza near the end of Book I is Horace's tribute to Cleopatra, whom he admired for her courageous, queenly demise. Although he begins on a dire note, describing Augustus Caesar's victory over the mad queen at Actium, he changes his tone in the closing lines and openly admires her nobility and pluck:

Yet she, seeking to die a nobler death, shows for the dagger's point no woman's fear . . . courageous, too, to handle poisonous asps, that she might draw black venom to her heart, waxing bolder as she resolved to die . . .

True to her royal upbringing, Cleopatra, ever the queen, preferred death to being paraded, as was the Roman custom for captured royalty, through the streets of Rome during a show of military triumph.

The third ode in **Book II** is an appropriate send-off to Virgil, Horace's close friend and colleague, who is embarking on a difficult voyage to Greece. Drawing analogies to great travelers from mythology, including Daedalus and Hercules, Horace makes one of his most enduring comments about human hardiness: *"Nil mortalibus ardui est"* (Nothing is too hard for man).

Another memorable theme is found in stanza 11, in which the poet urges the reader to make the most of life. "Show wisdom! Busy yourself with household tasks, and since life is brief, cut short far-reaching hopes!" He builds to a resounding climax, *"Carpe diem!"* (Seize the day), a phrase that often appears today in the original Latin, strong evidence that Horace's words are heard by listening ears.

Perhaps the most Roman of Horace's verses in **Book II** is the tenth ode, commonly called "The Golden Mean." In these six well-known stanzas, he lauds a sensible lifestyle and reminds the reader, "Although Jupiter brings back the unlovely winters, he also takes them away. If we fare ill today, 'twill not ever be so." As Horace often states, the best way to enjoy life is to take good times with caution and to endure lean times with greatness of heart. In simpler words, "nothing in excess," as the Romans were fond of saying.

Again, in the fourteenth ode, Horace, like Omar Khayyám in the *Rubáiyát*, dwells on the speed with which the "moving finger" of the years passes by: ". . . nor will righteousness give pause to wrinkles, to advancing age, or Death invincible . . ." Every person must reckon with the evanescence of life. Too soon the poet will abandon his wife and home, leaving behind his wealth and store of choice wine, which he once guarded under lock and key. The final lines of the eighteenth ode echo this same theme: "Why strive for more and more? For all alike does Earth unlock her bosom—for the poor man and for the prince's sons."

Book III tempers the harsher, grimmer poems with gentler themes. In the sixteenth ode, Horace sings of his contentment. Freed from a consuming lust for wealth, he declares to Maecenas that "the more a man denies himself, so much the more will he receive from the gods." Using his own experience as an example, he explains how the husbandry of his farm is reward enough:

> My stream of pure water, my woodland of few acres, and
> my trust in my crop of corn bring me more blessing than the
> lot of the dazzling lord of fertile Africa, though he know it not.

Rounding out his philosophy on the pursuit of money, Horace's summation echoes the sentiments of Aesop, Thoreau, and a host of other poets and philosophers who have considered their earthly lot: "To those who seek for much, much is ever lacking; blest is he to whom the god with chary hand has given just enough."

Horace ends Book III with a declaration of his fame. Pleased that he has carved out a niche "more lasting than bronze and loftier than the Pyramids' royal pile," he seems almost smug, safely immortalized where "no wasting rain, no furious north wind can destroy, or the countless chain of years and the ages' flight." Immortality is his reward. In his estimation, "I shall not altogether die, but a mighty part of me shall escape the death-goddess."

The odes of **Book IV** continue Horace's two-pronged theme — the shortness of life and the glory of immortality through poetry. In the third ode, he enjoys his fame:

> The children of Rome, queen of cities, deem it meet to rank
> me among the pleasant choirs of poets; and already am I less
> attacked by Envy's tooth. . . . I am pointed out by the finger
> of those passing by as the minstrel of the Roman lyre.

Cautious to praise the goddess who is responsible for his success, Horace thanks the muse Melpomene that he is "filled with the breath of song."

___ ARS POETICA (THE ART OF POETRY) ___

In a terse plea for simplicity and uniformity in poetry, Horace captures the reader's attention with a graphic opening sentence:

> If a painter chose to join a human head to the neck of a horse,
> and to spread feathers of many a hue over limbs picked up
> now here, now there, so that what at the top is a lovely
> woman ends below in a black and ugly fish, could you, my
> friends, if favored with a private view, refrain from laughing?

With a cursory nod to the Piso family, to whom this work is dedicated,

Horace turns his attention to the subject at hand: how to write. Attempt a manageable subject, he advises, and weave your words tastefully and carefully. Moreover, he adds, use a style suited to the nature of the piece.

Crucial to the writing itself is sincerity, consistency, and an understanding of the audience:

> If you want an approving hearer, one who waits for the cur-
> tain and will stay in his seat till the singer cries, "Give your
> applause," you must note the manners of each age and give
> a fitting tone to the shifting natures and their years.

To insure that the audience experiences the plot as vividly as possible, the poet should show rather than tell the story. Horace notes that a wise playwright sticks to the traditional five-act format and limits the actors to no more than three. In addition, a good playwright restrains himself from reliance on the *deus ex machina* technique, by which a deity arrives onstage at a crucial moment and solves human problems.

Horace offers more sage tidbits. For example, the chorus should follow its traditional role, singing songs that relate to the plot:

> It should side with the good and give friendly counsel; sway
> the angry and cherish the righteous. It should praise the fare
> of a modest board, praise wholesome justice, law, and peace
> with her open gates; should keep secrets, and pray and be-
> seech the gods that fortune may return to the unhappy, and
> depart from the proud.

The whole effect of dramatic art depends upon small conventions, including the careful wording of each line according to an iambic cadence.

In general, Horace tells the neophyte writer, "Of good writing the source and fount is wisdom." To acquire wisdom, the beginner should "look to life and manners for a model and draw from thence living words." Poems, he declares, should benefit or amuse. If they instruct, they should be brief. Once written, he warns, a work deserves careful criticism and a long period of rest before it is published. "What you have not published," Horace explains, "you can destroy; the word once sent forth can never come back."

❧

───────── MINOR POEMS ─────────

Less notable, but no less refined and memorable in their faithful record of Roman ways, are Horace's minor poems, the *Epodes* of his early years and the long, formal *Carmen Saeculare,* the hymn which he wrote as poet laureate of Rome. Published in 30 B.C., in the early years of the Roman Empire, the *Epodes* have a youthful grace and innocence that seem appropriate to the poet's stage of life. The *Carmen Saeculare,* on the other hand, represents a stylized form of occasional verse that is meant to sound traditional, sonorous, and predictable.

The first of the seventeen epodes, suitably dedicated to Maecenas, Horace's patron, asks, "Shall we, as bidden, devote ourselves to ease that is not sweet except with thee? Or shall we bear your hardships, alongside you, with such resolve as befits stalwart men?" In answer to his rhetorical question, the poet declares, "Bear them we will." With fitting thanks and a forthright promise, Horace declares, "Enough has thy bounty enriched me and more; I will not lay up treasure." But neither does Horace intend to waste anything.

The second epode is a winsome paean to country joys, the poet's greatest pleasure. He opens with a characteristic vigor, "Beatus ille" (Happy/Blessed he), and lists ample evidence of a country dweller's blessings – invigorating labor, lofty trees, productive cattle and swarms of bees, bountiful harvests of fruit, and the richness of nature. In the poet's estimation, "Amid such joys, who does not forget the wretched cares that passion brings?"

When rumors of civil war reach Horace, he is haunted by memories of the ten-year period that followed the assassination of Julius Caesar in March, 44 B.C. Short-tempered with young upstarts who fan the flames of war, he asks, "Whither, whither are you rushing to ruin in your wicked frenzy?" He reminds them how much Roman blood has already flowed during the Punic Wars, when Rome barely escaped the wrath of Carthage and returned to sow the city in salt; likewise in Britain, many young men died when Julius Caesar led his conquering forces across the channel to face the perversity of Celtic warfare. Horace declares that these hawkish upstarts are worse than wild beasts because even the fiercest of animals never turn their savagery against their own kind. He regrets that Rome was cursed by her founder, Romulus, who murdered a blameless brother.

Horace is capable of extremes of emotion, as is obvious by the pendulum swings of his verse. Epode XI, in contrast to the heavier verses, reveals Horace's response to puppy love, which kindles in him an insistent passion. In a similar vein, Epode XIII flaunts revelry and song as Horace turns from bad times with a hopeful outlook:

> Let us snatch our opportunity from the day my friends, and while our limbs are strong and the time is fitting, let serious-ness be banished from the clouded brow! . . . lighten every ill with wine and song, sweet consolations for unlovely sorrow!

However, the *palinode,* or retraction, in the last epode counters all preceding lightheartedness as Horace returns to serious thoughts. When he contemplates death, he cries out in anguish, "Shall I lament the issue of my craft, futile against you alone?"

In contrast to the intensity of Horace's lyric verse, the staid, tradi-tional intonation of the *Carmen Saeculare,* written for a public per-formance in 19 B.C., shows another side of the poet. Filled with apostrophe, allusion, and historical fervor, the lines achieve a notable elegance suitable to the occasion. He begins with a resounding, rev-erent line:

> O Phoebus and Diana . . . grant the blessings that we pray for at the holy season when the verses of the Sibyl have com-manded chosen maidens and spotless youths to sing the hymn in honor of the gods who love the Seven Hills.

Calling up images of worthy matrons and stout-hearted Roman fathers, he praises "wedlock and the marriage law, destined, we pray, to be prolific in new offspring . . ." Perpetuating this theme of fertility, Horace refers to Mother Earth, Ceres, Luna, Aeneas, and the allegorical virtues that undergird Rome's greatness:

> Already Faith and Peace and Honor and ancient Modesty and neglected Virtue have the courage to come back, and blessed Plenty with her full horn is seen.

Ending as he began, Horace closes his formal prayer with a devout hope that Phoebus and Diana will bless his homeland.

OVID

- *Metamorphoses*

- *Amores (Love Poems)*

- *Ars Amatoria
  (The Art of Love)*

- *Fasti (Holidays)*

- **Lesser Works**

OVID

LIFE AND BACKGROUND

Although he was reared in the Abruzzi region of the Apennine Mountains, ninety miles due east of Rome, Publius Ovidius Naso, was no bucolic bumpkin. Lightheartedly referring to himself as "Naso" in his autobiographical verses, he quickly became the darling of big city intelligentsia, and he eventually was recognized as the most outstanding love poet of his era.

Fortunately for modern readers, his bent toward autobiography, along with biographical bits from Seneca, has left the world a fairly clear picture of his life and times. Ovid was born on March 20, 43 B.C., a year after Caesar's assassination, to old money, upper-middle-class parents. He had an older brother, also born on March 20, and both boys were aware at an early age that their practical, middle-aged father intended for them to study law.

Accordingly, when Ovid was a teenager, he went to Rome and studied Greek and Latin literature and rhetoric under the tutelage of an Asian, Arellius Fuscus, and a Spaniard, Porcius Latro. Later, as was expected of good students who were monied, Ovid studied philosophy in Athens and even visited the site of ancient Troy. His older brother, also a law graduate, eventually practiced in the Roman basilica, and Ovid, when he wound up his tour of the sites of Greek civilization, also entered the courts, often delivering his legal arguments in verse, to the amusement of the audience.

When Ovid was nineteen, his brother died, and Ovid rebelled, quit his job as a lower court judge, abandoned a sure path to the rank of senator, and dedicated his life to poetry. Freed from surreptitious scribbling (lawyers were not supposed to be serious poets), he began giving frequent public readings of his work. His first collection was published about 20 B.C. under the patronage of Messalla and became an immediate best-seller. Thus, Ovid achieved notoriety early in his career. All of Rome was quoting his erotic verses.

Ovid, as we have noted, was an inveterate traveler before he returned to Rome to practice law. He spent over a year in Athens, traveling along the coast of Asia Minor and in Sicily, journeys which influenced his writing. A voracious reader, Ovid memorized and imitated the works of his contemporaries, especially Tibullus, Propertius, and Aemilius Macer, his traveling companion. Back in Rome, however, his life rapidly altered his personality as he conformed to the ways of fashionable, fast-paced literati, who set the standards of behavior in the infancy of the Empire. Although he lived by less opulent standards, Ovid, too, courted many young women and cultivated gaiety and wit, the hallmarks of Rome's evolving court, in contrast to his contemporary, Virgil, who disdained the pose of bon vivant.

Ovid married three times; the first two marriages, arranged by his father, quickly proved to be mistakes, but the third, to Fabia, was a lasting joy. Despite ten years' separation, when Ovid was in exile, his wife remained steadfast during her husband's most difficult times. Although Ovid was a winsome, lovable character, he fell out of favor with Augustus in 8 A.D. and was exiled to Tomis, a desolate Roman outpost south of the mouth of the Danube River, on the northern shores of the Black Sea. In addition, his books were banned from Rome's three public libraries. However, he felt fortunate in two respects: his property was not confiscated, and his parents did not live to see their youngest son shamed.

Ovid never reveals the nature of his crime in specific detail. On the surface, Augustus (who was a cranky seventy-one when he banished Ovid) labeled Ovid's poetry as indecent, particularly the sensual *Ars Amatoria (The Art of Love)*, a treatise on how to win the love of a mistress, published ten years previous to Ovid's exile. It is more likely that the emperor banished Ovid out of personal spite; Ovid hints at such an explanation in the *Tristia (Sadness)*:

> You [Augustus] avenged on me, as is right, a quarrel of your own. . . . Because my eyes unknowingly beheld a crime, I am punished. To have had the power of sight—this is my sin . . . it was my mistake that led me astray; my purpose was foolish, but not wicked.

A likely explanation is that Ovid knew of, and possibly took part in, the illicit escapades of Augustus' granddaughter Julia with Decimus Junius Silanus. This affair caused such a scandal that it led to Julia's expulsion, occurring about the same time as Ovid's own expulsion.

At Tomis, a dismal land populated by boorish people, Ovid saved himself from the insanities of grief, loneliness, and frustration by writing poems, including a eulogy in the local dialect about Augustus and Tiberius, a work that is regrettably lost. His major output during the final ten years of his life includes five books of the *Tristia* and four books of *Epistulae ex Ponto (Letters from the Black Sea)*, elegies to his wife, Fabia, to his friends, and to the emperor. In the *Tristia,* he reveals genuine remorse:

> When in my mind of that night the sorrowful vision arises,
> Which was the end of my life spent in the city of Rome,
> When I remember the night when I parted from all that was
>   dearest,
> Sadly a piteous tear falls even now from my eyes.

Although his work was a direct appeal for clemency, or at least, a plea for a less miserable place of exile, Ovid failed to move Augustus or his successor, Tiberius. He attempted to bear his burden manfully, but died, wretched and alone, far from Fabia, his daughter, Perilla, and his two grandchildren.

In contrast to his more pensive works written in exile, Ovid's greatest achievements were completed in the early part of his career. The three books of the *Amores (Loves)* contain forty-nine poems and describe the poet's relationship with Corinna, possibly a pseudonym for one of his early sweethearts, whom he describes as tall, slim, auburn-haired, and pale. The twenty-one love letters known as the *Heroides (Demigoddesses)* represent lines imaginatively composed, as it were, by fifteen women of the Heroic Age, including Phaedra, Ariadne, Medea, Dido, Sappho, Helen, Hero, and Penelope.

Other works that detail the nature of physical passion include a hundred-line fragment, *De Medicamine Faciei (The Care of the Face),* which includes exacting recipes for cosmetic preparations; the three books of the *Ars Amatoria,* a manual on seduction; and the *Remedia Amoris (Cures for Love).* He also penned a tragedy, *Medea,* now lost, which Quintilian labeled the finest in Greece or Rome, and two minor poems—*Ibis,* a scurrilous attack against an unnamed enemy in Rome, and *Halieutica (On Fishing),* a rather dull poetic treatise about fish, left uncompleted at his death.

Ovid's least characteristic verse is found in the *Fasti (Holidays)* and in the fifteen-book *Metamorphoses (Transformations)*, his masterpiece. Both works are products of the Christian era and contain a breadth of scope and subject matter unlike his other poems. The *Metamorphoses*, which was published shortly before his exile, is an unbroken series of two hundred and fifty stories from Greek mythology, beginning with primeval chaos and ending with the transformation of Julius Caesar into a star. The volume has influenced the major Italian and English poets, notably Chaucer, Boccaccio, Tasso, Petrarch, Dante, Marlowe, Spenser, Shakespeare, Milton, and Dryden, as well as the great painters of the Renaissance. The *Fasti*, a twelve-book work, six of which were never polished for publication, covers the origins of Roman holidays and contains stories from Roman mythology and early history.

Although Ovid lacked depth of characterization, he is remembered and loved for his ease of rhythm, carefree point of view, sparkling innovation, and command of narration. He predicted, at the end of the *Metamorphoses*, that the work would make his name immortal. He had high hopes for the book and intended to dedicate it to the emperor, and after his death, to Germanicus, Caligula's father. Later, from exile, he speaks with bitterness and dissatisfaction in the autobiographical *Tristia*, Book I, verse 7:

> On departing from Rome, I burned this poem [*Metamorphoses*] as well as many others of my works, either because I was disgusted with poetry which had proved my bane, or because this poem was still rough and unfinished.

Later, he relented and asked his friends to publish their copies. The work rose to prominence and for centuries was known as the textbook of classical mythology.

METAMORPHOSES

Written at the height of Ovid's power as a poet, the *Metamorphoses* combines in one smooth, intertwined narration the whole of Greek and Roman mythology. It begins in the murky era that precedes creation. Before describing the gods' taming of the elements, the poet calls on divine assistance to "breathe on these my undertakings, and bring down my song in unbroken strains from the world's very beginning even unto the present time." He describes the shapelessness of earth, wind, and water before Nature imposed order.

In **Book I,** when humanity appears, the earthly ages rank in descending adherence to Nature's dictates—first, the Golden Age, a time when righteous people had no need of law to restrain them from sinful actions; next, the Silver Age, less comfortable with the advent of winter; then the Bronze Age, a time of "sterner disposition"; followed by the Iron Age, when "all evil burst forth." Ovid delves into early lore—the coming of giants, the flood—and he ends with the promise of Phaethon, child of the sun.

Book 2 finishes the story of Phaethon, the unfortunate boy, struck from Hyperion's rightful seat in the sun-chariot and hurled through the heavens to a remote spot below where Naiads mark his tomb with a suitable epitaph: "Though he greatly failed, more greatly dared."

Book 3 turns to more intriguing tales, particularly the story of Teiresias' transformation from male to female for a period of seven years and the tragic experiences of Echo and Narcissus. All three undergo metamorphoses, or changes: Teiresias, because of an error in judgment; Echo, on account of her distracting chatter; and Narcissus, for the sacrilege of mocking nymphs. After Teiresias strikes a blow at two mating serpents, he is punished for impiety. Echo, who detains Juno whenever Jupiter is keeping company with the nymphs, suffers the wrath of her mistress, who rails, "That tongue of thine, by which I have been tricked, shall have its power curtailed and enjoy the briefest use of speech." Echo pines away until nothing remains but her voice.

Narcissus, who mocks Echo, receives his chastisement from Nemesis, who decrees that Narcissus may "himself love, and not gain the thing he loves!" Distraught with unrequited passion, Narcissus gazes at his reflection in a spring and collapses on the grass. As Echo and the dryads lament his going, Narcissus disappears. "In place of his body, they find a flower, its yellow center girt with white petals," another example of the graceful transformations that are Ovid's focus.

Book 4 contains one of literature's most famous love stories—that of Pyramus and Thisbe—which Shakespeare used as a play-within-a-play in *A Midsummer Night's Dream*. The handsome pair, who are next-door neighbors in Assyria, fall in love, but disapproving parents forbid them to marry. To continue their daily communication, Pyramus and Thisbe whisper through a chink in the garden wall. When Pyramus mistakenly assumes that a lion devoured his love, he cries out:

> Oh, I have been the cause of your death, poor girl, in that
> I bade you come forth by night into this dangerous place and
> did not myself come hither first. Come rend my body and
> devour my guilty flesh with your fierce fangs, O all ye lions
> who have your lairs beneath this cliff!

After Pyramus kills himself with his sword, Thisbe, who is not dead after all, finds her lover's corpse and, in despair, follows his example, killing herself with the same weapon. According to Ovid's version, "Her prayers touched the gods and touched her parents; for the color of the mulberry fruit still darkens to blood-red when it is ripe, and all that remained from both funeral pyres rests in a common urn."

Book 5 contains another important myth, Pluto's abduction of Proserpina, which takes place in Sicily. In this tale, Proserpina, Ceres' daughter, is gathering flowers when Pluto sees her and falls prey to love. Without hesitation, he snatches her up and "sped his chariot and urged on his horses, calling each by name and shaking the dark-dyed reins on their necks and manes." Striking downward with his scepter, he creates a fissure in the earth and plunges deep within, toward Tartarus.

Ceres mourns the loss of her fair, innocent child and demands Proserpina's return. Because Pluto remains adamant, Jove intervenes in their argument and mediates a settlement:

> Now the goddess, the common divinity of two realms, spends
> half the months with her mother and with her husband, half.
> Straightway the bearing of her heart and face is changed; she
> who but lately even to [Pluto] seemed sad, now wears a joyful
> countenance; like the sun, long concealed behind dark and
> misty clouds, reveals his face.

Thus, Jove effects a change in the earth itself: when Proserpina is on earth with her mother, Nature rejoices, but when Proserpina returns to the underworld, winter covers the landscape with leafless boughs and barren fields.

Another mournful tale of mother love, the story of Niobe, appears in **Book 6.** Niobe, proud beyond measure of her children, angers Latona by demanding that Latona's worshippers turn their hymns of praise to Niobe. Boasting, Niobe proudly points out:

> Surely I am happy. Who can deny it? And happy I shall remain. This also who can doubt? My very abundance has made me safe. I am too great for Fortune to harm. . . . Away with you, you have sacrificed quite enough, and take off those laurels from your hair.

As surely as pride is (usually) punished in classic literature, Niobe suffers dire pain. Her children, one by one, die torturous deaths. Niobe desperately begs that the least one be spared, but her prayers earn her no mercy. Finally, Niobe is metamorphosed into a waterfall atop a mountain peak, where her tears continue to cascade to the land below.

Books 7 and **8** relate more involved heroic tales – the tale of Jason and Medea, and that of Theseus and the Minotaur. An offshoot of Theseus' triumph over the Minotaur is the punishment of Daedalus, who is banished to Crete because he knows too much about the scandal of Queen Pasiphaë's lust for a bull. A well-crafted story of a father's love for his son, the poem details how Daedalus, an inventive genius, makes wings so that he and Icarus may fly home:

> He laid out feathers in order, first the smallest,
> A little larger next it, and so continued,
> The way that pan-pipes rise in gradual sequence.
> He fastened them with twine and wax, at middle.
> At bottom, so, and bent them, gently curving,
> So that they looked like wings of birds, most surely.

Wary of the dangers of flying, Daedalus warns his son to "fly a middle course," the Golden Mean of classic philosophy.

Unfortunately, the temptation to reach heaven's heights is too great for so immature a child. As he soars above a fisherman, shepherd, and plowman below, he exults, "'This is wonderful!' and left his father/Soared higher, higher, drawn to the vast heaven . . . " Too late, he realizes his error. He calls for his father as he tumbles downward "until the blue sea hushed him. . . . And Daedalus, father no more," realizes that his great engineering feat has cost him the life of his son.

Book 9, which contains similar feats of daring, ends (for the moment) Ovid's series of heroic tales with the twelve labors of Hercules.

In **Book 10,** Ovid once again turns his attention to tender tales of human love, notably that of Orpheus and Eurydice, Hyacinth, Venus and Adonis, and – one of the most influential of Ovid's stories – his retelling of the story of Pygmalion, the sculptor who falls in love with his own work. Pygmalion devotes himself to art, never taking the time to find a wife. Instead, he sublimates his desire for women by creating the ideal maiden out of ivory.

Smitten by her beauty, he caresses her and presents her with gifts – flowers, birds, jewelry, and rich robes. On the day of Venus' annual festival, he prays hesitantly at the love-goddess's altar:

> "Please, Goddess, if you can grant all human requests," He barely breathed his prayer, "If it is not profane to utter it, I would choose for wife a girl just like my ivory maiden."

Returning to his workshop, he again strokes the smooth surface of the statue. To his amazement, it feels soft, warm, and strangely yielding to his touch. He detects a hint of pulsation within the veins. Joyfully, he kisses her lips, and she proves herself human – she blushes.

In **Books 11** through **15,** Ovid returns to more heroic stories, here featuring human weaknesses, including those of Midas and the Golden Touch, Achilles and the Trojan War, Polyphemus and Ulysses, Aeneas' voyage to Italy, Hippolytus and Phaedra, and many lesser known tales. Ovid ends his work with a tribute to Augustus' family. At the conclusion of Book 15, he describes how Julius Caesar, "glorious in peace and war," is turned into a star. After linking the ruling house of the Roman Empire with the major myths of Greece and Rome, Ovid confers greatness on himself: "For wheresoever the Roman eagles spread their conquering wings, I shall of all be read."

❧

_____AMORES (LOVE POEMS)_____

Ovid, who wrote his worldly, but charming *Amores (Love Poems)*
while in a good-natured, light-hearted mood, appends a prefatory note
to **Book 1:**

> Once five, now three slim volumes,
> We are Naso's preference.
> Even if we give no pleasure
> The pain will be two books less.

He claims that he intended to write an epic, but that Cupid
scratched out a section. The poet tries to brush the meddler aside:

> You young savage . . . poetry's none of your business.
> We poets are committed to the Muses . . .
> You've a large empire, my boy – too much power already.
> Why so eager for extra work?

Cupid makes his standard reply and shoots Ovid with a mono-
grammed arrow. Overpowered by love, Ovid tosses in his bed and
aches all over. Finally he relents:

> I'm your latest victim
> Standing here with my hands up.
> The war's over. I'm suing for peace and pardon.
> There's no glory in shooting an unarmed man.

The poet joins forces with the winged god, and, with Cupid's aid,
begins his famous book of amorous verse.

Ovid vows to his beloved that he is "faithful" – that is, he remains
true to one girl at a time. Then he turns to specifics: learning that
her husband is going to the same dinner party which they plan to
attend, Ovid says that he hopes her husband chokes. He concocts a
plan: she should arrive first, join her husband at his couch, but maintain communication with Ovid by means of secret signals, nods, and
winks, each of them having an above-suspicion, prearranged meaning with "someone." Ovid urges her not to succumb to intimacies with
her husband lest Ovid have to watch at a distance and suffer. To keep
her husband's mind off love, she should get him drunk so that she
and Ovid can make a hasty exit.

Stanza 5 introduces the female persona of the work – Corinna, who wears a short dress and unbound tresses. Ripping away her filmy garment, Ovid admires her slender body before making love in the sultry afternoon heat. Sated with passion, the two fall asleep.

In contrast to this rapturous mating, Ovid beats his beloved in Stanza 7 and makes her cry. Then, as angry at himself as "Homeric Ajax when he massacred the flocks," Ovid begs his friends to bind his limbs until his fit is over. He castigates himself for his atrocious behavior and asks, "If I struck the humblest citizen I'd pay for it; have I any more right to strike my mistress?" He urges her to take sweet revenge by digging her nails into his face.

Stanza 9, which is suffused with a military motif, declares that love is the province of the young:

> Lovers too keep watch, bivouac, mount guard —
> At their mistress' door instead of H.Q.
> They have their forced marches,
> Tramping miles for love,
> Crossing rivers, climbing mountains,
> Trudging through the snow.

They resort to strategy to outwit sleeping husbands, and the results are a gamble. Like war, love has its "ups and downs. In both, apparent heroes can collapse." For best results, lovers must be courageous and enterprising — like Ovid, who claims to have been "born in a dressing-gown."

In Stanza 10, Ovid evaluates passion as it applies to males and females. He concludes that love is an equal venture, with gains and losses for both sides. A grateful lover will repay favors with kindness, loyalty, and gifts. Ovid's gift, his verses, are special in that they can confer fame: "Dresses tear, jewels and golden trinkets break, but poetic fame is a lasting present." He scorns his girlfriend for demanding payment in cash.

In the next pair of stanzas, Ovid sends a love letter by means of Napë, Corinna's hairdresser, who serves as go-between. He urges Napë to wait for a reply, hoping that it will be a long letter. Then, impatient with desire, he changes his request and asks for one simple word: "YES will do, in huge block capitals." His lover's answer blunts his ardor — "Can't manage today." In a fit of pique, he damns the wooden tablets on which the messages are written: "God rot their wood with worm and their wax with white mildew!"

Stanza 14 contains a direct message from Ovid to his love – stop tinting your hair before it falls out! Ovid likes its natural color: "It wasn't dark and it wasn't golden – it was both and neither . . ." In a cascade of admiring lines, he ponders the flow and delicacy of his sweetheart's hair. He exhorts her to look into her mirror with a different attitude and realize that she is naturally beautiful and needs no adornment.

Book 2 begins on an autobiographical note, "Another collection of verse by the man from Sulmona, that embarrassingly personal poet Naso." He admits that love is more important to him than piety:

> But while I was busy with Jupiter standing on a storm cloud,
> Thunderbolt at the ready to defend his heaven,
> Corinna slammed her door. I dropped the thunderbolt
> And even forgot the Almighty.

He begs forgiveness for his lust, which causes him to write verses.

In Stanza 2, a new woman catches his eye. He sends a message by her chaperone, Bagoas, and he attempts to bribe him so that dalliance will be easier. Ovid advises Bagoas to save the bribes so that he may someday buy his freedom. Informers, he assures the slave, end up in chains. Ovid's cynical words push for an alliance of seducer and chaperone: "Why fight against odds? You're bound to be beaten, in both senses."

Stanza 3 is an abrupt shift to a pitiable situation, the nameless state of the eunuch. Ovid insists that the castrator "should have suffered the wound he inflicted." With surprising agility and a generous dollop of crassness, Ovid changes the subject from "pity" to "money," urging Bagoas to "serve her well" so that he might obtain a generous reward. Such foresight, the poet notes, could become a "good investment."

Responding to his own self-seeking behavior in Stanza 3, the poet now castigates himself for his weak character and for his lack of self-discipline. Yet, he seems at ease with his clay feet:

> A graceful walk can step into my life.
> Awkwardness requires male relaxation.
> A silvery soprano tempts me
> To steal a coloratura kiss.

Listing the feminine traits and wiles that never fail to ensnare him, he admits that he loves all kinds of women, short and tall, young and "not so young," dark and light. "Put it like this –," he concludes, "there's beauty in Rome to please all tastes, and mine are all-embracing."

In imitation of Catullus' "sparrow poems," Ovid's Stanza 6 employs the mock epic technique to mourn the passing of Corinna's pet:

Parrot is dead – the Indian mimic.
Flock, you birds, to his funeral.
Good birds all, with wings and talons
Tear your hackles, beat your breasts.

Raising the bird to immortality with his verses, the poet mourns the loss of the bird's emerald feathers, his purple beak "with saffron spots." Ovid maintains that Fate, out of envy, snatched the bird away.

Stanza 9 returns to Ovid's favorite topic – passion. He pities men who enjoy a full night's sleep:

Offered a sexless heaven I'd say No thank you –
Women are such sweet hell.

In contrast to this light banter, Stanza 13 shows the poet in a somber mood:

My foolish love, being pregnant, tried to end it
And now she lies at death's door.
How could she take that risk without telling me?
I ought to be angry but I'm only afraid.
Still, the child was mine, or at least I think so.

At the end of the stanza, Ovid is willing to forego his usual adolescent ardor and assume a mature role in the relationship: if only Corinna survives, he says, he will do anything.

Ovid continues his jovial, life-loving hexameters into **Book 3,** but he makes an abrupt shift in Stanza 9 to mourn the death of his contemporary, the poet Tibullus:

Your poet laureate
Is burning on the tall pyre,
And Cupid's bow is broken,
His quiver reversed,
His torch burnt out.

Ovid sadly notes that "Death mocks dedication with the laying on of invisible hands." He comforts himself that all due ceremony is observed, that the ashes rest in a small urn, that Tibullus' mother and sister have performed the proper obsequies, and that Delia whispers over his grave, "My love gave you life." As Tibullus is greeted by Catullus and other notable Roman literati in Elysium below, the earth falls lightly on his remains. "To these rare spirits," Ovid asserts, "Tibullus brings grace."

Ovid's parting verse sums up his opinion of his own poetic talent. Placing himself among Rome's great lyricists, he claims:

> The Mantuans have Virgil, the Veronese Catullus,
> But I shall be the pride of the Peligni . . .
> Picture the future tourist, among these streams,
> Sizing up Sulmona:
> 'How tiny to produce a major poet!
> I call that great,' he'll say.

Grateful for his talent, which, more than fame or honor, brings him personal satisfaction, Ovid rounds out his verses with a farewell to the Muse, who inspires his "labour of love – these immortal remains."

ARS AMATORIA (THE ART OF LOVE)

Ovid begins his famous treatise on love with energy and purpose. First, to reassure the reader of his expertise, he establishes his method:

> The more violently Love has pierced and branded me, the better shall I avenge the wound that he has made: I will not falsely claim that my art is your gift, O Phoebus [the god of prophecy], nor am I taught by the voice of a bird of the air . . . experience inspires this work: give ear to an experienced bard; true will be my song: favor my enterprise, O mother of Love.

In order to practice lovemaking, one must find someone to love. Thus,

Ovid outlines "the pursuit" in one-two-three order: first, find an in-experienced girl; then, woo her; and finally, "make love long endure."

The poet declares that there is no dearth of choice women in Rome – they can be found on city promenades, at temples, even in law courts. They are particularly plentiful around theaters, where "they come to see; they come that they may be seen . . ." Another possibility, the Circus Maximus, is an auspicious spot to initiate casual conversation and gain audience with a likely candidate. At this point, Ovid inserts a forty-two-line digression honoring Augustus Caesar's victories in the eastern Mediterranean. Returning to his subject of where to meet girls, Ovid notes that banquets, too, are rife with nubile maidens.

Having completed the first part of his task, the poet deals with pursuit, the second stage in the art of love. He assures his reader that "all women can be caught; spread but your nets and you will catch them." With a sprinkling of allusions to familiar love stories from mythology, Ovid justifies his basic tenet: women like passion as much as men. Regardless of their marital state, "whether they grant or deny you, they are pleased to have been asked. . . . In fields not ours, the crops are ever more bounteous, and the neighboring herd has richer udders."

As a means of strategy, Ovid suggests that the pursuer make friends with the object's handmaiden. Any ruse, he says, is fair: "Corrupt her [the servant] with promises, or corrupt her with prayers; if she be willing, you will gain your end with ease." He urges the lover to avoid buying his love a flood of gifts, but instead, "let wax [tablets] go first to show your mind." The words should first inspire trust; then one can coax his beloved into a liaison.

Other mild flirtations may also prove fruitful – following milady's sedan chair into the market, drinking from her cup, ordering the same food she orders, and even attempting to please her husband. When the time is right, the next step is "to ensnare the mind with crafty flatteries, as the water undermines an overhanging bank." Another possibility is tears, which Ovid claims "can move iron." In some cases, the pursued may also yield to force, for "they often wish to give un-willingly what they like to give."

Some additional admonitions add polish to the lover: he might profitably remain pale and lean and keep his pursuit a secret from other men lest they move in on his territory. Ovid sums up his advice on a hopeful note: ". . . various are the hearts of women; use a thousand means to waylay as many hearts. . . . Here fish are caught with spears, there with hooks; here they are dragged with taut ropes in hollow nets. Let not one method suit all ages . . ."

Now that Ovid has the lover triumphant and exulting in his conquest, he attacks a key issue—how to maintain a love affair. Harshness, he declares, is treacherous. Instead, the lover should "keep far away from quarrels and bitter-tongued affrays; with soft words should love be fostered." Fighting, he contends, is the province of married couples. Lovers maintain their joyous state by persevering during mood fluctuations and complying with the love object's state of mind, however perverse or unpredictable.

Although the path seems smooth, the way to a lady's heart is anything but easy. "Love is a kind of warfare; avaunt, ye laggards! These banners are not for timid men to guard. Night, storm, long journeys, cruel pains, and all kinds of toil are in this dainty camp." To assure a place in his beloved's affections, the lover should ingratiate himself with her household by sending gifts of fruit, nuts, or live pigeons. For the lover herself, poetry, unfortunately, falls second to gold, the preferred gift.

Once having gained the beloved's attention, the lover must change his tactics: ". . . the wind to which you spread your sails when leaving the shore should not be used when once you have won the open sea." Small separations may be useful, although lengthy departures are certain death to love affairs. If the lover dallies with another mistress, he should hide all traces of his affair and carry out his affairs discreetly, destroying all love letters. If caught, he should deny his guilt, even though it is undeniable. While his beloved rages over his infidelity, the lover should continue to caress and soothe her, allowing her a brief moment to vent her emotion before renewing his ardor.

Although Ovid counsels the pursuer to tolerate rivals, he admits that he himself has slim patience when his mistress eyes another. Yet, he perceives that a mistress is newly inflamed with passion when she believes that she has duped her lover. Citing the example of Mars and Venus, who are caught in Vulcan's net while making love, Ovid concludes that the lover should forego suspicion: "Devise no toils for your rival, nor lie in wait for letters written in a secret hand." It is advisable to keep silent and bear all calumny. Accusing one's beloved will yield only a quick dismissal.

Ovid ends this section with a promise to young women that his next effort will be on their behalf. True to his word, his next section is dedicated to "you, Penthesilea [the mythic female warrior], and to your troop." Women, he begins, are armed with weapons that differ from the male arsenal. Whereas men often deceive, women are less often inclined to perfidy. So that women can protect themselves from faithless lovers, Ovid divulges the secret of lasting love: "Shall I tell what led you all to ruin? You knew not how to love; it was skill you lack; skill makes love unending." A bit rueful that he is betraying his own sex, he nonetheless chooses to obey Venus, his muse, and tell all.

In recognition of the brevity of life, Ovid warns women to use their wiles and beauty as long as they can, for old age will lessen their capabilities:

> That day will come when you, who now shut out your lovers,
> will lie, a cold and lonely old woman, through the night; nor
> will your door be broken in a nightly brawl, nor will you find
> your threshold strewn with roses in the morning.

Women fall prey to gray hair and other signs of aging because of rigorous childbearing, or, as Ovid phrases it, a "field grows old by continual harvesting." To make the most of beauty and vigor, women should eat wisely, groom themselves fastidiously – particularly their hair – and dress in flattering colors, namely sky-blue, golden yellow, turquoise, lavender, white, or gray.

Each woman's beauty regimen should be hidden from men; her toilette should be conducted in private. She should guard herself from stubbly legs and underarms and from bad breath, and she should hide her faults with artful posture, textured or padded clothing, facial masks, studied gestures, and a winsome laugh. To enhance her beauty, she should cultivate an alluring walk, exposing a bit of shoulder or upper arm for good measure.

Ovid covers a full list of accomplishments necessary to the well-versed coquette, including dancing and dicing (gambling). He warns women to beware the too-elegant male who mouths a glib line, thus betraying too great a knowledge of the mating game. In addition, the worldly woman should conceal her flirtations from her husband by artful deceit or outright fraud. In conclusion, Ovid commends the daring woman's pursuit of love, by whatever method is necessary to assure her pleasure.

FASTI (HOLIDAYS)

In a letter to Emperor Augustus, Ovid indicated that his book of holidays would comprise twelve books; however, he completed only six. Still, his frequent references to rituals and celebrations throughout the Roman calendar adequately covers the subject of Roman holidays. Ovid begins with January and continues through June, where he breaks off abruptly with the first week of July. (Note that the Roman month was divided into thirds, each marked by a significant day, either the *calends, ides,* or *nones.* Dates were expressed in the number of days before or after each point, as in "two days before the ides of April.")

Book I gets right to the point — Ovid intends to explain the system, purpose, and astrological underpinnings of the Roman calendar. He dedicates his poem to Germanicus, Tiberius' nephew and adopted son, and grandson of Augustus, who streamlined the Roman calendar. The original Roman calendar, established by Romulus, Rome's legendary first monarch, contained ten months in recognition of the approximate human lifespan before birth and the time of mourning which widows observed to honor their deceased husbands.

Romulus originally named the first month after Mars, the god of war and Rome's patron, and the second after Venus, mother of Aeneas, Rome's founder. The third and fourth months were named old and young — that is, *Maius* and *Junius;* the remaining six months were numbered. Numa, Rome's second king (715–673 B.C.), prefixed two months, the first in honor of Janus, the two-faced god. For business purposes, days were divided into three categories — religious, half-religious, and non-religious.

Following these prefatory remarks, Ovid sings a paean to Janus, herald of the new year and god of all beginnings and endings. Engaging the divine being in an imaginary conversation, Ovid learns the nature and purpose of new year celebrations, including reading of the omens and propitiating the gods with incense and wine to assure good fortune throughout the year. After a thorough discussion of the astrological signs that mark January, Ovid ends his description with a prayer for peace.

The second month of the Roman calendar is named for *februa*, the "instruments of purification":

> When houses are swept out, the toasted [grain] and salt which
> the officer gets as means of cleansing are called by the same
> name. The same name is given to the bough, which, cut from
> a pure tree, wreaths with its leaves the holy brows of priests.

Ovid notes that ancient people believed that the February ritual purged Rome of "every sin and every cause of ill." A major religious festival of February, the Lupercal, mentioned in the opening scenes of Shakespeare's *Julius Caesar*, honors Rome's early beginnings and the cave where the she-wolf, or *lupa*, suckled Romulus and Remus. From February 18–21, Ovid emphasizes, Romans traditionally honor the dead. On the last day, the Parentalia, they bring small gifts to their ancestors' tombs. Parentalia commemorates Aeneas' pious offerings to his father, Anchises, who died during the voyage from Troy to Italy. February ends with signs of spring's approach.

In describing the third month, which is dedicated to Mars, Ovid retells the legend of Rhea Silvia, the Vestal priestess whom Mars impregnated: "Sleep left her; she lay big, for already within her womb there was Rome's [legendary] founder." Amulius, the tyrant king, feared the twin boys would rob him of his ill-gotten throne and had them "sunk in the river." But the waters withdrew, leaving the infants safe on dry land.

In his discussion of March, Ovid makes a case for the month of Mars as a likely beginning of the "true year," because it brings fresh laurel branches and other signs of spring. He duly notes the date of Julius Caesar's assassination, which Vesta insists that he acknowledge out of respect for her "priest." (Note: Julius Caesar held the rank of *pontifex maximus*, or chief priest, a significant political post.) Ovid justifies the violence that followed Caesar's death and declares that Augustus performed "his duty, his first task by righteous arms to avenge his [adoptive] father."

March ends with lengthy festivals in honor of Minerva, and April continues the spirit of worship with the rites of Venus, Aeneas' mother. Ovid notes:

> In the time of our forefathers, Rome had fallen from a state of chastity, and the ancients consulted the [Sybil] of Cumae. She ordered a temple to be built to Venus, and when that was duly done, Venus took the name of Changer of the Heart [*Verticordia*] from the event.

Following her rituals come the games in honor of Ceres, goddess of the bountiful harvest, apparently one of Ovid's favorite times of year. Later in April, Romans celebrate the Parilia, or Palilia, the shepherds' festival in honor of the discovery of fire and Rome's founding.

The poet then explains the derivation of May. He calls upon Polyhymnia, the muse of sacred poetry, who explains how Majesty, or *Maiestas*, was born of the union of Honor and Reverence. Seated on Olympus beside Modesty and Fear, the worthy goddess rules heaven: "Straightway respect for dignities made its way into their minds; the worthy got their due, and nobody thought much of himself." A protector of Jupiter, she "assures to him his scepter's peaceful tenure."

The subject matter of the next book momentarily puzzles Ovid. He sits in a sacred grove and muses a bit—when suddenly Juno appears at a distance and says:

> O poet, minstrel of the Roman year, you who have dared to chronicle great things in slender couplets, you have won for yourself the right to look upon a celestial divinity by undertaking to celebrate the festivals in your numbers . . . know that June takes its name from mine.

Freed from his quandary, Ovid describes the festivities that mark June, particularly weddings, which interest him because his daughter is about to marry. He completes his almanac through June 30, looking forward to the "birthday of the Calends of July."

LESSER WORKS

Because they comprise a major portion of his canon, it is perhaps inexact to refer to Ovid's *Tristia, Ex Ponto,* and *Heroides* as "lesser," or "minor" works. Yet, in comparison to the lofty themes of the *Metamorphoses* and the scintillating verses of his love lyrics, they run a poor second. Certainly, there is much to learn about Ovid the poet from these lesser known works.

The *Heroides,* published in 15 B.C., is a product of a happy period in Ovid's life. Although artificial and a bit mechanical in construction, these fictional letters from famous women are disarming but, in their own way, believable. Because the poet refers to familiar love stories, he appeals to the romantic tastes and interests of the casual reader, rather than the more erudite literati of Rome.

The opening lines, from Penelope to Ulysses, in contrast with Homer's masculine point of view, reveal an anxious, fearful wife: "This missive your Penelope sends to you, O Ulysses, slow of return that you are—yet write nothing back to me; yourself come!" Although she has received rumors of his activities and whereabouts, fantasies and alarms plague her mind because of his long, unexplained delay.

Another intriguing liaison, Achilles' love affair with Briseis, suggests that the girl, whose abrupt departure initiated Achilles' divisive feud with Agamemnon, regrets their enforced separation. Doubly cursed in her slavery, she wails:

> Ah me! I had to go, and with no farewell kiss; but tears without end I shed, and I rent my hair—miserable me, I seemed a second time to suffer the captive's fate!

She indicates that her relationship with Achilles was triply satisfying, for she, in the absence of family and friends, considered him master, husband, and brother.

In contrast to the chaste, naive love babblings of Briseis, Phaedra's voice smolders like a mature woman, inflamed by an illicit passion for her stepson, Hippolytus. Burdened with the fact that she can never acknowledge her love for her husband's handsome son, she says, "Love has come to me, the deeper for its coming late—I am burning with love within; I am burning, and my breast has an unseen wound." Likewise, Queen Dido succumbs to passion in her riper years and plunges into a doomed affair. Like Phaedra, she refers to the heat of love: "I am all ablaze with love, like torches of wax tipped with sulphur . . ."

Both women speak without hope, relieving their tensions through the futile act of putting words on paper.

Later in Ovid's life, the mournful verses that he penned express his own complaints at the terms of exile which denied him access to Rome, his friends and family, and the rhythms of life that at one time filled his days. He opens the *Tristia,* a compendium of letters sent from his home on the Black Sea, with an explanation of his circumstances:

> Little book, you will go without me – and I grudge it not – to the city [Rome]. Alas, that your master is not allowed to go! Go, but go unadorned, as becomes the book of an exile. . . . Be not ashamed of blots; he who sees them will feel that they were caused by my tears.

Ovid's former, charming way with words does not fail him in exile, for he notes, "Go, my book, and in my name greet the loved places: I will tread them at least with what foot I may," a witty reference to the metrical feet of his verse.

He describes in chilling detail his emotional response to stark reality, the fact that he must pay the price for his unidentified crime:

> No time had there been or spirit to get ready what might suit best; my heart had become numb with the long delay. . . . I was as dazed as one who, smitten by the fire of Jove, still lives and knows not that he lives.

Ovid remembers how he clasped his friends, one by one, and his sobbing wife. His daughter, living in Libya, knew nothing about his abrupt departure. As he walked away, he looked back at his former home: "Men and women, children too, grieved at this funeral of mine; in my home, every corner had its tears."

In similar style, the *Epistulae ex Ponto (Letters from the Black Sea)* follow a pattern of mournful regret as Ovid writes to the Roman sources of power, his only hope. He commends his poetry to Brutus; to Germanicus, he exults over a recent victory against the Dalmatians; to Graecinus, he pleads:

> But in [Augustus Caesar's] leisure from the more pressing cares of state add both your prayers, I beseech you, to mine, and if the breeze shall belly any sail, loosen the cables that my bark may set forth from these hellish waters.

Naturally preoccupied with his banishment, Ovid is reduced to begging, a humbling that is moving in its dignity, yet grating in its repetitiveness.

To his wife, friends, and ex-friends, he chastises, "As long as my bark rested firmly upon its keel among all who wished to sail with me, you were first." His letters home are filled with details of the barren landscape that fills his eyes: ". . . to you [Pontus], autumn extends no clusters of grapes; but all seasons are in the grip of excessive cold." Although he refrains from denying his guilt, urging all to "defend not my deed," his constant plea to his wife and friends is that they do all in their power to release him from his hateful exile. Clearly, many of Ovid's lesser known works have an emotional power that is worthy of admiration.

Other examples of noteworthy lesser works capture a timeless charm and sophistication – for example, Ovid's *De Medicamine Faciei Liber (The Care of the Face)*, a work written before his *Art of Love*. This book is little more than a list of recipes for cosmetic treatment; yet, in its hundred lines, it captures a hedonistic desire to extend youth as far as possible by judicious use of jewelry and formulas for home beauty treatments.

Before offering his homey advice about bags under the eyes or spots on the face, Ovid urges women to

> . . . look to your behavior. The face pleases when character
> commends. Love of character is lasting: beauty will be ravaged
> by age, and the face that charmed will be plowed by wrinkles
> . . . Goodness endures and lasts for many a day, and through-
> out its years love securely rests thereon."

The poem breaks off abruptly with a formula for rouge: pound poppies with drops of cool water and rub them on the cheeks.

As a balance to his many tips on how to woo a fair maiden, Ovid produced a single treatise of 810 lines – written, most definitely, from a masculine viewpoint – on how to recover from love gone sour. He notes, ". . . if any endures the tyranny of an unworthy mistress, lest he perish, let him learn the help my art can give. . . . He who, unless he give o'er, will die of hapless love, – let him give o'er . . ."

His initial advice is practical – to recover from lovesickness, "first of all, shun leisure." In a stanza reminiscent of one of the best-known Puritan admonitions – that is, "An idle mind is the Devil's workshop" –

Ovid urges the erstwhile lover to forego moping, sleeping, gambling, and wine. To justify this sweeping dictum, he claims that "where sloth is, that Boy [Cupid] is wont to follow; he hates the busy: give the empty mind some business to occupy it." Like a modern advice-to-the-lovelorn columnist, the poet suggests that the victim of love should sublimate his desires with fresh country air and clean living. "Count not the days," he advises, "nor be ever looking back at Rome; but flee: by flight, the Parthian is still safe from his foe."

As he indicates in *The Care of the Face,* Ovid scorns the use of love potions, magic spells, and amulets: "He best wins freedom for himself who has burst the bonds that hurt his soul, and once and for all o'ercome the smart." In place of the supernatural, the poet suggests self-control. To break old habits, he advises the victim to "unlearn your loving . . . you must be taught by me."

He appends a lengthy list of possibilities for putting the offending lover in her place – using, for example, ridicule and revelation of her flaws, all of which will destroy the victim's desire to worship her. In order to supplant idealism, Ovid urges the lover to

> . . . turn to the worse your girl's attractions . . . call her fat, if she is full-breasted, black, if dark-complexioned; in a slender woman, leanness can be made a reproach. If she is not simple, she can be called pert; if she is honest, she can be called simple.

He promises the victim that if he follows this advice, he will be made whole again.

A bold departure from Ovid's usual ebullience is the *Ibis,* a melancholy work inspired by his miserable exile. He initiates the diatribe with a simple request for peace as he pursues his writing career, but he claims that a certain unnamed miscreant in Rome

> . . . vexes the wounds that crave repose and shouts my name in all the Forum, nor allows her who is joined to me in the perpetual union of the marriage-bed to weep for her husband's living corpse. . . . He strives that my exiled old age may lack sustenance: Ah! how much worthier is he himself of my distress!

Wrapping himself in layers of self-pity, the poet enumerates the standard curses that Romans employed to assuage a festering spirit. He would deny the offender the fruits of the earth, sun, wind, health, comfort, sexual pleasures, esteem, and even the release of death. He summons an array of mythic and literary allusions and promises to write more, at which time he shall name names.

The most un-Ovidian of works attributed to his authorship is the *Halieutica (On Fishing)*, which Pliny assures us is truly Ovid's verse. Although only a scant one hundred and thirty-five lines remain of the original, it seems reasonable to assume that Ovid wanted to explain the nature and purpose of fishing and to describe the types of fish that swam in the Mediterranean. In his usual dramatic fashion, Ovid details the emotions of the squid:

> . . . when caught perchance beneath the clear water (and every moment his entrails fear the clutching hands) he vomits dark blood from his mouth and stains the sea; then turns from his track baffling the eyes that follow him.

Likewise, the pike leaps from the net, the polypus clings to the rocks, the eel bites, and the anthias cuts the fisherman's line with the sharp spines on its back. There is not enough development, however, to indicate how Ovid planned to conclude this series.

THE SILVER AGE

- **Seneca**
- **Longinus**
- **Pliny the Elder**
- **Pliny the Younger**
- **Josephus**
- **Martial**
- **Plutarch**
- **Tacitus**
- **Epictetus**
- **Juvenal**
- **Suetonius**
- **Minor Writers**

SENECA

- *Moral Essays*
- Tragedies

SENECA

LIFE AND BACKGROUND

A prolific writer, philosopher, and consummate politician, Lucius Annaeus Seneca, son of Lucius Annaeus Seneca Senior, was born in Corduba (now Cordoba), Spain, around 4 B.C. to an upper-class family of means and influence. His family ties are notable for a variety of reasons: his father was a well-known rhetorician and his mother, Helvia, a model of virtue and cultivation; his elder brother, Novatus (or Gallio, as he was later called), is remembered for presiding over St. Paul's arraignment; and his younger brother, Mela, was the father of the brilliant, but ill-fated poet Lucan. All his family suffered in one way or another from the machinations of Rome's corrupt emperors.

Like other children of equestrian rank, Seneca came to Rome in infancy to be educated for a career in law and the military. His rise through the ranks to senator and *quaestor* was predictable, owing to his ease with public speaking and debate. Caligula, who called Seneca's speeches "sand without lime," is said to have condemned Seneca to death out of jealousy for his eloquence in the senate; fortunately, Caligula relented, supposedly because Seneca suffered ill health.

Intrigue, however, in the corrupt family of Claudius and Caligula resulted in Seneca's banishment to Corsica for an alleged adultery with Julia Livilla, Caligula's sister. During his eight-year exile, Seneca wrote his plaintive *Consolation* and sent it to his mother, Helvia. In 49 A.D., Agrippina, Claudius' new empress, had Seneca recalled so that he could serve as tutor and adviser to her eleven-year-old son, Domitius, later known as Nero.

It was during this period that perplexing inconsistencies appear between Seneca's beliefs and his practices, probably because of the tensions, jealousies, and power struggles that existed in the royal family. By careful financial maneuvers, Seneca turned his era to his

own benefit and became one of the wealthiest men in the Mediterranean world and served as virtual ruler of the Roman Empire by
means of his influence with Nero.

When Nero was crowned emperor after Claudius' death, Seneca
wrote "The Pumpkinification," a ribald satire based on the deifications
of earlier emperors. Seneca and Sextus Afranius Burrus, chief of the
Praetorian Guard, allied to keep Nero in check, but Agrippina concocted numerous schemes to rule through her impressionable son.
Long a buffer between Nero and Agrippina, these two precipitate,
cataclysmic forces, Seneca wrote a letter to the senate justifying Nero's
murder of Agrippina.

After Burrus' death, however, Seneca's political influence began
to crumble as Nero turned to Poppaea, his second wife, for guidance.
Seneca realized his tenuous position, and, before falling prey to Nero's
avarice and cruelty, he retired to the country with the emperor's blessing. After three years, he was implicated in the abortive conspiracy
of Gaius Calpurnius Piso and was ordered to kill himself. In 65 A.D.,
he and his wife, Paulina, slit their veins and awaited death. Slaves
rescued Paulina, but Seneca, who dictated a lengthy deathbed treatise
on morality, suffered protracted agony, which ended in suffocation
in the bath.

Despite his compromising political strategies, Seneca was un-
doubtedly the most brilliant thinker of his day. His broad learning
and his terse, epigrammatic style served as a model to later generations. His philosophy was grounded in stoicism, although early Church
fathers incorrectly suspected that he was a Christian and a confidant
of St. Paul and attempted to canonize him.

Of his extant works, the most memorable include twelve dialogues
on moral precept, three books on clemency, twenty books of correspondence, and seven books on physics entitled *Natural Questions*.
His nine tragedies—closet dramas, intended for dramatic recitation
rather than for the stage—greatly influenced French, Italian, and
English playwrights of the sixteenth century. The Spanish "tragedy
of blood" had its beginnings in the spectacle and bombast of Seneca's
theatrics. Likewise, he influenced Shakespeare, Webster, Abelard, and
Roger Bacon.

His greatest strength lay in the revival of philosophy in Roman
literature and the humanization and vitalization of stoicism. Seneca
espoused a belief in humanism and the brotherhood of man. He de-

plored gladiatorial contests, slavery, and cruelty, for which his era was notorious.

_____*MORAL ESSAYS*_____

Seneca's initial comments cover a subject that has long plagued human thought – why good people suffer. Seneca maintains that the world "does not endure without someone to guard it . . ." A deity, which Seneca calls Providence, "does not make a spoiled pet of a good man; it tests him, hardens him, and fits him for his own service." Like a cherishing parent, Providence looks beyond the trivialities of everyday life to a moment of crowning success, which comes when a person is able to "triumph over the calamities and terrors of mortal life."

In a later treatise dedicated to the Emperor Nero, Seneca discusses mercy as a means of instructing the young ruler in the "greatest of all pleasures." His argument is strong and appealing:

> . . . just as medicine is used by the sick, yet is held in honor by the healthy, so with mercy: though it is those who deserve punishment that invoke it, yet even the guiltless cherish it.

Cruelty, he notes, is unseemly in a monarch's behavior. To show himself worthy of rule, a wise monarch emphasizes his power to grant life:

> To save life is the peculiar privilege of exalted station, which never has a right to greater admiration than when it has the good fortune to have the same power as the gods, by whose kindness we all, the evil as well as the good, are brought forth into the light.

Mercy, Seneca concludes, rises above the law in that it injects fairness and beneficence into civic affairs. Like the nurseryman, the merciful ruler tends all the trees in the orchard, the weak as well as the strong, to enable them all to produce good fruit.

TRAGEDIES

Seneca's tragedies, which are the antithesis of his gentle, human essays, are noted for their emphasis on revenge, violence, and calamity. Written between 49 and 65 A.D., the plays, most of which are based on similarly titled works by Euripides, were not performed in the playwright's lifetime. It was not until the birth of Renaissance theatre that they were enacted on the stage.

The Mad Hercules, based on Euripides' *Heracles,* follows a predictable plotline: Hercules, returning to Thebes to save his wife, Megara, their childen, and his father, Amphitrion, from the tyrant Lycus, murders the usurper, but collapses in a frenzy and kills his wife and children. He recovers, realizes his crime, and contemplates suicide. He is persuaded to take refuge in Athens at the court of Theseus.

Seneca colors the tragedy with long, melodramatic speeches, such as Hercules' admission of wrongdoing:

> I haste to purge the earth of such as I. Now long enough has
> there been hovering before my eyes that monstrous shape
> of sin – so impious, savage, merciless, and wild. Thus come,
> my hand, attempt this mighty task, far greater than the last.

Comforted by his friend, Theseus, Hercules yearns to hide from his guilt in a place where lenience promotes mercy.

Seneca's *Trojan Women,* in imitation of a favorite Greek theme, features the multiple sufferings of Troy's noble women, particularly Polyxena, Hecuba, and Andromache. Andromache, falling before Ulysses, begs a reprieve for her doomed son and dredges up memories of home within the staunch Greek leader:

> So may you see again your faithful wife; so may Laertes live
> to greet you again; so may your son behold your face, and . . .
> excel his father's valor and the years of old Laertes. Pity my
> distress: the only comfort left me in my woe is this my son.

Andromache realizes that Ulysses intends to kill her son, an heir to the throne of Troy and a threat to Greek power. He leads the boy away, muttering that Andromache's grief is endless and that the fleet is being detained while they discuss mercy.

Seneca considered *Phaedra* and *Medea* his two most successful plays. His Medea, differing from Greek versions, sympathizes with the hero, Jason, whose evil wife murders her children; Seneca stresses the diabolical magic of the main character. In Act V, when Jason is about to seize Medea, she crows in victory:

> Now, now have I regained my regal state, my sire, my brother!
> ... And by the magic of this hour I am a maid once more.
> O heavenly powers, appeased at length! O festal hour! O
> nuptial day! Oh, no! Accomplished is the guilt, but not the
> recompense.

Medea's rationalizing is chilling proof of her mental aberration, which allows her unrestrained freedom in carrying out vile plots.

In *Phaedra*, too, Seneca dwells on the psychology of an unhappy woman. Her stiff, formal speeches belie the emotion of earlier versions, as is evident in her admission of an unspeakable passion for her stepson:

> Full consciously my soul goes headlong on its downward way,
> ofttimes with backward glance, sane counsel seeking still,
> without avail. So, when the mariner would sail his ship
> against the boisterous waves, his toil is all in vain until, van-
> quished quite, the ship drifts onward with the hurrying tide.

When Phaedra views the mangled corpse of Hippolytus, she makes an equally wooden atonement, vowing to "plunge the avenging sword within my sinful breast" and to follow Hippolytus "through Tartarean pools, across the Styx, through streams of liquid fire."

LONGINUS

- *On the Sublime*

LIFE AND BACKGROUND

Because of the great time span that separates the current age from antiquity, variances in names, dates, birthplaces, titles, and even authorship are not unexpected. A most puzzling conundrum, however, is an undated work of great sensitivity and excellence, *On the Sublime*. Although this treatise is one of the most useful critical manuscripts to have survived from the Mediterranean world, scholars know little about its origins. Even the term "sublime," which scholars have debated since Nicholas Boileau's translation in 1674, has received so many interpretations that it, too, proves elusive.

The first extant evaluation of *On the Sublime*, by Marc-Antoine Muret, a French poet and literary critic, occurred in 1554. For more than four centuries, *On the Sublime* has been widely translated, sparking scholarly debate among academicians around the world. A spirited, uplifting work, it has challenged and inspired later authors, including Gibbon, Dryden, Addison, Goldsmith, Fielding, Sterne, and Pope.

The manuscript was written in Greek and was at first assigned to Dionysius of Halicarnassus, a Greek historian of the first century B.C., and then to Cassius Longinus of Palmyra, a Syrian rhetorician and philosopher of the third century A.D. It appears from textural evidence—mainly because the author mentions no literary work written after Augustus' time—that both guesses were wrong and that the mysterious "Longinus" lived about the first century A.D., possibly during the time of Nero's reign.

The lack of sufficient documentation has resulted in neglect by later scholarly inquiries into ancient literature, yet the intrinsic value of *On the Sublime* argues for its inclusion. Unfortunately, the original document exists in eleven manuscripts, over a third of which are missing. To complicate matters further, some parts are nearly indecipherable.

Still, there are verifiable data among the host of unknowns. That the work is addressed to Postumius Terentianus is certain, although his identity is obscure. The reference to "Cecilius' little treatise on the Sublime," a work by a Jewish Sicilian grammarian who taught in Rome during the first years of the Empire, provides a second link to fact. Another reasonable assumption is that the author himself was a Hellenized Jew, probably a follower of Theodorus of Gadara, Tiberius' teacher, who believed that art, by nature of its creative spark, could not be controlled by rules. A second reason for assuming that Longinus was a Jew is his quotation of the opening lines of Genesis, a remarkable inclusion of Hebrew literature in so classic a treatise.

ON THE SUBLIME

Written in the form of an informal letter, Longinus' critical study of poetry opens with the author's refutation of Cecilius' treatise, which Longinus insists is "too trivial to satisfy the full demands of the subject." The recipient of the letter, Postumius Terentianus, appears to be a bright young Roman who studied literature with Longinus. Because the author illustrates the importance of second-person singular as a means of enlivening the experience of narration, one might conclude that Postumius Terentianus is a fictional persona created for the sake of focus.

Longinus' commentary offers practical advice on the creation of readable, meaningful literature. For example, he advocates the use of the historical present tense as a means of putting the reader in the front row of the action. To convince and enlighten the audience, Longinus recommends common language as opposed to forced elegance. To prove his point, he employs the comparative method, citing Herodotus as a model because his *Histories* involve the reader through vivid detail and immediacy.

In an attempt to define the "sublime," Longinus speaks familiarly to his young friend and student, who has already convinced the author of his appreciation for great literature. The sublime, Longinus contends, does not so much persuade as it transports the reader:

> Inevitably what inspires wonder casts a spell upon us and is always superior to what is merely convincing and pleasing. Our convictions are usually under our own control, while such passages exercise an irresistible power of mastery and get the upper hand with every member of the audience.

In Longinus' view, this "transport" implies a mystical power not unlike an enchantment that possesses the reader in a trancelike spell.

The irresistible force which holds its audience in thrall comes not in a steady stream like a magnetic force, but in bold flashes which illuminate the work at crucial or opportune moments and adhere indelibly to the mind, turning the reader's thoughts inward to ponder the very meaning of existence. By nature of their importance to the organic whole, these flashes of enlightenment are the products of inborn genius. They defy the humdrum, stultifying criteria laid down by merely mundane critics.

Punctuating his remarks with frequent quotations from fifty Greek masters, including Plato, Homer, Sophocles, Demosthenes, Xenophon, Thucydides, Sappho, and Herodotus, whose works he treats with reverence, but not with the overawed adoration of some critics, Longinus illustrates the most common violations of the sublime. Tumidity exists where the author allows pompous phrases and puffy, pointless stodginess to overcome creativity. The opposite extreme, puerility or frivolity, results from straining for effect, and wrecks its efforts "upon the tinsel reefs of affectation." The third violation, misapplication of emotion, disjoints the whole with its tedious display of subjectivity.

Longinus describes a test for sublimity in literature. If, upon subsequent readings, "its effect does not outlast the moment of utterance," the work fails in its aspirations. On the other hand, if a work continues to nourish the mind with wholesome reflection, it deserves to be labeled sublime:

> For what is truly great gives abundant food for thought: it is irksome, nay, impossible, to resist its effect: the memory of it is stubborn and indelible. . . . For when men who differ in their habits, their lives, their tastes, their ages, their dates, all agree together in holding one and the same view about the same writings, then the unanimous verdict . . . makes our faith in the admired passage strong and indisputable.

This lasting quality, Longinus concludes, possesses universality, the ability to please "all people at all times."

The source of grandeur in literature is "full-blooded ideas" and "vehement emotion." To achieve these aims, creators must have a command of the art, particularly energetic figures of speech, noble diction, and dignified, elevated composition. Authors must possess what Longinus calls "judgment in literature . . . the last fruit of ripe experience"—an inner sense of what is suitable, where it should appear, and how much emphasis is necessary to make it meaningful and memorable. Each work, to achieve sublimity, must cohere in a oneness that forbids the removal of a single part.

One of the most remarkable accomplishments of Longinus' text is his preservation of a Sapphic ode which Catullus translated, but which was unread in the original Greek until the sixteenth century. The poem, which describes a lover consumed with passion while watching his beloved smile into the face of another person, excels other love poetry in that it enlarges on the physical symptoms of love. The speaker suffers a broken spirit, quivering heart, loss of voice, a final rush of desire, and diminution of the senses. The speaker's conclusion summarizes the merciless grip of passion: "I can feel that I have been changed; I feel that death has come near me."

Longinus lets Sappho's skill speak his message. In sixteen lines, she achieves what he has been describing:

> Is it not wonderful how she summons at the same time, soul, body, hearing, tongue, sight, color, all as though they had wandered off apart from herself? She feels contradictory sensations, freezes, burns, raves, and reasons—for one that is at the point of death is clearly beside herself. She wants to display not a single emotion, but a whole congress of emotions. Lovers all show such symptoms as these, but what gives supreme merit to her art is, as I said, the skill with which she chooses the most striking and combines them into a single whole.

For Longinus, Sappho's skill equals that of the great orators, philosophers, historians, and epic poets because she grasps a totality—the sudden illumination of meaning in a universal situation. At the moment of truth, the speaker of the poem feels humanity in all its contradictory power, the simultaneous realization of love and death.

Longinus' advice to would-be writers is to employ the touchstone method. By reading and imitating Homer or Plato or Demosthenes, authors avail themselves of the best teachers. As Longinus phrases it, "Emulation will bring those great characters before our eyes, and like guiding stars they will lead our thoughts to the ideal standard of perfection." Authors who shrink from writing literature that must stand the test of the ages conceive "some blind, half-formed embryo, all too abortive for the life of posthumous fame."

By way of summary, Longinus notes that even the greatest authors make mistakes, but that "they are all more than human." Although these masters readily demonstrate their humanity, "sublimity lifts them near the mighty mind of God." But literary achievement, he contends, may not receive immediate recognition. The laurel which signifies greatness comes, not from contemporaries, but from succeeding generations, who award the true "crown of victory."

In the final surviving paragraphs, Longinus ponders the "worldwide dearth of literature." He quotes a contemporary who surmises that literature must suffer when democracy declines. The philosopher censures the "equitable slavery" which assails the minds of his contemporaries:

> We never drink from the fairest and most fertile source of literature, which is freedom, and therefore we come to show a genius for nothing but flattery.

Longinus, on the other hand, proposes a different form of thralldom as the prime suspect:

> It is the love of money, that insatiable sickness from which we all now suffer, and the love of pleasures that enslave us, or rather, one might say, sink our lives, soul and all, into the depths; for love of gold is a withering sickness, and love of pleasure utterly ignoble.

He concludes that apathy saps the spirit of its innate urge to excel, suppressing the "honorable and admirable motive of doing good to the world."

PLINY THE ELDER

- *Natural History*

PLINY THE YOUNGER

- *Letters*

PLINY THE ELDER
PLINY THE YOUNGER

LIFE AND BACKGROUND

One of Rome's most literate aristocratic families, the Plinius name belongs to two distinguished writers. The first, Gaius Plinius Secundus, known today as Pliny the Elder, was an energetic, somewhat rigid, but multi-talented man of letters, interested in military history, biology, biography, geography, rhetoric, and oratory. He was the forerunner of the Renaissance man. His encyclopedic knowledge and command of language made him the perfect surrogate father for his orphaned nephew, Gaius Plinius Caecilius Secundus, now known as Pliny the Younger.

The elder Pliny, born in Como, in the Po Valley on the Italian-Swiss border in 23 A.D., led a well-rounded life. He immigrated to Rome in his teens to study rhetoric, served as a military cavalry prefect in Germany from 47 to 57 A.D., and practiced law before establishing a literary career. An expert on the deployment of cavalry, he became the confidant and trusted adviser of two emperors, Vespasian and Titus.

According to his nephew, the elder Pliny was an insatiable reader who made use of every book he read and let nothing stand in the way of his studies. Even a five-year term as governor in Spain, Gaul, and Africa and as *prefect* of the Roman navy at Naples during the last five years of his life did not deter him from daily observation, meditation, research, and note-taking. On the day he died, August 24, 79 A.D., he was viewing at close range the eruption of Vesuvius, for humanitarian and academic reasons. He left 160 papyri crammed with notes on both sides.

A prolific writer with varied interests, the elder Pliny's first publication, *De Iaculatione Equestri,* is a weapons manual on the javelin. His second book, a biography of the poet Pomponius Secundus, his commanding officer, was followed by the *Bella Germaniae,* a twenty-book study of Rome's wars with the Germans. Next, he wrote *Studiosus,* a three-book treatise on the training of orators. In 67 A.D., he completed *Dubius Sermo,* an eight-book study of ambiguous language. Then he turned to history, compiling a 31-book history of Rome as a complement to an earlier history written by Aufidius Bassus. Unfortunately, of these early works, only bits of the *Dubius Sermo* survive.

In 77 A.D., Pliny the Elder produced the first Roman encyclopedia, a 37-book compendium dedicated to Titus and covering 35,000 topics and collected from over 4,000 writers. Entitled *Natural History,* the carefully organized work covers the universe, geography, astronomy, meteorology, ethnology, anthropology, physiology, psychology, zoology, botany, pharmacology, minerology, and metallurgy. Pliny's young nephew describes his uncle at work, utilizing a staff of readers and note-takers during brief, idle moments at noontime and during wakeful periods in the night. He praises his uncle's "diffuse, erudite, and varied" compilations, despite the obvious jumble of fact, opinion, and occasional misreadings of source material. To his detriment, the elder Pliny appears to have worked quickly, without allowing himself time for reflection or corroboration of his source materials. Yet, his enjoyment of curiosities made him a favorite of readers well into the Middle Ages.

After the death of his father, Lucius Caecilius Cilo, the younger Pliny, who was born in Como to a wealthy, notable family in 62 A.D., lived under the guardianship of Verginius Rufus, the distinguished general. Eventually the boy was adopted by his maternal uncle. Like the elder Pliny, he traveled to Milan and Rome to study law, which proved an auspicious choice for his talents, for his command of forensic oratory catapulted him to success.

Following military service as a tribune, or financial manager, in Syria, Pliny made his mark first as *praetor,* or judge, then as *quaestor* in 89 A.D., *consul* and *augur* in 100 A.D., and in 110 A.D., business manager and governor of Bithynia, a tricky diplomatic post requiring the utmost discretion and tact. Because of the abrupt halt in his writing, he is assumed to have died at a place that was some distance from Rome, probably while he was working in Bithynia, in 112 A.D.

The young Pliny learned early from his uncle's example to use his spare moments for reading and self-improvement, even while riding in a sedan chair. Spurred by his uncle's love of literature and the influence of Quintilian, his teacher, young Pliny chose Cicero as his model and made oratory and composition his chief goals. One of the most learned men of his day, he early made a name for himself in the law courts. Unfortunately, none of his speeches have survived.

Although young Pliny's early fame rests on his *Panegyricus,* which he addressed to the Emperor Trajan in thanks for a consulship, his most enduring work is a collection of 370 epistles, a veritable autobiography in letters, the last book of which is directed to Trajan. His charming vignettes capture the cultured life of first-century Rome and include sports, relaxation, literature, public life, religious ceremonies, ghost stories, financial advice, travel, friends, dining, news and gossip, Christianity, and the government of the Empire. Of letter-writing, Pliny recommends that the finished product be *pressus purusque* (succinct and unembellished), advice which he apparently followed.

His most famous letters, Book VI, numbers 16 and 20, written to Tacitus, describe the eruption of Vesuvius in 79 A.D. and the death of Pliny the Elder from the combined effects of asthma, fatigue, overweight, and poisonous fumes while attempting to evacuate civilians trapped by the engulfing smoke and cinders. On the day that the volcano erupted, the elder Pliny invited his nephew to go along on a sea voyage, but the younger Pliny, like his studious uncle, preferred to finish reading an assignment in Livy.

Young Pliny's epistolary style is quite readable – brief, unified, and fluent. In addition, it seems obvious that he intended to publish his letters in a collection, for seemingly he styled them for the ages rather than for the moment. They reveal a probing, intellectual man, childless, thrice married, somewhat vain, obsessed with a desire for immortality, but cheerful, engaging, and punctilious, especially in matters of courtesy and deportment. Pliny's most valuable service is not only self-revelation, but also his descriptions of notable contemporaries, including Tacitus, Suetonius, Martial, and Trajan.

In his lifetime, Pliny the Younger acquired enormous wealth, which he put to philanthropic use in his hometown. There, he built a library, funded a welfare program for poor children (in part, because there were no teachers in Como), and established an annual town banquet in his honor. He was surrounded by numerous friends and seemed extremely fond of his third wife, Calpurnia, to whom his last letter is addressed. Strangely enough, papers found in Domitian's desk after his death implicated Pliny in a scandal, which might have ruined him had Domitian lived to pursue the matter.

Like his uncle, the younger Pliny practiced stoicism. A survivor in shaky times, he understood how to bide his time, avoid confrontation, and wait for more favorable circumstances. His compact essays are pithy commentaries on the vicissitudes of life, particularly Roman life in the first century.

NATURAL HISTORY

In calculated, businesslike fashion, Pliny the Elder organizes his encyclopedia into logical units. His extensive preface, which dedicates the work to the Emperor Vespasian, warns that there is little opportunity in such a work for niceties:

> . . . a work of a lighter nature, as it does not admit of talent, of which in any case I possessed only quite a moderate amount, nor does it allow of digressions, nor of speeches or dialogues, . . . matters interesting to relate or entertaining to read.

Pliny acknowledges that he has left the well-traveled path of most authors to pursue arcane bits of lore, and he takes pride that his accomplishment outstrips the Greeks, who are usually first with innovations.

Book I, he explains, is an index, complete with sources. Users need not bother reading straight through it, but may employ it merely as a means to locate the subjects they wish to pursue. So begins the world's first encyclopedia:

> Book II. Contents:
> (i-iii) The world—is it finite? is it one? its shape; its motion; reason for its name.
> (iv) The elements.
> (v) God.

(vi) The planets – their nature.
(vii) Eclipses, solar and lunar. Night.

With a startling resemblance to modern versions of encyclopedic arrangement, Pliny lists subject and source for each topic, through Book XXXVII.

In contrast to the objective tone of current encyclopedists, Pliny inserts his opinions at frequent intervals, such as in Book XIV, which deals with winemaking. He describes the degradation of drunkards whom

> . . . we see getting themselves boiled in hot baths and being carried out of the bathroom unconscious, while others actually unable to wait to get to the dinner table, no, not even to put their clothes on, but straight away on the spot, while still naked and panting, they snatch up huge vessels . . . and pour down the whole of the contents, so as to bring them up again at once, and then drink another draught . . .

Drunkenness, he warns, leads to early death, or, at the very least, telltale symptoms of indulgence, including shaky hands, jowly faces, bloodshot eyes, restless sleep, and reeking breath. He is particularly scandalized that Mark Antony published a book boasting about his prowess with the cup.

Frequently, Pliny's essays include matter, method, and history, as found in his discussion of Egyptian papyrus. He credits Alexander with founding the paper industry in Alexandria, Egypt. Papyrus, which is indigenous to the stagnant pools that flank the Nile, as well as parts of Syria along the Euphrates, has multiple uses. The flowers can be made into garlands; the roots can be made into timber, firewood, or wooden utensils; and the stalks into plaits, which are woven into boats, mats, sails, blankets, and rope. The inner portion can be chewed like chewing gum.

To form paper, craftsmen split the stalk into strips with needles, reserving the tender inner fibers for the highest grade product, and weave them on a board moistened with muddy river water, which acts as a glue. After the excess moisture is pressed out, the layered fiber is dried, then joined into a single long roll. It is then smoothed out with ivory or shell, or is beaten with a mallet. He concludes that paper has become so essential that, during Tiberius' reign, a paper shortage led to rationing in order to prevent general chaos.

In his last entry, Pliny considers the most valuable resources of the earth—animal, vegetable, and mineral. The pearl he puts in first place, followed by crystal, gemstones, silk, spices, and amber. Among animal products, he lists the elephant's tusk and the shell of the sea turtle. Also, he mentions the costly purple dyes made from shellfish. Of precious metals, he says:

> We must not forget to mention that gold, for which all mankind has so mad a passion, comes scarcely tenth in the list of valuables, while silver, with which we purchase gold, is almost as low as twentieth.

His conclusion reflects the Roman character—a peculiar mixture of pride and humility: "Hail, Nature, mother of all creation, and mindful that I alone of the men of Rome have praised you in all your manifestations, be gracious unto me."

LETTERS

Eager to preserve himself for posterity in his letters, Pliny the Younger opens Book I with a statement of purpose:

> You [Septicius] have frequently pressed me to make a select collection of my letters (if there be any which show some literary finish) and give them to the public. I have accordingly done so . . .

With this thought in mind, Pliny arranged his correspondence with an eye toward some future readership. True to his intent, he supplied later generations with an accurate picture, not only of himself, but of the Roman world during Trajan's reign.

Pliny's most famous commentary covers the events of August 24, 79 A.D., when Mount Vesuvius erupted, killing his Uncle Pliny. Explaining that his letter (VI, xvi) is a reply to Tacitus, who requested more information about the elder Pliny's death, he suggests that the noted historian "transmit a more exact relation of it to posterity," thereby assuring his uncle of immortality. Pliny describes the family setting: his uncle, after sunbathing and eating lunch, is engaged in study. Pliny's mother disturbs her brother to urge him to "observe a cloud of very unusual size and appearance." The elder Pliny complies, putting on his shoes and climbing to a vantage point to examine the phenomenon.

Intrigued by the pine-shaped cloud, which is at one moment white and then dotted with cinders, the elder Pliny halts his examination to read an urgent note from Rectina, a neighbor who implores him to rescue her from the ominous cloud. Instantly, he abandons scientific observation and sets out on a heroic mission:

> He ordered large galleys to be launched, and boarded one himself, with the intention of assisting not only Rectina, but many others . . . he steered his direct course to the point of danger . . .

Pliny stresses his uncle's courage by quoting the elder Pliny's famous quotation, "Fortune favors the brave," which he remarks to the captain of the vessel.

To reassure the terrified passengers, Pliny's uncle makes a great show of tranquility, even stretching out for a nap, which is punctuated with vigorous snores. When violent tremors shake the houses and pumice fragments rain down, they tie pillows to their heads with table napkins. Because rough seas prevent their departure, the elder Pliny reclines upon a sail, but is unable to rise when shaken. Pliny assumes that his uncle was asphyxiated rather than crushed, for "his body was found entire and uninjured . . . its posture was that of a sleeping, rather than a dead man."

A follow-up letter to Tacitus (VI, xx) gives additional information. Having assumed the role of man of the house, Pliny the Younger, like his audacious uncle, seeks to reassure his mother by making a show of bravery. While he reads a volume of Livy, a family friend visits the house and chastises young Pliny and his mother for "her patience and my indifference." Unruffled, Pliny continues reading. When the thick cloud begins to descend, Pliny yields to his mother's pleading, takes her hand, and leads her to safety.

The scene that greets them outside their villa causes Pliny to realize the full impact of the panic and hysteria of his countrymen:

> You could hear the shrieks of women, the crying of children,
> and the shouts of men; some were seeking their children,
> others their parents, others their wives or husbands, and only
> distinguishing them by their voices. . . .

The ominous sounds ring in his ears as some people pray to the gods
and others insist that "there are no gods" and that the world is coming
to an end. Pliny is proud that, although he is not quite eighteen years
of age, he makes no outcry, but takes strength from the fact that he
is "perishing with the world itself."

Other letters deal with domestic matters of a more mundane
nature. To his wife, Calpurnia (VI, iv), Pliny expresses his displeasure
in being too busy to escort her to Campania during her sudden bout
of illness. His devotion to her is obvious:

> Were you in sound health, yet I could not feel easy in your
> absence; for there is harassing suspense in being every now
> and then wholly ignorant of what is happening to a most
> dearly loved one . . .

He urges her to write often, "every day, and even twice a day," to
keep him informed of her progress. In a subsequent letter (VI, vii),
he comments on Calpurnia's claim that she reads his works while they
are apart as a means of assuaging her loneliness. He, too, uses her
letters as consolation, but grieves: ". . . they serve only to make me
more strongly regret your absence."

In a letter to Calpurnia's aunt, Calpurnia Hispulla, Pliny describes
his wife's character: "She is incomparably discerning, incomparably
thrifty, while her love for her husband betokens a chaste nature." He
praises her love of reading and her constant support for his career.
His outlook for their marriage is rosy; he predicts that the "harmony
between us will increase with our days, and be as lasting as our lives."
Buoyed by her confidence, Pliny pledges to "become all that my wife
now thinks I am."

Some of Pliny's letters are more reflective, turning to examples
of moral and physical courage and providing philosophical commentary on their meaning. In his letter to Nepos (III, xvi), Pliny uses the
exemplary actions of Arria, a well-known counsul's wife, to justify
his belief that "those which have been most celebrated have not always

been the most illustrious." While Arria nurses both her son and Paetus, her husband, through a deadly illness, she suffers the loss of her son, but keeps his death a secret so that Paetus will not grow disheartened. Arria further displays her nobility and honor by attempting to follow her husband to prison, where she offers to serve as his body servant.

In a more reflective mood, Pliny draws on his considerable experience in governing distant provinces (VIII, xxiv) and advises the governor of Achaia to remember that Greece is the place "where civilization, literature, even agriculture were born." He urges constraint and respect for "their antiquity, their marvelous deeds, even for their myths . . ." His advice echoes his personal philosophy:

> Authority makes a poor test of its own force if it flouts others;
> it is a poor sort of homage that is won by terror; affection
> gives a far stronger guarantee for holding what you want than
> does fear.

Employing a memorable turn of phrase, Pliny stresses the principles that made him a success. This letter is the quintessence of a gentleman scholar who was comfortable with himself and with his administration of governmental affairs.

JOSEPHUS

- *Vita (Autobiography)*

- *Bellum Judaicum
  (The Jewish War)*

- *Against Apion*

LIFE AND BACKGROUND

A unique hybrid, Flavius Josephus (37–*ca.* 100 A.D.), Jewish scholar and Roman historian, is an amalgam, a historical improbability. A native of Jerusalem, the second son of a priest, and an offspring of royal lineage on his mother's side, Joseph ben Matthias was a child prodigy who studied Hebrew and Greek. At the age of fourteen, he consulted with scholars and also spent three years with Bannus, a desert hermit, in an effort to choose among three sects, the Essenes, Sadducees, and Pharisees. At the age of nineteen, he chose the latter. In 64 A.D., as a delegate to Nero, he journeyed to Rome, where he met the empress, Poppaea.

Impressed by Rome's invincibility, one of his first acts as governor of Galilee was to warn his people of the dangers of war; in 66 A.D., however, Josephus led a handful of freedom fighters in a revolt against Roman occupation forces, and for forty-seven days, his band held out at Jotapata, fifteen miles west of the sea of Galilee, but ultimately yielded to Vespasian's legionnaires, who led a surprise attack during the night. Vespasian ordered the city burned and the males massacred. Josephus escaped by hiding in a pit with forty other Jews and living off a cache of supplies. When Vespasian's troops discovered the pit three days later, Josephus made a momentous decision, accepted a proffered safe conduct, and, avoiding the mass suicide plotted by his compatriots, he survived the terrible ordeal.

When his prophecy that Vespasian would one day become emperor came true, Josephus was set free. He adopted the name Flavius in honor of his liberator, Titus Flavius Vespasianus, and allied himself fully with Rome, accepting citizenship, a pension, and an estate in Judea. Josephus' career was secure from the start because he was in constant demand as an interpreter and mediator. His personal life, however, suffered; his first wife, a war prisoner from Caesarea, left him. Later, he divorced his second wife, a native of Alexandria and the mother of his eldest surviving son, Hyrcanus, because of her improper behavior.

As a member of Titus' staff, Josephus was distrusted by both the Jews and Romans alike for good reason. For example, when Josephus returned to Judea, he assisted the Roman high command at the siege of Jerusalem, but offered what help he could to hard-pressed Jews. Some he freed from prison, and he had three removed from crosses, only one of whom survived the experience.

Josephus was married a third time—this time, to a famous Jew from Crete, and he fathered two sons, Justus and Simonides Agrippa. In the security of his position as protege of the emperor, he devoted his life to writing and study. He drew on ample resource material from the palace library and employed two assistants to translate his work from Aramaic into Greek.

Josephus' best-known works, the *Bellum Judaicum* (*The Jewish War,* 76 A.D.) and *Jewish Antiquities,* a history of the Jews from creation until 70 A.D., (94 A.D.), are an outgrowth of his inner compunction to square his name with fellow Jews. Haunted by the label of traitor, which Justus of Tiberias attached to him in a rival history of the Jewish War, Josephus seeks to justify his actions in his writings, some of which have led historians to wonder if his lengthy protestations are indeed the truth.

Josephus' final work, *Against Apion,* published at the beginning of the second century, is an attempt to reconcile Jews and gentiles. In hostile revolt against the anti-Semitic propaganda written by Apion, a notable Egyptian scholar, Josephus argues that stories of human sacrifice and other equally absurd fiction cause needless friction between Jews and other nations.

Despite his scholarly triumphs, Josephus lived apart from the two worlds which he sought to merge. He was honored with dedicatory statues, erudite Greeks and Romans read his works, but he never rose to the higher levels of the emperor's entourage, nor was he quoted as an expert on Roman history. St. Jerome singled him out as the Greek Livy, but his own people withheld all honors, refusing even to mention his name.

જ⋑

_____ VITA [AUTOBIOGRAPHY] _____

Josephus opens his autobiography with a description of his eminent ancestors and declares that his maternal ancestry sprang from the Hasmoneans, nicknamed the Maccabees, or Hammerers. He describes his father, Matthias, as "esteemed for his upright character, being among the most notable men in Jerusalem, our greatest city." In reply to some unnamed foe, the historian claims, "With such a pedigree, which I cite as I find it recorded in the public registers, I can take leave of the would-be detractors of my family."

Josephus allies himself with the Pharisees, a sect that resembles the Greek stoics. At the age of twenty-six, he travels to Nero's court to speak in defense of a party of priests who were imprisoned. On the way, his ship sinks in the Adriatic Sea, and he and six hundred others have to swim to safety. He, along with eighty survivors, boards a Cyrenian vessel, lands at Puteoli, and is befriended by Aliturus, an actor and a favorite of the emperor. Through this connection with the royal family, Josephus curries favor with Poppaea, Nero's wife.

Returning home to an incipient revolution, Josephus attempts to make peace, but is unable to stem the unrest of his countrymen. He casts himself in the role of a hero and natural leader with his description of a delegation to Galilee:

> My colleagues [Joazar and Judas], having amassed a large sum
> of money from the tithes which they accepted as their priestly
> due, decided to return home; but, on my request, consented
> to stay until we had brought matters into order.

When a party of dissidents massacres the Greeks in Tiberias, Josephus attempts to recover the plunder and return it to the emperor.

Josephus also arranges a workable solution to the local uprising and tries to keep his name clear of corruption and injustice. Although his intentions are honorable and his following large, he is caught up in a plot. A rumor implicates him in an attempt to betray Galilee to the Romans. One morning Josephus awakens to find his bodyguard gone and a howling mob demanding his death. At a critical moment, he makes a tearful plea to the populace and extricates himself from certain death.

At a low point in his administration of Galilean affairs, when he considers giving up his commission, Josephus has a prophetic dream:

> . . . I thought that there stood by me one who said: 'Cease, man, from your sorrow of heart, let go all fear. That which grieves you now will promote you to greatness and felicity in all things. Not in these present trials only, but in many besides, will fortune attend you. Fret not yourself then. Remember that you must even battle with the Romans.'

The next day, the grateful residents implore Josephus to stay. He accedes, using their outpouring of loyalty as leverage to extract five thousand armed men to add to his forces.

When Josephus is captured by Vespasian's legions at the siege of Jotapata, his fortune alters considerably. Although he no longer finds himself at the center of a potential revolution, he becomes a man without a country:

> . . . my life was frequently in danger, both from the Jews, who were eager to get me into their hands, to gratify their revenge, and from the Romans, who attributed every reverse to some treachery on my part . . .

Working through diplomatic channels, Josephus frees what Jews he can, including his older brother and fifty friends and a few relatives in a captive band of women and children bound for slavery. In addition, through the emperor's favor he manages to preserve the sacred books of his faith.

Josephus receives privileged treatment under three emperors — Vespasian; his successor, Titus; and Domitian. Under the third emperor, Josephus enjoys additional honors. Domitian punishes Josephus' Jewish accusers, including his son's tutor. Josephus receives an exemption from property tax, "a mark of the highest honor to the privileged individual." In addition, the empress, Domitia, showers him with favors.

_____ BELLUM JUDAICUM (THE JEWISH WAR) _____

Josephus' history of the war between Rome and Judea is a detailed study of two ideologies in conflict. The struggle begins with a series of minor border skirmishes and develops into a major battle for survival. In his glimpses of ill-equipped Jews fighting the sophisticated Roman war machine, Josephus evens out the two sides, balancing Roman might with a vivid description of the Temple of Jerusalem, the stronghold which symbolizes the Jews' only chance for self-preservation.

Jerusalem itself, nearly four miles in circumference and fortified by three walls, steep ravines, and a single rampart, lies on "two hills separated by a central valley." The most ancient wall dates back to the time of David and Solomon. Turrets of great strength and beauty rise at intervals, "square and solid as the wall itself, and in the joining and beauty of the stones is in no wise inferior to a temple."

Within lies Herod's palace, "baffling all description: indeed, in extravagance and equipment no building surpassed it." The walls are fitted with rare stones from foreign lands; the ceilings feature exposed beams, decorated with surface detail. Inner apartments boast silver and gold appointments, contrasting columns, and an inner courtyard with groves of trees "bordered by deep canals, and ponds everywhere studded with bronze figures . . ." Josephus, in mourning the destruction of such grandeur, assures the reader that it is brigands and not Romans who set the roof afire and burned the palace to the ground.

The historian next turns his attention to the dimensions and craftsmanship of the temple. Before the inner doors hangs a "veil of Babylonian tapestry, with embroidery of blue and fine linen, of scarlet also and purple, wrought with marvelous skill." The color scheme denotes the universe, composed of fire, earth, air, and water. Depicted across it is a "panorama of the heavens, the signs of the Zodiac excepted." Only the undefiled are allowed access – that is, women and lepers are denied even a glimpse of the inner chambers. Only priests are allowed to penetrate the screen that conceals the holy of holies.

After incessant battering by Roman siege weapons, the Jews face a losing battle. Josephus is appointed to walk the length of the endangered inner wall and implore his comrades "to spare themselves and the people, to spare their country and their temple" by surrendering before a final assault brings collapse of the whole structure and carnage among innocent people. He recounts the lessons of history and declares that God is on the side of the Romans. Yet his country-men reject his advice and fight doggedly on.

Before military might decimates their numbers, the Jews fall prey to famine, infighting, and various forms of torture and mayhem. Titus allows mass crucifixions, hoping that survivors will surrender to stop the killing:

> The soldiers out of rage and hatred amused themselves by nailing their prisoners in different postures; and so great was their number, that space could not be found for the crosses nor crosses for the bodies.

The confrontation between Jews and Romans continues, but the famine within the walls is more telling than war.

> The roofs were thronged with women and babes completely exhausted, the alleys with the corpses of the aged; children and youths, with swollen figures, roamed like phantoms through the marketplaces and collapsed wherever their doom overtook them.

Burial becomes impossible as hunger and disease sap the strength of the living. To add to their woes, the survivors are beset by looters. Even Titus is moved by the rotting carcasses, and he groans to heaven that he is not to blame.

Book VI contains the poignant conclusion to armed resistance, **The Defense of Masada,** in which dissident Jews attempt to hold out and commit mass suicide when overtaken by the forces of Flavius Silva. The last survivors, led by Eleazar, a "descendant of the Judas who . . . induced multitudes of Jews to refuse to enroll themselves, when Quirinius was sent as censor to Judea," elect a remote spot atop a huge, high rock fortress accessible only by two meandering goat paths up treacherous slopes.

The level plain above, a pet project of Herod a century before, is fitted out with a sumptuous palace, reservoirs for water, and boun-tiful supplies:

> . . . here had been stored a mass of corn, amply sufficient to last for years, abundance of wine and oil, besides every variety of legume and piles of dates. . . . There was also found a mass of arms of every description, hoarded up by the king

and sufficient for ten thousand men, besides unwrought iron, brass, and lead . . .

Herod, who feared that Cleopatra would inflame Antony, her Roman lover, to assault and overrun Judea, stocked Masada against the day that he had to protect himself from Roman legions. The Jews believe that, with these royal stores, they can survive a protracted siege.

When Silva completes an earthwork and breaches the seemingly impregnable wall around Masada, Eleazar realizes that their hopes are false. He assembles his followers and offers them a noble end to the ill-fated revolt:

> At this crisis let us not disgrace ourselves; we who in the past refused to submit even to a slavery involving no peril, let us not now, along with slavery, deliberately accept the irreparable penalties awaiting us if we are to fall alive into Roman hands.

His band replies with whimpers and misgivings, to which he responds with a noble appeal outlining the relief of death, which he describes as a twin of sleep.

The power of his exhortation is immediate. The Jews vie to be among the first to die, "deeming it a signal proof of courage and sound judgment not to be seen among the last." The numbers left alive dwindle down to one; the last warrior surveys the pitiable scene, torches the palace to deprive the Romans of booty, and plunges his sword into his own entrails. Two old crones and five children out of a total of nine hundred and sixty conceal themselves in underground aqueducts and survive to tell the tale.

The vanguard of the Roman legion climbs to the top of the earthwork and is stunned by the sight and the chilling silence:

> Here encountering the mass of slain, instead of exulting as over enemies, they admired the nobility of their resolve and the contempt of death displayed by so many in carrying it, unwavering, into execution.

The Romans have little difficulty completing their subjugation of Judea for, after Masada falls, there is no force left to oppose their power.

AGAINST APION

Josephus' commentary on Jewish custom and practice begins with a description of his race's reverence for holy scripture. Unlike the Greeks, he says, who practice selective memory in preservation of historical records, the Jews are scrupulous in their devotion to the past:

> Not only did our ancestors in the first instance set over this business men of the highest character, devoted to the service of God, but they took precautions to ensure that the priests' lineage should be kept unadulterated and pure.

He describes the sacred writings in three distinct categories: the five books of Moses, or law (Genesis, Exodus, Leviticus, Numbers, and Deuteronomy); the thirteen books of history (Joshua, Judges and Ruth, Samuel, Kings, Chronicles, Ezra and Nehemiah, Esther, Job, Isaiah, Jeremiah and Lamentations, Ezekiel, the minor prophets, and Daniel); and four books of hymns and proverbs (Psalms, Song of Songs, Proverbs, and Ecclesiastes).

Contrasting Jews with Greeks, Josephus insists that Jews are willing to sacrifice and suffer in order to preserve the past:

> Time and again ere now the sight has been witnessed of prisoners enduring tortures and death in every form in the theaters, rather than utter a single word against the laws and the allied documents.

The Greeks, however, are content to accept their lore as "mere stories improvised according to the fancy of their authors."

Josephus defends his accuracy in the *Antiquities,* which "certain despicable persons have essayed to malign." These books, he declares, were written not only by a priest well-versed in Hebraic philosophy, but by an eyewitness. In defense against attacks on his veracity, Josephus concludes with assurance, ". . . nothing whatever was said or done of which I was ignorant."

After detailing Jewish history from unimpeachable sources, including the Egyptians, Phoenicians, and Greeks, Josephus begins a defense of his people. It was the Egyptians, he maintains, who first vilified the Jews with false accounts of their arrival to and departure from Egypt. So eager were the Egyptians to concoct specious histories that "they did not hesitate to contradict their ancient chronicles, nay, in the blindness of their passion, they failed to perceive that in what they wrote they actually contradicted themselves."

Against Apion himself, an Egyptian who studied at Alexandria and taught grammar in Rome during the first century A.D., Josephus is most vociferous. Some of Apion's allegations he calls "pure buffoonery" which display the "gross ignorance of their author." Josephus calls Apion a "man of low character and a charlatan to the end of his days." Outraged that Apion calls Moses a native of Heliopolis and that he derives the word "sabbath" from "sabbo," the Egyptian word for disease of the groin, Josephus declares that "sabbath" originates from the Jewish word "sabbaton," denoting "cessation from all work."

Against Cleopatra, whom the Jews are said to have mistreated, Josephus outlines a series of sins:

> . . . [she] committed every kind of iniquity and crime against her relatives, her devoted husbands, the Romans in general, and their emperors, her benefactors, . . . owing her throne to the first Caesar, dared to revolt against his son and successor, and corrupting Antony by sensual passion, made him an enemy to his country and faithless to his friends, robbing some of their royal rank, discharging others, and driving them into crime.

He further accuses Cleopatra of deserting Antony at Actium and ultimately committing suicide as a result of the "cruelty and treachery which she had practiced towards all." Josephus rounds out his denunciation of the Egyptian queen by exclaiming that the Jews should be proud that she refused them corn in time of famine.

Josephus concludes his spirited diatribe against Apion with assertions of Jewish belief:

> What, then, are the precepts and prohibitions of our law? They are simple and familiar. At their head stands one of which God is the theme. The universe is in God's hands; perfect and blessed, self-sufficing and sufficing for all, He is the beginning, the middle, and the end of all things.

With a noble firmness and grace, Josephus propounds the philosophy of monotheism, emphasizing the need for reverence, obedience, sobriety, and cleanliness in all human affairs, particularly the sacred rite of marriage. Honor to parents, second in importance to the first commandment, requires respect for all elders, of whom "God is the most Ancient."

Inherent in Jewish standards is charity, respect for all life, mercy, and honesty in all human dealings. As a reward for uprightness, ". . . God has granted a renewed existence and in the revolution of the ages the gift of a better life." In his closing arguments, Josephus contrasts the piety of Jews with the paganism of the anthropomorphic Greeks. He concludes that the Jews have given the human race an admirable ideology. He questions, "What more beneficial than to be in harmony with one another . . . and to be convinced that everything in the whole universe is under the eye and direction of God?"

MARTIAL

- *Liber Spectaculorum*
  (Book of Spectacles)

- *Epigrammata (Epigrams)*

MARTIAL

Marcus Valerius Martialis, the salty, impudent cosmopolite, though of humble, rural origin, made quite a splash in Rome, possibly because he received the sponsorship of three literary giants, Lucan, Seneca, and Quintilian. With their help, he gained renown as a prolific producer of epigrammatic poetry, the short, pungent verses which were inscribed on monuments, tombs, gifts, and temple offerings. It was Martial who raised this form of literary expression to a high art; he created seemingly unassuming verses that caught his readers unaware when the poem climaxed in an unforeseen stinger.

The son of Valerius Fronto and Flaccilla, Martial, named for March (his birth month), was born in Bilbilis, Spain, a mining town famed for its armor, about a hundred miles west of Barcelona. He received a literary education there and immigrated to Rome in 64 A.D. to practice law.

Of his early existence little is known. Disdaining the law courts, he lived the hand-to-mouth life of the stereotypical starving poet in a garret on the third floor of a rickety rooming house on the Quirinal. Later, he acquired a farm near Nomentum, fifteen miles north of Rome, possibly a bequest from Lucan's widow or from Seneca, a fellow Spaniard. Although Martial owned slaves, his living was meager on his barren scrap of land, which he describes as small enough to hide under a cricket's wing.

Martial is accused of obsequiousness and amorality in that he tailored his views and practices to suit the times and flattered whoever was in power, particularly Domitian, although such behavior was common in writers who lived by patronage. Martial appears to have despised work, preferring to make his living by attaching himself to people of wealth and influence, poor-mouthing his way to dinners and, like a stand-up comic, ingratiating himself with clever repartee and sparkling one-liners. Ragged, but proud, he never hesitated to compare himself to Rome's best poets and boasted openly that his early poems, which have not survived, were equal to those of Lucan and Catullus.

Under the Emperor Titus, Martial rose to the honorary titles of military tribune, knight, and "father of three children," although he appears to have been a bachelor. Even these moderate successes, however, could not stave off his disillusionment with city life, particularly when a change in the power structure made his fulsome praise of Domitian unpopular. The change in Martial, which he claims grayed his thick crop of black hair, forced him home to Spain. In 98 A.D., after thirty-five years in Rome, he returned to Bilbilis, with the help of Pliny the Younger, who paid his passage. On his small country estate, he lived out his life with Marcella, the Spanish patroness whom he may have married shortly before his death.

Martial's works include the *Liber Spectaculorum (Book of Spectacles)*, a collection of thirty-three short poems published in 80 A.D. commemorating the opening of the Flavian Amphitheater, now known as the Colosseum. The next two books of poems, *Xenia (Guest Gifts)* and *Apophoreta (Party Favors)*, published in 84–85 A.D., contain a total of three hundred and fifty *distichs,* or couplets, to accompany gifts on Saturnalia, the Roman harvest festival celebrated December 17–23.

The last and by far most important of Martial's publications, his *Epigrammata (Epigrams)*, which appeared from 86 to 102 A.D. in twelve books, contains 1,172 short, snappy verses, the last of which were mailed to Rome from his Spanish retreat. Of his salient wit, Martial says, "My page smacks of human life." Indeed, his range of subject matter encompasses Rome's seediest, most outrageous characters, from panhandlers to noblemen, pompous professionals to slaves, and fortune-hunters to hussies, whom he describes objectively, warts and all.

A marvelously facile wordsmith, Martial survives in the modern world because of his ease with phrasemaking. His insouciant verses, sometimes no more than twelve or fifteen words in length, lampoon the high and the high-minded, the humble and the dregs of society. One victim of his rapier-sharp tongue is Statius, a rival poet whose long-winded epic poems bored Martial. Although rightly accused of prurience and smut, which affects only one tenth of his work, Martial excels other satirists in his scorn of hypocrisy and his liberality and tenderness toward friends.

Martial's skill with terse, witty words requires patience and a natural gift for expression. With the right turn of phrase or the caustic *mot juste,* he manages snide put-downs, plays on words, pithy commentaries, and coarse belly laughs with each inscription. He composed in a variety of moods, yet it is his satiric verses which influenced later authors, particularly Juvenal and more recent epigrammatists, notably Oscar Wilde, Ogden Nash, and Dorothy Parker.

Two facts indicate that Martial was an enterprising poet, although he probably earned a scanty living from his books. It appears that he was the first poet in the Western world to publish his works in bound volumes instead of the more traditional Roman scrolls. Also, he laced his creative efforts with advertisements, including price, binding, and the book shop where they could be purchased.

LIBER SPECTACULORUM
———————*(BOOK OF SPECTACLES)*———————

Martial's timely glimpse of the Colosseum, one of the world's seven wonders, is a rare gift to modern times – a brief bird's-eye view of the opening ceremonies:

> Let not barbaric Memphis tell of the wonder of her Pyramids,
> nor Assyrian toil vaunt its Babylon; let not the soft Ionians
> be extolled for Trivia's fame; let the altar wrought of many
> horns keep hid its Delos; let not Carians exalt to the skies
> with boundless praise the Mausoleum poised on empty air.
> All labor yields to Caesar's Amphitheatre: one work in place
> of all shall Fame rehearse.

His vignettes of thronging spectators, mangling attackers, treacherous beasts, and bloody sand detail the savagery for which the Empire is famous. In verse XIV, a brood-heavy sow falls, and from her fatal wound spring live piglets. Equally crowd-pleasing are the mock sea battle and troops of sea nymphs swimming in unison.

EPIGRAMMATA (EPIGRAMS)

Martial introduces his first book of epigrams with a succinct warning to the squeamish or overly fastidious reader:

> . . . if there be anyone so pretentiously prudish that to his mind it is permissible to speak plain Latin, he may content himself with the introductory epistle, or rather with the title.

In grandiose Roman style, Martial opens with an over-confident boast, that he is "known through the whole world for his witty little books of epigrams." His next comment, equally self-serving, suggests that the size and style of the book is perfect for travelers, who may locate copies at the bookstall of Secundus, "behind the entrance to the temple of Peace and the Forum of Pallas."

Martial mixes his verse, combining wit with humor, lampoon with social commentary. For one victim, he offers four lines of ridicule:

> If I remember right, you had, Aelia, four teeth: one fit of coughing shot out two, and another two more. Now you can cough in peace: a third fit has nothing left to discharge.

In another, he snickers at Milo, whose wife cuckolds him while he travels:

> Milo is not at home:
> Milo has gone away, and
> His fields are neglected;
> Yet his wife is not less fruitful.
> Why his land is sterile and his wife fertile,
> I will tell:
> His land lacks a cultivator,
> But his wife doesn't.

To others, only a few lines are necessary:

> He who fancies that Acerra reeks
> Of yesterday's wine is wrong.
> Acerra always drinks till daylight.

> . . . .

> Diaulus has been a doctor,
> He is now an undertaker.

He begins to put his patients to bed
In his old effective way.

. . . .

Philaenis always weeps with one eye.
Do you wonder how
She accomplishes that feat?
She is one-eyed.

Whether long or short, Martial's epigrams move quickly to the gist of the matter, saving the punch line for last. At intervals, he reminds scandalized aunties, boys, and virgins that his poems are not meant for bluestockings or the faint of heart.

Occasionally, Martial surprises the casual reader by tucking a soulful lyric or pleasant nature poem among the more scathing epigrams. One poem that reflects Horace's influence is No. 58, in Book III, a short work praising country life:

Nor does the country visitor come empty handed:
That one brings pale honey in the comb,
And a pyramid of cheese from Sassina's woodland;
That one offers sleepy dormice;
This one the bleating offspring of a shaggy mother;
Another, capons debarred from love.
And the strapping daughters of honest farmers offer
In a wicker basket their mother's gifts.

For Martial, sickened by Rome's unhealthful ostentation, the openhandedness of rustic folk is preferable to the lavish tables of society matrons. Even the slaves are well-fed. The profusion of "cabbages, eggs, fowls, apples, cheese" leads him to ask, "Ought this to be called a farm, or a townhouse away from town?"

Martial gives us a brief glimpse of his tender side in a graveside farewell to tiny Erotion, a six-year-old girl who faces the "Tartarean hound's stupendous jaws. " He regrets that she did not complete her "sixth cold winter" and notes that she spoke with a charming lisp. The crusty exterior of the bon vivant poet hides a sympathy for children, as evidenced by his intercession at her burial:

"And let not hard clods cover her tender bones,
Nor be thou heavy upon her, O earth:
She was not so to thee!"

In Book X, Martial summarizes for his friends his advice on how to get the most out of life:

> The things that make a better, happier life, most agreeable . . . are these: Money not earned but inherited; a farm not unproductive, a hearth ever warmed by a cozy fire; never a lawsuit, rarely a business suit; a mind at peace; inborn strength, a healthy body; prudence and honesty, friends like one's self; informal pleasures, a simple table; a night not besotted but free from care; a bed not puritanical yet decent; sleep that makes the night go fast; wish to be what you are and ask for nothing more; neither fear nor wish for your last day.

The lines capture his insouciance, yet there is no doubt that he observed enough of city turmoil and stress to make him happy to return to the slower rhythms of country life. To Juvenal, his protege, Martial expresses his delight in Bilbilis, where he sometimes sleeps until nine to shake off the bone-weariness that Rome instilled in him:

> Perhaps, my Juvenal, your feet stray
> Down some noisy Roman street, . . .
> While after many years of Rome, I
> Have regained my Spanish home.
> Bilbilis, rich in steel and gold,
> Makes me a rustic as of old.

After a lapse of three years, he completed his last book of epigrams in 102 A.D. The volume, rich in food imagery and kitchen lore, suggests the profusion of tempting fare that a country larder is apt to store.

Pliny the Younger eulogizes Martial in 104 A.D., noting that he was talented, energetic, and subtle, mixing wit with candor. Martial's self-analysis reflects a similar attitude. In Book V, xiii, he compares himself to Callistratus, a rich man whose "roof rests on a hundred columns." Admittedly, the poet says, "I have always been poor," but his notoriety is pay enough. As Martial characterizes his career, "I am widely read, and my fans say of me, 'There he is!'"

PLUTARCH

- *Parallel Lives*

- *Morals*

LIFE AND BACKGROUND

Although he was a native of Chaeronea, Boeotia, a country town on the north end of the Isthmus of Corinth, Lucius Mestrius Plutarchus (the Latinized version of his name) contributed immensely to Rome's knowledge of itself. A forerunner of the neo-Platonists, he lived between 45 and 120 A.D.; the fourth son in a line of witty, cultured men, he was born to a family rich in landholdings.

Plutarch studied rhetoric, science, and philosophy in Athens and Smyrna. From his illustrious teacher, Ammonius, Plutarch learned the value of amalgamating intellectual and civic interests, for his own good as well as that of the community. Consequently, Plutarch married a hometown girl, Timoxena, who bore him four sons and a daughter, and he settled down in Chaeronea, eventually becoming town mayor.

Plutarch traveled widely—throughout Greece, Asia Minor, Egypt, and Italy—and he cultivated friendships in many cultures. During a ten-year diplomatic mission to Rome, from 69 to 79 A.D., he taught philosophy and traveled to Milan and the Po Valley to view famous battle sites. Although he enjoyed the intellectual ferment of Rome, particularly the well-stocked libraries, and received Roman citizenship, he missed his homeland. Upon his return to Chaeronea, he served as *archon,* or chief magistrate; *agoranome,* or market commissioner; and *Boeotarchos,* or magistrate, of Boeotia. In recognition of his literary contributions, he was made an honorary citizen of Athens.

A devout and ethical man, Plutarch made frequent horseback journeys to Delphi, his second home, where he performed priestly duties at the temple of Apollo, served as director of the games, and discussed philosophical issues with illustrious visitors. At his death, Delphians honored him with a statue. He opened a school in Chaeronea and lectured on Greek and Roman institutions, saving his private time for reading, writing, and conversation. By nature an optimist, Plutarch garnered bits of useful information, chiefly from Greek sources, to use in his writing.

Although Plutarch was a prolific writer, fewer than one third of his 300 volumes survive. His major works, *Parallel Lives* and *Morals,* exist in pieces. His philosophical essays, of which only 78 of the original 187 are extant, have earned him the nickname "physician of the soul" for their uplifting, consoling qualities. His style varies from monologue and dialogue to lecture and essay.

Because Plutarch cultivated interests in many fields, his essays touch on the whole of human wisdom – archeology, education, music, philology, politics, history, zoology, psychology, mathematics, physics, astronomy, geography, religion, and folk tales. Although he appears at times to dwell on trivia, such as whether water or fire is more useful, his charm and enthusiasm make up for minor shortcomings. His appeal to subsequent great minds, including Boswell, Franklin, Beethoven, Montaigne, Emerson, and Napoleon, attest to his lasting popularity and classic wisdom.

As a biographer, Plutarch's most valuable asset is his emphasis on the humanity of each subject, which he reveals through juxtaposition, mixing Greeks with Romans and commenting on one pair at a time, although modern editions tend to ignore his original plan. Because he is unable to encompass the history of an entire single life, he recreates enough dramatic detail through anecdote and quotation to enliven each sketch. His work is even, lacking extremes, but of his fifty character studies of famous Greeks and Romans, only a few stand out – notably, the lives of Themistocles, Pericles, Aristides, Alexander, Sulla, Caesar, Cicero, and Cato the Younger.

Plutarch lived in an era of goodwill, when Hellenism was merging with Roman influences, a positive atmosphere that suited his own platonic outlook. In general, he approved of the Roman Empire and its attempt to control an unwieldy outlay of lands and peoples, but he maintained the right to criticize. His philosophy, based on the Greek belief that "power will show the man," undergirds each evaluation, revealing the stuff from which character is made. Because of Plutarch's integrity in applying the principle of character under stress of pressure and temptation, his writing received the public acclaim of both Trajan and Hadrian and, later, formed the basis of three Shakespearean tragedies – *Coriolanus, Julius Caesar,* and *Antony and Cleopatra.*

Quick to claim himself a philosopher, not a historian, Plutarch nevertheless reveals a reverence for history:

> . . . I began to write these Lives to give pleasure to friends, but I have persisted with the project for my own sake, and I delight in it. For me, history is like a faithful mirror in which I observe these great men in order that I may seek to model my own life on their virtues.

As a true eclectic, he performed a single great service to the modern world — by reading, analyzing, and digesting the great literary works of antiquity, he preserved the thought and wisdom of works long since lost.

PARALLEL LIVES

A forerunner of the modern psychological biographer, Plutarch sets out to describe pairs of corresponding lives — for example, Scipio Africanus, Rome's great military man, with Epaminondas, his Greek counterpart; and Camillus, savior of Rome, with Themistocles, savior of Athens. In all, he wrote biographies of fifty men, intermingling the great with the near-great, although only twenty-two pairs of these essays of contrasts and similarity have survived. Of these, eighteen possess the formal comparison that Plutarch appended as a means of drawing together parallel lives while commenting on the inter-relatedness of career and character.

In introducing his comparison of Theseus and Romulus, founders of Athens and Rome, respectively, Plutarch admits his inability to separate fact from myth so far back in time:

> May I therefore succeed in purifying Fable, making her sub-mit to reason and take on the semblance of History. But where she obstinately disdains to make herself credible, and refuses to admit any element of probability, I shall pray for

kindly readers, and such as receive with indulgence the tales of antiquity.

By means of this ingenuous disclaimer, Plutarch reveals his real strength—his disarming and thoroughly delightful tone, neither pedantic nor ponderous, but rather curious and contemplative.

He justifies his choice of Theseus and Romulus, stating that both are of obscure parentage, are reputed to have descended from gods, and combine strength with brilliance. Meticulously, he pursues more similarities:

> . . . each resorted to the rape of women. Besides, neither escaped domestic misfortunes and the resentful anger of kindred, but even in their last days both are said to have come into collision with their own fellow-citizens . . .

At this point, Plutarch begins the examination of the individual life of each man before summing up his appraisal.

Plutarch's detailed study of Romulus owes much to Livy, whom Plutarch read in the original, although he makes no claim to being an expert at the Latin language. He repeats Livy's linguistic supposition that the she-wolf that suckled Romulus and his twin, Remus, might have been a hired nurse of easy virtue, since the Romans referred to prostitutes by the animal term *lupa* (she-wolf). But Plutarch maintains his individuality in other passages, notably the lenience in his description of Remus' murder:

> . . . as Romulus was digging a trench where his city's wall was to run, [Remus] ridiculed some parts of the work, and obstructed others. At last, when he leaped across it, he was struck down, some say, by Romulus himself, and fell dead there.

Whereas Livy emphasizes Romulus' lack of constraint and violent anger, Plutarch softens the blame somewhat with the use of a passive verb, "was struck down," as well as an equivocation as to who really struck the fatal blow.

Plutarch utilizes the comparative essay as a means of moralizing, for he considers himself primarily a philosopher and moralist. Of Theseus and Romulus he concludes that,

> . . . although [they] were both statesmen by nature, neither

maintained to the end the true character of a king, but both deviated from it and underwent a change, the former in the direction of democracy, the latter in the direction of tyranny, making thus the same mistake through opposite affections.

In this instance, Plutarch reveals the Greeks' longstanding bias against tyranny. Having witnessed firsthand the workings of the Roman Empire, he was not altogether in favor of Rome's loss of the civil liberties that flourished during the Republic.

Yet, this very perspective, so heavily tinged with Hellenism, has provided the modern world with its keenest view of eminent Romans, especially those who were alive near the end of the Republic—the younger Cato, Pompey, Crassus, Antony, Brutus, and Julius Caesar. The Caesar whom Plutarch describes seems familiar to readers of Shakespeare, for even minute incidents from the essay, such as the savage murder of Cinna the poet and Calpurnia's bad dream, assume major importance in Shakespeare's tragedy, *Julius Caesar*.

A remarkably fair observer, Plutarch evenly matches praise with blame in his character sketch, which contains lesser known exploits, such as Caesar's vengeance on the pirates who kidnapped him, as well as the thrilling, positive moments in his life:

Caesar was born to do great things and had a passion after honor; the many noble exploits he had done did not now serve as an inducement to him to sit still and reap the fruit of his past labors, but were incentives and encouragements to go on; they raised in him ideas of still greater actions and a desire for new glory, as if the present were all spent.

With the same even-handedness by which Plutarch describes Romulus, he blends Caesar's overweening ambition with his innate greatness, thereby extending to Caesar the benefit of the doubt.

As a balance from Greek history, he probes deeply into the cause and effect of Alexander's impressive career. By way of introduction to his task, he comments,

. . . my design is not to write histories, but lives. And the most glorious exploits do not always furnish us with the clearest discoveries of virtue or vice in men; sometimes a matter of less moment, an expression or a jest, informs us better of their

characters and inclinations, than the most famous sieges, the
greatest armaments, or the bloodiest battles.

Ironically, Plutarch proceeds with a discussion of Alexander's descent
from Hercules.

Eventually, however, Plutarch turns his attention to the "matters
of less moment" in Alexander's life. One of the most endearing, and
certainly the most repeated, of these episodes is the story of how Alexander subdues Bucephalus, which Plutarch puts in the form of a
dialogue:

> . . . Alexander, who stood by, said, 'What an excellent horse
> do they lose for want of address and boldness to manage
> him!' . . . 'Do you reproach those who are older than yourself,
> as if you knew more, and were better able to manage him
> than they?' Replied Philip to his son. 'I could manage this horse
> better than others do.' . . . 'And if you do not, what will you
> forfeit for your rashness?' said Philip. Answered Alexander,
> 'I will pay the whole price of the horse.'

Thus begins the famed comradeship between a young conqueror and
his steed. After Alexander steadies Bucephalus by turning him away
from his shadow, Philip realizes his son's potential: "O my son, look
you out a kingdom equal to and worthy of yourself, for Macedonia
is too little for you."

To counter passages of praise, Plutarch inserts just enough evidence of human frailty to suggest clay feet, even in the great Alexander. After the unforeseen death of his constant companion and
lover, Hephaestion, Alexander flies into an epic rage:

> . . . he immediately ordered the manes and tails of all his
> horses and mules to be cut and the battlements of the neigh-
> boring cities to be overthrown. The poor physician he [liter-
> ally] crucified, and he forbade playing on the flute or any other
> musical instrument in the camp a great while . . .

Through these telling glimpses of Alexander, Plutarch achieves his
intent: "to give my more particular attention to the marks and indications of the souls of men. . . ."

MORALS

A grab bag of thoughts, observations, anecdotes, and narration, Plutarch's *Morals* reveal more of the man himself than do *Parallel Lives*. One worthwhile piece which calls to mind *Poor Richard's Almanac* or Bartlett's *Familiar Quotations* is his "Sayings of Kings and Commanders," which he dedicates to Trajan. Plutarch begins pleasantly enough, offering "trifling gifts and tokens of friendship, the common offerings of the first-fruits that come from philosophy." His purpose is clear, to reveal through quotation the "characters and predilections of men in high places."

Plutarch's assortment of anecdotes and epigrams from world leaders covers much territory—from Cyrus to Semiramis, Philip to Lysander. Some indicate pride, as does Alexander's comment, "the earth could not tolerate two suns, nor Asia two kings." Others denote good advice, such as the words of Aristides, who remains a political independent, vowing that "influence derived from friends encourages wrongdoing." Some merely denote presence of mind in difficult situations, such as Brasidas' thoughtful comment upon being bitten by a mouse: "There is nothing so small that it cannot save its life, if it has the courage to defend itself . . ."

An equally pithy collection is Plutarch's "Sayings of Romans," some of which, in contrast to Greek eloquence, tend toward more economy of words. Chief among Roman phrase-makers is the elder Cato, assailing his profligate countrymen; Cato declares that "it is hard to talk to a belly with no ears." Equally succinct is Cicero's blatant criticism of Voconius' three ugly daughters: "Phoebus forbade when he his children got." And Plutarch repeats Caesar's famous pair, "The die is cast" and "I came, I saw, I conquered." But to be fair, Plutarch ends with a tribute to Roman eloquence in Augustus' encomium to his contractor: "You make my heart glad by building thus, as if Rome is to be eternal."

A curious essay, "The Bravery of Women," results from a friendly debate between Plutarch and Clea, a priestess at Delphi. Plutarch demonstrates a generosity toward females that is both refreshing and heartening, considering the overall chauvinism of the ancient world. He lauds the Roman custom of eulogizing women as well as men. Before listing worthy heroines, he expresses faith in the method by which he composed *Parallel Lives:*

. . . it is not possible to learn better the similarity and the difference between the virtues of men and of women from any other source than by putting lives beside lives and actions beside actions, like great works of art . . .

TACITUS

- *Annals*

- *Histories*

TACITUS

LIFE AND BACKGROUND

Judged by critics as Rome's most illustrious historian, Publius Cornelius Tacitus, whom Thomas Jefferson revered as the "first writer in the world without a single exception," was probably born about 55 A.D. in Gallia Narbonensis, near modern-day Narbonne, France, although there is little evidence to support the date or place. There is much conjecture about other details of his life, including his *praenomen* (the first of the usual three names of a Roman), which Apollinaris gives as Gaius.

Tacitus' family was of the equestrian rank, and his father was probably the Cornelius Tacitus who served as governor of Belgian Gaul. Tacitus evolved into a decent, god-fearing man and a devout follower of republicanism and the aristocracy. In 78 A.D., he married the daughter of Gnaeus Julius Agricola, Domitian's ablest general, and enjoyed the favor of three emperors, Vespasian, Titus, and Domitian, although he came to despise Domitian's oppression of Rome.

Tacitus received the standard Roman education in rhetoric and launched a brilliant career in law. Known for his vigorous, incisive rhetoric, he established a noteworthy reputation for oratory in the law courts. In 88 A.D., Tacitus served as *praetor,* or judge, and was probably promoted to provincial *praetor,* for he and his wife were absent from Rome at the time of his father-in-law's death. In 97 A.D., Tacitus was appointed consul to succeed Verginius Rufus, whom he eulogized in a memorable speech. A close friend of Pliny the Younger, whose letters detail some of his accomplishments, Tacitus rose to the governorship of Asia, a signal honor for a member of the senatorial rank.

Tacitus' earliest manuscript, the *Dialogue of Orators,* was composed in the reign of Titus (79–81 A.D.), but was probably published about 105 A.D. Written in the classic style, the discussion centers on the decline of eloquence. Tacitus maintains that the development of oratory depends upon freedom of speech, which can flourish only in a republican setting. (Because of Tacitus' distaste for emperors, Napoleon Bonaparte, one of his more notable detractors, called the historian a "sensation-monger.")

During the terrifying years of Domitian's reign, Tacitus published nothing, but early in 98 A.D., he completed both his *Agricola* and *Germania*. The former, a biography of his father-in-law, whom Tacitus admired and revered, is generally accepted as the most distinguished biography in Latin. Written in terse, fast-paced prose, it contrasts with Tacitus' earlier, more ponderous work, which reflects Cicero's influence. The *Agricola* is also marked by a lengthy digression on the history of Britain, an area which Tacitus claims Agricola explored and pacified.

The latter work, *Germania,* a two-part treatise on German lifestyle and customs, discusses a subject matter which interested Romans greatly. The first part, **Books 1–27,** deals with the Germans as a whole, while the last portion, **Books 28–45,** covers the individual tribes. Because *Germania* failed to incorporate up-to-date information, critics have speculated that Tacitus intended his work as a commentary on the freedom-loving barbarians, in contrast to the corrupt, cynical Romans of his day.

The *Histories* and *Annals,* which are major contributions to world history, are conscientious and accurate and concentrate upon cause and effect and the nature of autocracy. The *Histories,* a fourteen-book work which describes the era from 68 to 96 A.D., from the death of Nero to that of Domitian, contains information supplied by the letters of Pliny the Younger. The *Annals,* which extend from the death of Augustus into the events of 116 A.D., suggest that the historian may have died in 117 A.D., leaving unfinished his plans for a thorough study of the Augustan age and the reigns of Nerva and Trajan.

Although Tacitus grew bitter toward the Flavian emperors during Domitian's reign and emphasized the weaknesses of the imperial system, his credibility is impeccable. His extensive commentary on tyranny, injustice, and debauchery has colored the thinking of succeeding generations about imperial Rome. In contrast with his idealized "noble savage" in *Germania,* the harsh tone with which Tacitus characterizes the Roman citizen of the first century leaves no doubt that the historian felt the imminent demise of a noble civilization.

ANNALS

In his introduction to the *Annals,* Tacitus gives a brief overview of Rome – from the monarchy, established in 753 B.C., to the beginnings of the Empire in 31 B.C. He determines his task to be a description of the "rising tide of sycophancy" under Augustus' four successors – Tiberius, Gaius (generally referred to as Caligula), Claudius, and Nero. To the younger generation, those born after the Battle of Actium, he notes, Rome little resembled its early greatness. Because of the decimation of the civil war,

> . . . few indeed were left who had seen the Republic. It was an altered world, and of the old, unspoiled Roman character not a trace lingered. Quality was an outworn creed, and all eyes looked to the mandate of the sovereign. . . . So long as Augustus remained in control, all was well; however, his advancing age and ill health caused Roman leaders to consider a successor.

In his youth, Tiberius, bred to the arrogance of the Claudian family, already gave evidence of his cruel, lascivious character. Following Augustus' death, which Tacitus implies was hastened by Livia, the emperor's wife, Tiberius murdered his kinsman and rival, Agrippa Postumus, on the pretense that it was Augustus' dying wish, and he seated himself securely upon the throne. Tacitus refers to Rome's second emperor as an "interloper who had wormed his way to power with the help of connubial intrigues and a senile act of adoption."

The towering villain during Tiberius' reign was Sejanus, the captain of the Praetorian Guard, whom the emperor both loved and feared. During Tiberius' last years, he withdrew to the island of Capri and made Sejanus his spokesman. In complete control over the emperor's contacts with the outside world, Sejanus manipulated events and people to his own tastes. Yet, Sejanus provided some small rein on Tiberius' famed sexual license. Upon Sejanus' death, Tiberius allowed his debauched temperament to run riot, committing innumerable acts of cruelty. Unfortunately, most of the fifth book of the *Annals* is missing, leaving a serious gap in information about Tiberius.

Books XI–XVI detail the reigns of Claudius and Nero. In contrast to the willful guile of his predecessor, Claudius, halting in both gait and speech, seems half-witted. In a significant personal digression, Tacitus comments:

The more I study past and present history, the more I perceive the mockery of all human hopes and dreams, for in reputation, expectation, and general respect, anybody was a more likely candidate for the purple than the man whom Fortune was hiding in reserve as emperor of the future.

According to Tacitus, Claudius was as easily managed by the palace staff as he was by his lustful wife, Messalina, notorious for sexual escapades, which led to her execution.

Book XII describes the maneuvering of Agrippina, Claudius' niece and last wife, who manipulated the political situation in order to put her son, Nero, on the throne. A different sort from his forebears, who pursued excellence in rhetoric, the Roman ideal of the educated man, Nero, even in his childhood, turned his lively mind to other interests:

> . . . he carved, painted, practiced singing or driving, and occasionally in a set of verses showed that he had in him the rudiments of culture.

In contrast to Tiberius, Nero opened himself to the people and let his excesses speak for themselves: "It was an old desire of his to drive a chariot and team of four, and an equally repulsive ambition to sing with a lyre in the stage manner." The Roman public, inured to vice, longed for spectacle and encouraged Nero's exhibitionism.

Book XIV opens with a description of the unnatural relationship between Nero and his ambitious mother. As Tacitus describes the situation, ". . . all men yearned for the breaking of the mother's power; none credited that the hatred of the son would go the full way to murder." In her attempt to assure her influence over Nero, Agrippina often dressed and acted the part of the coquette, engulfing her son in endearments and kisses, prefatory to incestuous relations. Nero, wishing to end her iron-fisted control of his career and personal life, lured Agrippina to Baiae, disarmed her with passionate kisses, and sent her on a fatal boat trip.

Agrippina, possibly forewarned of her son's treachery, evaded the trap and swam to shore. Before a concerned mob could rush to her villa and congratulate her on the narrow escape, Nero dispatched hired killers to cordon off the area and murder his mother. When her executioner drew a sword to end the attack, Agrippina dramatically pointed to her lower abdomen and cried out, "Strike here." Although Nero neglected her funeral rites, her servants honored her with a humble tomb. Tacitus ends the account with an oft-repeated story that Agrippina knew her son would reign and slay his mother, to which she replied, "Let him slay, so that he reign."

Nero's grasp of reality began to slip away as greater fantasies demanded a public staging. He invited the entire city to banquets, one of the most extravagant of which featured a table floating on a raft in the Pool of Agrippa:

> He had collected birds and wild beasts from the ends of the earth, and marine animals from the ocean itself. On the quays of the lake stood brothels, filled with women of high rank; and opposite, naked harlots met the view.

The sequence of events moves at a quickened pace spiraling downward, from mere obscenity to depravity and abomination. A few days after the feast, Nero observed full rites in a traditional Roman wedding ceremony, at which he assumed the role of the "wife of one of that herd of degenerates, who bore the name of Pythagoras."

Shortly after this bizarre affair, Rome caught fire, beginning in the Circus Maximus and reaching the Palatine and Caelian Hills. As the homeless fled in terror, despairing of their livelihood:

> None ventured to combat the fire, as there were reiterated threats from a large number of persons who forbade extinction and others were openly throwing firebrands and shouting 'they had their authority'—possibly in order to have a freer hand in looting, possibly from orders received.

Although Nero offered the victims temporary shelter in the Campus Martius and his own gardens, he forever muddied his reputation by mounting a stage and singing verses about the destruction of Troy.

In order to prevent rumors that the fire was set by order of the emperor, Nero chose the Christians as scapegoats and pursued them with unstinting malice:

> Derision accompanied their end: they were covered with wild beasts' skins and torn to death by dogs; or they were fastened on crosses, and when daylight failed, they were burned to serve as lamps by night.

Dressed in the garb of a charioteer, Nero rode among the gathered spectators. Yet, this abysmal spectacle proved injurious to his popularity, for the Romans, while angry that the Christians burned the city, perceived Nero's sacrifice of the Christians to be cowardly, a means of placating a monster.

HISTORIES

In strict annalistic form, Tacitus begins his *Histories* on January 1, 69 A.D., a cataclysmic year which saw the reigns of four emperors, beginning with Galba and ending with Vespasian. Tacitus attaches a disclaimer to his book, noting that

> . . . while men quickly turn from a historian who curries favor, they listen with ready ears to calumny and spite; for flattery is subject to the shameful charge of servility, but malignity makes a false show of independence.

To set the record straight, he claims to have had no direct dealing with Galba or with either of his two successors, Otho and Vitellius.

Tacitus does acknowledge his debt to the next three emperors, Vespasian and his two sons, Titus and Domitian. Looking toward future volumes, Tacitus plans to save the histories of the reigns of Nerva and Trajan for his old age, although no evidence exists that he ever wrote them. He looked forward to the more peaceful conditions of the later emperors, "a richer and less perilous subject . . . in which we may feel what we wish and say what we feel."

By way of contrast, Tacitus introduces the earlier era, "a period rich in disasters, terrible with battles, torn by civil struggles, horrible even in peace." In a torrent of disgust, he summarizes a wretched span of years in which arson, desecration, adultery, cruelty, and corruption held sway:

> The rewards of the informers were no less hateful than their crimes; for some, gaining priesthoods and consulships as spoils; for others, obtaining positions as imperial agents and

secret influence at court made havoc and turmoil everywhere, inspiring hatred and terror.

Slaves were corrupted against their masters, freedmen against their patrons; and those who had no enemies were crushed by their friends.

Despite this cheerless preface, he offers a slim paean to those few Romans who remain untainted. Quickly returning to his grim theme, he insists that the gods give due warning in signs and portents, such as lightning and prophecies.

Tacitus devotes thirty-eight chapters to Galba's reign and reveals how Galba's choice of Piso Licinianus as heir to the throne inspired Otho to plot with the Praetorian Guard to overthrow the emperor. Weak and old, Galba was unable to strengthen the tottering Empire. Otho's supporters lured Galba from his stronghold with fraudulent news of Otho's death. As the palace guard rallied around their chosen leader, Otho

. . . stretched out his hands and did obeisance to the common soldiers, threw kisses, and played in every way the slave to secure the master's place.

The scene quickly changed to the expected bloodbath as the bodies of Galba's supporters lay in heaps, their heads displayed on poles alongside the standards of the Roman legions.

Tacitus is loath to end his narration, carrying the horror to greater heights through several chapters before describing the desecration of the emperor himself:

Galba's body was long neglected and abused with a thousand insults. . . . Finally Argius, his steward, one of his former slaves, gave it humble burial in his master's private garden. Galba's head, which had been fixed on a pole and maltreated by camp-followers and servants, was finally found the next day . . . and was placed with the body, which had already been burned.

The historian summarizes the good and bad of Galba's character. He died at age seventy-three and had been happy, fortunate, and wealthy. Although born of a noble lineage, he was "of mediocre genius, being rather free from faults than possessing virtues."

His successor, a fat, lazy sybarite, depended upon the Praetorian Guard, which held him a virtual hostage of its capricious will. But the same restlessness that brought down Galba proved too much for Otho's meager powers. As Vitellius crowded his authority, Otho had little choice but to kill himself:

> Then two daggers were brought him; he tried the points of both and placed one beneath his head. After learning that his friends had gone, he passed a quiet night, and . . . even slept a little. At dawn he fell on the steel.

Tacitus' description of the "Roman way of death" seems much too peaceful and merciful for a usurper who caused such carnage only a few months before. Yet, Otho died nobly and honorably at the age of thirty-seven and received a military funeral and modest tomb.

Book III is the high point of horror in this single year in Rome's history. While Vitellius hid away in his garden, bloated like a "torpid beast" from his stockpile of food, the situation outside Rome worsened. For the third time, Rome's fickle mob caressed a new hero, Vespasian, an able field commander, who sanctioned the sack of Cremona, a city pledged to the emperor:

> Aged men and women near the end of life, though despised as booty, were dragged off to be the soldiers' sport. Whenever a young woman or a handsome youth fell into their hands, they were torn to pieces by the violent struggles of those who tried to secure them, and this in the end drove the despoilers to kill one another.

Their depravity led them to steal from the temples, burn, loot, and torture. As Tacitus summarizes their wantonness, "no two held the same thing sacred and there was no crime which was held unlawful."

Vitellius mobilized too late to stop mass defections to Vespasian. Convinced that his death was near, he led his family into the streets, held his small son out to anyone who would take him, and he offered his dagger as a token of his submission. The crowds refused his gesture and forced him back to the palace. Rumors of Vitellius' abdication spread quickly, and Vespasian followed a sure path to the throne. In the melee, the Capitol burned.

In Book XXII, Tacitus despairs over another even more senseless act of violence, the needless destruction of the temple of Jupiter Optimus Maximus:

This was the saddest and most shameful crime that the Roman state had ever suffered since its foundation. Rome had no foreign foe; the gods were ready to be propitious if our characters had allowed; and yet the home of Jupiter Optimus Maximus . . . this was the shrine that the mad fury of emperors destroyed!

The people, drunk with perverted pleasure and having no loyalty to either side, gathered to watch the slaughter, "as if they were at games in the circus." As pools of blood formed alongside heaps of corpses, prostitutes and pimps plied their trade.

Vespasian's reign, also stained red with gore, boasted the destruction of Jerusalem. Under the leadership of Titus, whom Vespasian sent to subjugate Judea, an allied force made up of Syrians, Egyptians, and Arabs joined against the Jews, about whom Tacitus knew little. In his discourse of rumor, half-truth, and outright lies, he vilifies the entire nation:

. . . the other customs of the Jews are base and abominable and owe their persistence to their depravity . . . [they] are extremely loyal toward one another and always ready to show compassion, but toward every other people they feel only hate and enmity.

His pathetic misinformation ends in Book XXVI in mid-sentence, the remainder of his *Histories* having been lost in antiquity.

EPICTETUS

- *Discourses*

EPICTETUS

LIFE AND BACKGROUND

Epictetus (*ca.* 55–135 A.D.), a crippled slave born in Hierapolis, Phrygia, in what is now the northern part of Syria, became a profound influence on Roman thought and life. How and why he was enslaved or maimed is unknown, although there is some evidence that he was tortured. His master, Epaphroditus, a freedman of Nero's and a member of the imperial bureaucracy, brought him to Rome at an early age and allowed him to attend the lectures of Gaius Musonius Rufus, a notable stoic teacher. After Epictetus obtained his freedom, he, too, taught philosophy until the emperor Domitian, fearful that stoicism posed a threat to his dynasty, banished all philosophers from Rome in 92 A.D.

Epictetus established a school in Nicopolis, Epirus, on the west coast of Greece and remained there until his death. At Epictetus' school, the sons of gentlemen and public notables came to be educated, and renowned visitors sought advice, for Epictetus had established his reputation by the time he came to Epirus. Even though he published none of his lectures, one of his pupils, Arrian, who later became a well-known Greek philosopher and historian, preserved his classroom conversations and precepts verbatim in eight books, four of which are extant. The thrust of Epictetus' philosophy is ethics, by which he exhorted his students to champion good and to value their kinship with other human beings.

Epictetus espoused a simple formula for everyday life: "endure and renounce." He maintained that affliction, suffering, and death are natural occurrences and that human beings are enriched by pain. Real happiness, he revealed, comes from the inner being, where peace of mind frees the individual to enjoy living. To Epictetus, each person has only to play the role dictated by God in order to find contentment. Later readers, impressed by the humble tone and pious outlook of his sayings, insisted that Epictetus must have come under the influence of Christian missionaries.

DISCOURSES

The opening lines of Epictetus' *Discourses* leave little doubt that the philosopher was a godly man. Like David, the Hebrew poet, Epictetus vigorously exhorts his hearers to honor the divine being.

> What else can I that am old and lame do but sing to God? Were I a nightingale, I should do after the manner of a nightingale. Were I a swan, I should do after the manner of a swan. But now, since I am a reasonable being, I must sing to God: that is my work. I do it and will not desert this my post, as long as it is granted me to hold it, and upon you too, I call to join in this self-same hymn.

From this premise springs Epictetus' concept of right actions. If man is born of the gods, "he would never conceive anything ignoble or base about himself." Such a divine birthright, he concludes, sets human beings free from sorrow and fear.

One of the certainties upon which Epictetus based his philosophy is that whatever happens is God's will—an idea which permeates the writings of Marcus Aurelius, Epictetus' most learned disciple. Epictetus takes hope in the realization that God is in charge of the universe.

> So when you have shut the doors and made a darkness within, remember never to say that you are alone, for you are not alone. God is within, and your Guardian Spirit, and what light do they need to behold what you do?

To foster a close association with God, he encourages his students to seek wisdom, for the real nature of God is "intelligence, knowledge, and right reason."

To illustrate his kernels of wisdom, Epictetus laces his discourses with humble metaphors from carpentry, the barnyard, the market-place, and military life, and he frequently refers to great thinkers of the Greek world, such as Diogenes, Heraclitus, Socrates, and Demos-thenes. In one graceful lesson, he notes:

> Our way of life resembles a fair. The flocks and herds are passing along to be sold, and the greater part of the crowd to buy and sell. But there are some few who come only to look at the fair, to inquire how and why it is being held, upon what authority and with what object.

To these students, Epictetus gives a dramatic, compelling definition of stoicism:

> Who then is a stoic – in the sense that we call that a statue of Phidias. . . . Show me a man who is sick – and happy; in danger – and happy; on his deathbed – and happy; an exile – and happy; in evil report – and happy! Show me him, I ask again. So help me heaven, I long to see *one* stoic!

Such an individual, the philosopher summarizes, lays no blame on God or man and suffers none of the negative emotions, neither dis-appointment, crossness, anger, envy, nor jealousy. "To a good man," he declares, "there is no evil, either in life or death."

Some of the more mundane admonitions that are credited to Epic-tetus sound true to the classroom teacher who chooses wisdom over punishment as a means of ameliorating student behavior:

> Nature has given men one tongue but two ears. . . . Keep neither a blunt knife nor an ill-disciplined looseness of tongue. . . . None is a slave whose acts are free. . . . Chastise your passions that they avenge not themselves upon you. . . . No man is free who is not master of himself.

These epigrams of Epictetus, as well as his piercing rhetorical ques-tions and fuller statements of truth, have a single aim – to enlighten his pupils and present them with lofty goals. As he states in one of his most positive aphorisms:

> Even as the sun does not wait for prayers and incantations to rise, but shines forth and is welcomed by all: so you also

wait not for clapping of hands and shouts and praise to do your duty; no, do good of your own accord, and you will be loved like the sun.

JUVENAL

- *Satires*

JUVENAL

LIFE AND BACKGROUND

The most famous social critic of the Roman Empire, Decimus Junius Juvenalis lived from about 60 A.D. to about 140 A.D. He began writing late in life, possibly around 110 A.D., and published his scathing, pyrotechnic verses until 127 A.D. Most of the discontent which his work reflects centers on the reign of Domitian, a period which saw repression and absolutism carried to such lengths that members of the emperor's family, including his wife, carried out Domitian's assassination.

Although information about Juvenal is scanty and contradictory, it appears that he was born in Aquinum, seventy-odd miles southeast of Rome, the son or foster son of a wealthy freedman. He is remembered as a well-educated man—a stoic, a master declaimer, rhetorician, and poet. An intensely private individual, he appears to have suffered financial difficulties and an accompanying bitterness, although he later owned a farm at Tibur and hosted friends at his house in Rome.

Scattered bits of information place Juvenal at the head of a military mission in northern Britain. Also, he may have served as a minor magistrate and *flamen* (priest of Jupiter) in Aquinum. According to medieval sources, at the age of eighty, he was exiled to a minor military post in Egypt by Domitian as unofficial punishment for ridiculing Paris, a stage mime and the emperor's favorite. The satirist supposedly died there very shortly from grief and frustration, although there are other tales of his death in Rome, in despair over Martial's death.

His terse, epigrammatic style has left numerous quotable remarks for later generations to ponder, such as "Honesty is praised and shivers," "What man was ever content with one crime," "A sound mind in a sound body," "Bread and circuses," and "No man ever became extremely wicked all at once." In a particularly severe mood, he wonders aloud why Romans, who raise money to divine heights, have neglected to build an altar to wealth "to match their worship of Pax, Fides, Victoria, Virtus, and Concordia [peace, faith, victory, strength, and harmony]!"

Of his verse, only sixteen satires remain, the last being incomplete. The most quoted, his sixth, is a diatribe against women. Other favorites are "On Life at Rome" and "On Prayer." Juvenal attempts to expose Roman vice of the first century by presenting elements of social decay—graft, perversion, cynicism, disreputable business practices, flattery, discrimination, gluttony, parasitism, and, of course, the decline of the arts. Although marred by his prejudice and pessimism, his satire proved influential to later writers, particularly Chaucer, Boileau, Dryden, Pope, Johnson, Addison, Steele, and Byron.

SATIRES

Juvenal's ferocious, resentful complaints fade somewhat toward the end of his life, as though the author passed from a state of righteous indignation to the passivity associated with extreme age. Early in his career, he peopled his verse with identifiable dregs of Roman society— a eunuch, stripper, nouveau riche barber, flashy foreigner, sadists, gigolos, poisoners, and assorted frauds. Unfortunately, his cryptic references to the notorious of his day require extensive footnoting to have meaning for modern readers.

His first satire serves as an introduction to his career. In sardonic, rambling fashion, he leads up to his momentous announcement:

> But if you can give me time, and will listen quietly to reason,
> I will tell you why I prefer to run in the same course over
> which the great nursling of Aurunca [Lucilius, Rome's first
> satirist] drove his steeds.

His glib, facile verse runs on, lampooning first one absurdity, then another. He concludes that, with people like these buffoons walking the streets of Rome, "it is hard not to write satire."

A source of his derision, the nouveau riche who posture and take on airs seem particularly odious to him, probably because he suffers money troubles and bears them ill-will out of envy. A typical snipe asks:

> If then the great officers of state reckon up at the end of the year how much the dole brings in, how much it adds to their income, what shall we dependents do who, out of the self-same dole, have to find ourselves in coats and shoes, in the bread and fire of our homes?

A master of facetious naivete and the rhetorical question, his hand-wringing leads perpetually to dire warning. "So turn these things over in your mind before the trumpet sounds," he concludes, leaving little doubt that he believes the hour is already too late for repentance.

Juvenal puts his insistent, inflammatory gibes to work in Satire VI, his notorious invective against women. In mock consternation that Postumus, a hypothetical bridegroom, is about to marry, the poet-cum-misogynist unleashes his venom on women:

> Can you submit to a she-tyrant when there is so much rope to be had, so many dizzy heights of windows standing open, and when the Aemilian bridge offers itself to hand? . . . how much better to take some boy-bedfellow, who would never wrangle with you o'nights, never ask presents of you when in bed, and never complain that you took your ease and were indifferent to his solicitations!

Blustering on at length with examples of wives gone wrong, he assures the credulous victim that "every street has its Clytemnestra."

In a general thrust at the whole gamut of human folly, Juvenal ridicules piety, particularly the prayers offered by greedy Romans:

> Thus it is that the things for which we pray, and for which it is right and proper to load the knees of the gods with wax, are either profitless or pernicious.

The most inappropriate of prayers, he submits, is the prayer which requests longevity. This prayer is typical of youth and good times, before old age and disease render the face unrecognizable, the "pendulous cheeks and the wrinkles like those which a matron baboon carves upon her aged jaws in the shaded glades of [Numidia]."

What, then, should the petitioner ask for? Juvenal replies with disarming sincerity, "Leave it to the gods themselves to provide what is good for us," what will suit our needs. God, the poet insists, is benevolent to human beings. To him should go prayers for *"mens sana in corpore sano"* (a sound mind in a sound body) and for courage to face death. Divesting himself of jeering, snide humor, Juvenal pronounces a classic conclusion: the only road to serenity is through uprightness.

SUETONIUS

- *De Viris Illustribus*
  (Illustrious Men)

- *De Vita Caesarum*
  (Lives of the Caesars)

SUETONIUS

LIFE AND BACKGROUND

Gaius Suetonius Tranquillus lived during Rome's most prosperous and peaceful era, an era in which the superstructure of Roman bureaucracy expanded at an enormous rate because the so-called "good emperors" attempted to improve the lot of the average citizen. He was born in northern Africa, about 69 A.D., and his father, a military tribune of the thirteenth legion, brought him to Rome to be educated.

Early in life, as a member of the *equites,* or the moneyed middle class, Suetonius prepared himself for law. He turned from law, however, to schoolteaching for a brief stint. He says little about his personal life, although Pliny's letters indicate that he was married, but that he had either no children, or fewer than three, as he was ineligible for the *ius trium liberorum,* a government bonus for families with three or more children. According to further remarks from Pliny, Suetonius appears to have been of good character, but lacked any interest in the political intrigue of his day.

Around 100 A.D., Suetonius applied for a commission in a legion bound for Britain as the next stage of his carefully engineered career. He changed his mind almost immediately, however, and took a promising position as a court magistrate. Then he returned briefly to his hometown in Africa to assume the responsibilities of a priest.

For a time he traveled in Bithynia, part of modern-day Turkey, with the younger Pliny, his close friend and literary colleague. Upon his return to Rome, Suetonius served as a *studiis,* or staff aide, for Trajan, assuming the role of court researcher. He advanced to the post of court librarian, or archivist, and after Trajan's death, he subsequently took charge of Hadrian's official correspondence. As a member of the imperial council, Suetonius made the most of his close association with state documents by probing into the history of Rome, particularly into that era which saw the demise of Julius Caesar (and the Republic) and the rise of the Roman Empire.

Working from varied public and private sources, Suetonius was able to draw on a vast store of facts, anecdotes, curiosities, and gossip to enliven his writings. Unfortunately, he, along with Gaius Septicius Clarus, commander of the *praetorians,* or palace guard, was dismissed from his official duties around 122 A.D. for insulting the Empress Sabina, although the charge may have been a ruse for the emperor's displeasure with Suetonius' more intimate disclosures about the lives of Julius Caesar and Augustus Caesar. At this point, it appears that Suetonius retired from public life and withdrew in order to complete the antiquarian studies that have made him famous.

His work, painstakingly precise and scholarly, written intermittently in Greek, covers a variety of subjects, such as Greek and Roman entertainments, linguistics, the calendar, natural science, body deformities, literary symbols, Roman customs and clothing, famous courtesans, street language, bureaucratic red tape, and royalty. His lively, titillating approach to biography influenced Einhard, Charlemagne's secretary and biographer, and has colored later generations' ideas of the life and times of the first emperors of Rome.

Suetonius' style, in comparison with the genius of Tacitus and Pliny the Younger, suffers from severe shortcomings. He lacks depth in his inquiry, preferring personal estimations and occasional coarse commentary to more incisive political or historical inquiry. He follows a predictable sequence in each biography—birth, childhood, public career, personal qualities, and death. This tedious formula, along with a less-than-precise command of language, which he frequently salts with Greekisms, saps his writings of energy. His redeeming feature is an eye for detail—an unerring ability to capture a memorable tidbit, such as his account of Nero's fiddling while Rome burned.

DE VIRIS ILLUSTRIBUS (ILLUSTRIOUS MEN)

A valuable sourcebook for Jerome and other scholars, Suetonius' compendium of biographical data is particularly strong in references to Terence, Virgil, Horace, and Lucan. The work appears to have followed on the success of the *Grammarians* and *Rhetoricians*, his earlier publications. Under the influence of Marcus Varro, critic and biographer at the end of the Republic, Suetonius appears to have broadened the scope of his writing, particularly in his treatment of Terence. From an undistinguished compiler of data, he advanced to a respectable, if somewhat inept biographer.

The most memorable section of Suetonius' descriptions of famous men is the third section, which deals with poets. Generously laced with quotations, his description of Terence gives this account of the playwright's last years:

> After publishing these comedies before he had passed his twenty-fifth year, either to escape from the gossip about publishing the work of others as his own, or else to become versed in Greek manners and customs, which he felt that he had not been wholly successful in depicting in his plays, he left Rome and never returned.

Capitalizing on the mysterious disappearance, Suetonius quotes Cosconius to the effect that Terence drowned on a return voyage, along with the one hundred and eight plays that he had adapted from Menander. Another version has Terence dying of frustration and grief after his luggage, containing his most recent work, was lost.

Suetonius makes extensive commentary on the life and works of Virgil, including a popular legend of the poet's birth:

> While he was in his mother's womb, she dreamt that she gave birth to a laurel branch, which on touching the earth took root and grew at once to the size of a full-grown tree, covered with fruits and flowers of various kinds; and on the following day . . . gave birth to her child in a ditch beside the road.

He embroiders the personal commentary with a mishmash of data — that Virgil was tall, dark-skinned, rustic, and given to lust for young boys. In addition, according to Suetonius, Virgil suffered from throat and stomach ailments and had frequent hemorrhages.

Of Virgil's productivity, Suetonius notes that the *Bucolics* took three years to complete, the *Georgics* seven, and the *Aeneid* twelve. He declares that the *Aeneid* was an immediate success; allegedly, Sextus Propertius exclaimed: "Yield, ye Roman writers; yield, ye

Greeks; a greater than the *Iliad* is born." Suetonius reports Eros, Virgil's secretary, as saying that Virgil gave infrequent readings and that he used public reaction at these gatherings as a method of isolating and strengthening the weaker portions of his epic verse.

Of Horace, Suetonius has equally droll comments. He quotes an unflattering remark from one of Augustus' letters to the poet:

> . . . you seem to me to be afraid that your books may be bigger than you are yourself; but it is only stature that you lack, not girth. So you may write on a pint pot, that the circumference of your volume may be well rounded out, like that of your own belly.

Suetonius' accounts of Lucan's indiscretions are even more salacious. He describes how Lucan's squabble with Nero resulted in a prolonged assault by "words and acts of hostility to the prince, which are still notorious." A particularly coarse comment involves a bout of intestinal gas in a public toilet which inspired Lucan to quote, "You might suppose it thundered 'neath the earth'," a line from one of Nero's verses.

DE VITA CAESARUM
(LIVES OF THE CAESARS)

Suetonius' most influential work, the *Lives of the Caesars*, bursts with life through the blend of pertinent data, superstition, and trivial, sometimes caustic commentary that the biographer made famous. Sections of his physical descriptions have left believable portraits for later generations to savor. Concerning Augustus, Suetonius notes that he was handsome, somewhat short, with piercing eyes, curly blond hair, a thick nose, wide-spaced teeth, a noticeable limp, and smooth, dark skin. Tiberius, he says, had a wiry build and a tallish frame, was left-handed, and wore his hair long at the back. Claudius, according to Suetonius, was dignified except when he talked and startled people with his stuttering, his trembling head, and his braying laugh.

One of the most treasured of Suetonius' portraits is the "Divine Julius," although the truncated version apparently lacks an introduction, long since lost. Suetonius remarks that Julius Caesar was tall, fair-skinned, and keen-eyed. He was fussy about his appearance, "being not only carefully trimmed and shaved, but even having superfluous hair plucked out . . ." He had a taste for finery, particularly gemstones, pearls, and art objects. To conceal his weakness for handsome slaves, he had his accountants omit them from his ledgers.

In characteristic style, Suetonius indiscriminately mixes the sweet with the sour. He lauds Caesar's generosity to his soldiers as well as his visionary edicts, designed to improve the general welfare:

> He conferred citizenship on all who practiced medicine at Rome, and on all teachers of the liberal arts, to make them more desirous of living in the city and to induce others to resort to it.

Also, to discourage the rich from flouting the law, he increased the penalties for crime. Other deeds indicate that Caesar was "conscientious and strict" in matters of justice and that he wished Rome to grow and prosper.

On the other hand, Suetonius quotes scurrilous sources that mock Caesar's predilection for both sexes, such as Curio's disparaging gibe, "the brothel of Nicomedes and the stew of Bithynia," and Bibulus' equally unflattering epithet, "the queen of Bithynia." Despite its crudeness, Suetonius does not hesitate to repeat a bit of camp doggerel:

> All the Gauls did Caesar vanquish, Nicomedes vanquished him!
> Lo, now Caesar rides in triumph, victor over all the Gauls,
> Nicomedes does not triumph, who subdued the conqueror.

Also, he provides a list of the Roman matrons that Caesar is reputed to have despoiled, including the wives of Pompey and Crassus and especially Servilia, mother of Marcus Brutus, whom he rewarded with a costly pearl.

It is Suetonius who fostered the story of Caesar's love affair with Cleopatra and the birth of their son, who "was very like Caesar in looks and posture." The biographer's next remark, however, is more telling. In describing a bill promulgated by Caesar which would allow him to "marry what wives he wished and as many as he wished" in order to provide him with offspring, Suetonius suggests the reason for Caesar's assassination. Because he appeared to favor the return of monarchy, his rush to beget children had an ominous ring to Romans, whose earlier dealings with kings forever soiled the title of "rex."

The flow of detail, both positive and negative, continues. Suetonius describes Caesar's good manners, lack of respect for temples and shrines, profligacy, concern for friends, and eloquence. He describes Caesar's use of code, skill in weaponry and horsemanship, appreciation for fine horseflesh, and caution when in command of his legions. Interspersed with Caesar's flair for speedy, unforeseen movements, Suetonius notes that he never let religious sacrifices hold him back, for he had "no regard for religion."

In explanation of Caesar's ignoble death, Suetonius sides with the assassins, explaining that Caesar "allowed honors to be granted him which were too great for mortal man." Among his excesses were a golden throne, a chariot and litter in the procession at the circus, temples, altars, statues, a special priest, and the "calling of one of the months by his name." After considering several methods of killing him, including tossing him from a bridge, the conspirators decided to waylay Caesar in the Senate.

Suetonius describes the carnage in bold detail. At first, Caesar fought back, stabbing Casca in the arm with his stylus. But at last, realizing that he was outnumbered, he composed himself for death, wrapping his robe about his head and extending the edge decently over his feet. Suetonius notes with some pathos how, before giving up to the twenty-three stab wounds that killed him, Caesar saw Marcus Brutus rushing at him and said in Greek, "You too, my child?" His corpse lay undisturbed for some time before slaves found the courage to bear it away, one arm trailing limply over the side of the litter.

Caesar's will was read at Antony's house. It named his sister's grandson, "Gaius Octavius, to three-fourths of his estate." Also, it established that Octavius was to be considered his legally adopted son and to share the name "Julius Caesar." To Roman citizens, as Shakespeare noted, Caesar was most generous: "To the people he left his gardens near the Tiber for their common use and three hundred sesterces to each man." Mourners filed toward his bier from all parts of the city, some tearing their garments and hurling them into the flames, as did numerous women with their jewelry.

Suetonius' account of Augustus Caesar's life is no less stirring. Following a brief comment on his boyhood, Suetonius narrates the astounding career that took Augustus, a rather plain man, to the position of first Roman emperor. Packed with the same mixture of good and bad as the previous biography, Suetonius' sketch reveals a decisive and brutal personality:

> He allowed [Antony and Cleopatra] the honor of burial in the same tomb, giving orders that the mausoleum which they had begun should be finished. The young Antony . . . he dragged from the image of the Deified Julius, to which he had fled after many vain entreaties, and slew him. Caesarion, too, the son of Caesar and Cleopatra, he overtook in his flight, brought back, and put to death.

Yet, in a show of mercy and compassion, he spared the children of Antony and Cleopatra and raised them "as if they were his own kin."

Returning to the shambles of Rome after the devastation of civil war, Augustus considered reestablishing the Republic, but fearing that "it would be hazardous to trust the State to the control of the populace, he continued to keep it in his hands . . ." His idealism took precedence over egotism in his hopes for the "best possible government." Augustus despaired of the city's outward appearance and "so beautified it that he could justly boast that he found it built of brick and left it in marble."

Primary among his concerns were safety and function. He built to accommodate growth, which he envisioned for the peaceful years, named the "pax Romana," that were to follow. With particular attention to piety, Augustus constructed colonnades, basilicas, a theater, and temples, naming them in honor of family members. He was punctilious in matters of justice, sometimes reclining on a litter as court sessions extended far into the night. To restore honor and credibility to Rome's legislators, he winnowed out the weak among the senatorial class and restructured the entire law-making process.

Augustus was a devoted family man, both for private reasons and as a matter of state. He took an interest in his grandsons, teaching them

reading, swimming, and the other elements of education . . .
taking special pains to train them to imitate his own hand-
writing; and he never dined in their company unless they sat
beside him on the lowest couch, or made a journey unless
they preceded his carriage or rode close by it on either side.

Unfortunately, his attempts to produce a model family failed in his
daughter and granddaughter, the two Julia's, "guilty of every form of
vice," whom he banished.

Augustus himself was not free from scandal, as Suetonius reports,
and declined to deny the many accusations of adultery. He was casti-
gated for luxurious tastes, gaming, impiety, and waste. Yet, he showed
remarkable constraint in his simple home, where he often escaped
to a small workshop on the roof when he desired privacy. About the
house, he wore unassuming, homemade garments, modeled after the
traditional Roman garb, and he reserved his robes of state for the
public eye. In matters of diet, he was scrupulous to eat only plain
food in small quantity and to avoid overindulgence in wine.

Suetonius enumerates the flaws on Augustus' body, particularly
his birthmarks, which formed a pattern resembling Ursa Major. He
recounts how Augustus kept a *strigil,* or scraper, with which to scratch
himself. In addition, he suffered a characteristic weakness in his left
leg and hip, atrophy in his right forefinger, and kidney stones. Frequently in ill health from various internal ailments, including liver
and lung disorders, he disliked extremes of temperature and traveled
at night in a litter.

Suetonius concludes that Augustus was granted the one great wish
of his life—that he suffer a "euthanasia," or kindly death. On his
deathbed, he lay in the embrace of his wife, Livia, whom he addressed
tenderly with his dying words. Distracted and babbling in death
throes, he revived briefly and cried out that forty men were carrying
him away, a portent that superstitious Romans ascribed to the exact
number in his honor guard, which appeared to Augustus in a final
vision.

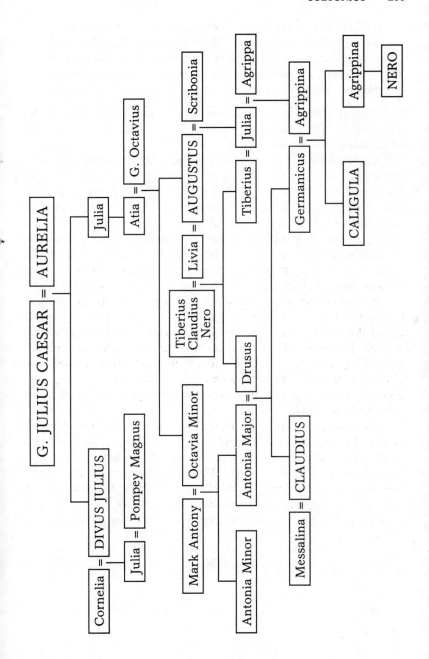

MINOR WRITERS

- **Statius**

- **Lucan**

MINOR WRITERS

STATIUS

Of far less literary stature than the previous examples is Publius Papinius Statius (45–96 A.D.), the court poet and friend of the Emperor Domitian. Although he ranked high among Rome's great epic poets during his lifetime, his works have failed to achieve lasting recognition.

A Neapolitan by birth and the son of a celebrated teacher, Statius earned fame around 90 A.D. because of his victory in a poetry contest established by the emperor. Statius quickly ingratiated himself among the elite of Rome and published many works to their liking.

His earliest surviving verse, *Thebaid,* is an energetic twelve-book epic detailing the conflict between Eteocles and Polyneices, Oedipus' ill-fated sons. The title is derived from the city of Thebes, where their final battle brought about great carnage, including the deaths of both central figures.

A second work, a two-book *epyllion* (short episode from an epic), is the *Achilleid,* describing the adventures in Achilles' life previous to the Trojan War. More pleasing, perhaps, are the thirty-two poems collected under the title *Silvae,* or the *Five Books of the Forests,* a compendium of occasional and court poetry. The most noteworthy of these minor poems is "To Sleep."

Statius was revered in the Middle Ages as one of Rome's greatest poets. Dante places him above Virgil in the *Purgatory* section of *The Divine Comedy.* In the fourteenth century, Chaucer imitates Statius' *Thebaid* in *Troilus and Criseyde*; he holds him in equal status with Virgil, Ovid, Homer, and Lucan. A revival of interest in Statius occurred in the eighteenth century, when Pope and Gray translated portions of his work into English.

303

_____ **LUCAN**

The son of a Roman cavalry officer and the nephew of the philosopher Seneca, Marcus Annaeus Lucanus was born in Cordova, Spain, in 39 A.D. Taken to Rome in infancy and educated in the stoic tradition, Lucan received a court appointment as *quaestor* before the age of twenty-five and became an augural priest. Because of his gift for witty conversation, he was made a member at court, whom Nero, jealous of his rival's precocity and brilliance, forbade to publish or recite in public.

Resentful of Nero's edict, Lucan wrote secret satires and fostered a personal enmity that boiled over into the public domain. Along with his teacher, Cornutus, Lucan joined the abortive Pisonian conspiracy against Nero and was condemned. Before he could be executed, however, he confessed his crime and begged for mercy, implicating even his mother in the plot. At the emperor's order, Lucan committed suicide in the Roman manner – dining first on sumptuous foods and afterward opening his veins. Tacitus reports that Lucan's final words were a recitation of his own poetry.

Of the thirteen works credited to Lucan, including court poems, satires, essays, speeches, panegyrics, letters, an epic, librettos, and a drama, only the ten-book *Pharsalia,* or *Civil War* has survived. An unpolished, obviously unfinished work, *Pharsalia* begins with an overblown dedicatory to Nero. The chronology follows fact, starting with Julius Caesar's crossing the Rubicon, and it outlines the events of Caesar's war against Pompey, including the Battle of Pharsalus. Lucan intended to cover events up to Caesar's death in 44 B.C., but he died when he was only thirty, leaving the details of Caesar's campaign in Egypt in obvious disarray.

Emphasizing liberty as a major theme, Lucan accentuates the heroism of Brutus and the younger Cato, to the detriment of both Pompey and Julius Caesar, although it is never quite clear whom he intended to be the central figure. Much of Lucan's verse is thinly veiled declamation, such as Cato's speech to General Labienus:

> Men who doubt and are ever uncertain of future events – let them cry out for prophets: I draw my assurance from no oracle but from the sureness of death. The timid and the brave must fall alike; the god has said this, and it is enough!

Although Lucan attempted to inject realism into his epic, he neglected to emulate real speech.

Despite his shortcomings, Lucan is remembered for writing about contemporary events and for breaking with earlier traditions by approaching history from the point of view of an orator. His emphasis on rhetoric and epigram avoids the Virgilian dependence on pomp, mythology, and divine inspiration. Although his poem contains frequent errors in historical fact, as well as logic, the work achieved great status in the Middle Ages and during the Renaissance because of its narrative power and its ebullient style. Marlowe, an admirer of Lucan, translated his poetry into blank verse.

THE LATE EMPIRE

- **Marcus Aurelius**
- **Apuleius**
- **St. Jerome**
- **St. Augustine**

MARCUS AURELIUS

- *Meditations*

MARCUS AURELIUS

Marcus Aurelius Antoninus (121–180 A.D.) distinguished himself by ruling Rome for twenty-eight years during a time when Roman legions no longer proved invincible against the great shaggy hordes of barbarian invaders; meanwhile, he maintained a notebook of some of the world's most profound and uplifting stoic philosophy. These two accomplishments seem mutually exclusive, but they appear to have resulted one from the other, for Marcus Aurelius espoused a simple, sincere belief in forbearance and moderation, whatever the situation.

Born Marcus Annius Verus of Spanish ancestry and named after his father, he was reared by his grandfather after his father's death. He came to the attention of the emperor Hadrian, who arranged the boy's education under the tutelage of an all-star cast of teachers, including the estimable Marcus Cornelius Fronto and Herodes Atticus. Later, the emperor appointed Aurelius to the priesthood and pledged him to marry the daughter of Lucius Aelius Caesar, who stood next in line to the throne. As a tribute to Aurelius' love of learning, Hadrian changed Marcus' surname from Verus (true) to Verissimus (truest).

After the deaths of Hadrian and Aelius in 138 A.D., Antoninus Pius succeeded Hadrian and adopted Marcus Aurelius, changing his name to Marcus Aelius Aurelius Verus Caesar, and, at the same time, he adopted Lucius Ceionius Commodus, who took the name Lucius Verus Caesar. Aurelius gained political ground with the acquisition of a *quaestorship* in 139 A.D., two consulships in 140 and 145 A.D., and the tribuneship in 147 A.D. He married well, securing his position in the emperor's favor by wedding Faustina II, Antoninus' daughter, in 138 A.D.

For fourteen years, Aurelius served as companion and confidant to the emperor and learned firsthand the responsibilities of the Empire. During this period, he developed his philosophical learning (partly through extensive correspondence with his teacher, Fronto, and partly from reading the works of Epictetus) and became one of the outstanding stoic philosophers of the ancient world. It was also during this period, from 147 to 161 A.D., that he composed the first of his *Meditations,* a series of twelve books of commentaries on morality and the good life.

When Aurelius became emperor in 161 A.D., he set a precedent by naming his adopted brother, Verus, as co-regent and ruling with him until Verus' death in 169 A.D. During his final four years as emperor, Aurelius shared the throne with his son, Commodus. The most prominent deed of Aurelius' career proved unfortunate, for he forever stained his name by blaming Christians for a severe pestilence that his returning legions brought home from the Parthian Wars. The resulting era of cruel persecution was one of Rome's last and most brutal efforts to check the advance of Christianity.

Fortunately, Aurelius established a great name for himself as a benevolent ruler, similar to the philosopher-king that Plato described during the Golden Age of Greece. Under the emperor's guidance, schools opened their doors to Rome's poor, orphanages and hospitals relieved the city of the hungry and diseased, and a general extension of humane law raised Rome's standards from earlier levels of semi-barbarity. However, his reliance on public service burdened the city with an unwieldy bureaucracy.

Marcus Aurelius died in the field in Vienna in 180 A.D., leaving Commodus, his dissolute, capricious son, as heir. The contrast in the two emperors greatly strengthened Marcus Aurelius' memory as Commodus' excesses quickly wiped out the gains of the Aurelian reign. Romans who could afford a copy of Aurelius' statue kept it in a place of honor among the household gods and spoke of him as though he were a saint. The modern world can contemplate Aurelius' military accomplishments, for they are represented on the Column of Marcus Aurelius in Rome's Piazza Colonna. His equestrian statue, which still stands on the Capitoline Hill, captures the attention of passersby with his benevolent hand outstretched.

ॐ

MEDITATIONS

Marcus Aurelius preserved quiet moments of contemplation and self-analysis in his *Meditations*, which he maintained in Greek in a private notebook over a period of nineteen years, possibly as a guide-book for his undisciplined son. The work, which he obviously never intended to publish, reveals not only his grasp of stoic philosophy, but also a conscientious, intellectual desire to rule the Roman empire with justice and enlightenment. The tone is modest, unassuming, at times almost abject as though the thinker were gazing at his own reflection and criticizing its shortcomings. In the words of John Stuart Mill, the *Meditations* is "almost equal in ethical elevation to the Sermon on the Mount."

He begins **Book I** with a tribute to his grandfather, who taught him morals and restraint. Continuing with a list of influences on his character, he credits modesty and manliness to his father, and piety, beneficence, and abstinence to his mother, Lucilla. Others who helped mold his nature were Diognetus, who encouraged the boy to "become intimate with philosophy," and Aurelius' brother Severus, who inculcated "consistency and undeviating steadiness in my regard for philosophy, and a disposition to do good, and to give to others readily, and to cherish good hopes, and to believe that I am loved by my friends . . ."

Book II sets forth the daily precepts that guided the emperor's life. With pragmatic wisdom, Aurelius exhorts himself to positive virtues:

> Begin the morning by saying to yourself, I shall meet with the busybody, the ungrateful, arrogant, deceitful, envious, unsocial. . . . I can neither be injured by any of them, for no one can fix on me what is ugly, nor can I be angry with my kinsman, nor hate him. For we are made for cooperation, like feet, like hands, like eyelids, like the rows of the upper and lower teeth.

He encourages himself to thank Providence for whatever comes his way and to "think steadily as a Roman and a man." As a reminder of the importance of the moment, he notes, ". . . the present is the only thing of which a man can be deprived, if it is true that this is the only thing which he has . . ."

The flow of simple admonition and practical advice defies outline.

Rather, the *Meditations* should be read as a bedside book of homilies, similar to *Poor Richard's Almanac,* or the Proverbs of Solomon. Richly scattered with nuggets of wisdom, their worth is serendipitous, striking the reader with truths of the moment. Some of these gems find repetition in modern philosophy, such as "The universe is change; our life is what our thoughts make it" and "Death, like generation, is a secret of nature." One of his strongest statements of the good life recalls Thoreau's doctrine of simplicity: "Remember this, – that very little is needed to make a happy life."

Overall, Marcus Aurelius consoles himself for the hard times of his life and reign – the deaths of his children, his wife's death in 174 A.D., defeats suffered by the Empire, and the physical disabilities that robbed him of the vigor to lead Rome's fighting forces – with a philosophy of wholeness reminiscent of Oriental mysticism:

> Constantly regard the universe as one living being, having one substance and one soul; observe how all things have reference to one perception, the perception of this one living being, and observe how all things act with one movement, how all things are the cooperating causes of all things which exist; observe, too, the continuous spinning of the thread and the contexture of the web.

In contrast to this detailed statement, other of his aphorisms are short and unadorned:

> Look within. . . . I consist of a little body and a soul. . . . Be not ashamed to be helped. . . . Retire into thyself. . . . Wipe out the imagination. Stop the pulling of the strings. Confine yourself to the present.

From stoicism, Marcus Aurelius finds the strength to confront difficult times, to avoid brooding and self-abnegation, to value intrinsic worth, and to treasure the moment.

His concluding entry concerns death, which he discerned as a natural end, not to be dreaded. His advice is straightforward:

> Man, you have been a citizen in this great state the world: what difference does it make to you whether for five years or three? . . . Depart then satisfied, for he also who releases you is satisfied.

It is remarkable that these words came from a Roman emperor whose life, in contrast to the voluptuaries and monsters who ruled the Empire during the preceding century, served as a model to his own time and to succeeding generations.

APULEIUS

- *The Golden Ass*

APULEIUS

LIFE AND BACKGROUND

Touted as Rome's greatest novelist, Lucius Apuleius Africanus was a restless traveler, a bilingual product of the Graeco-Roman empire. Because of his position in the canon of Latin literature, Apuleius has been called the "last voice of Rome," though, indeed, he could scarcely have been Romanized by his tenure in the city itself. Born in Madauros, Numidia, on the Gaetulian border around 125 A.D., to Theseus, a local dignitary, and Salvia, a distant relative of Plutarch, Apuleius was an attractive man—tall, blond, and gray-eyed. He was extremely proud of his birthplace, which he called a "settlement of the highest distinction."

Liberally educated at Carthage and Athens, Apuleius traveled in Greece and the Near East and lived for a time in Rome, where he practiced law and purified his provincial Latin. His inheritance from his father's estate enabled him to pursue eclectic interests for a time, but his well-documented generosity put a sizable dent in the two million sesterces he shared with his brother. After a year-long illness kept him at Oea (Tripoli) in the care of Sicianus Pontianus, a friend from their school days, Apuleius returned to North Africa, where he married Aemilia Pudentilla, Pontianus' rich widowed mother.

Shortly after their marriage, Pontianus died. As a result, Apuleius' in-laws had him arrested and tried at Sabratha for murdering Pontianus and bewitching Pudentilla in order to cheat her of her fortune. Despite his interest in magic, he obtained an acquittal by exposing the venality and vulgarity of the whole clan and returned to Carthage to live his life in peace.

Apuleius was a widely respected religious leader, lawyer, philosopher, writer, and lecturer. Several statues in his honor are still visible in North Africa and elsewhere in the Mediterranean world. He was named an honorary priest of Aesculapius, an important post in his day, and was initiated into the rites of Isis and Osiris.

319

His achievements reach into varied literary corners, from treatises on Platonism to theories of the universe, from speeches and essays to his novel, *The Golden Ass,* a heavily embroidered folk tale that ridicules the priesthood and human folly in general. Much of his more academic writing has fallen by the wayside, but his novel, particularly the episode of Cupid and Psyche, which occupies most of Books IV–VI, has influenced later writers, including Boccaccio, Cervantes, Rabelais, and Robert Graves.

_____ *THE GOLDEN ASS* _____

In the dedication to his son, Faustinus, Apuleius begs pardon for his greatest literary weakness – his baroque language, which is a blend of antiquarian Latin, provincial dialect, and artificial, studied prose. He characterizes his tale as a "pleasant Grecian jest," hoping that it will achieve his one goal, entertainment. As he explains his source material in Book I, Apuleius gives an encapsulated "autobiography."

The speaker, Lucius, falls in love with Fotis, a sorceress, who intends to change her lover into a bird. She reassures his last-minute fears by guaranteeing her ability to "turn again the figures of such as are transformed into the shapes of men." With a bit of razzle-dazzle, Fotis cleanses herself with herb water before producing the magic potion, which is in a coffer within her chamber. Lucius anoints himself generously and flaps his arms, expecting to lift himself into the sky.

Instead of wings and feathers, however, Lucius sees coarse hair, toughened skin, and appendages that form hooves. On one end, he sprouts a tail; on the other,

> . . . my face became monstrous and my mouth long and my nostrils wide, my lips hanging down, and my ears exceedingly increased with bristles. . . . I perceived that I was no bird, but a plain ass.

He attempts to blame Fotis, but he finds that he has no voice. She promises that all can be remedied, as soon as she can gather roses, an antidote to the ointment.

Lucius' trials are many. First, the stable boy bludgeons him with a cudgel; then a band of thieves breaks open the barn door and steals the ass and his fellow inmates. After a series of harrowing adventures, Lucius hears an old woman tell the story of Cupid and Psyche. According to the tale, Psyche is so beautiful and pure a maiden that worshippers neglect Venus and follow Psyche through the streets, strewing the way with flowers. The goddess, angered that her altars are deserted and barren, calls her son to wreak vengeance on the hapless girl.

Psyche is condemned to fall in love with a husband that she must never look upon. Her love for him is true, but her curious sisters coerce her into disobeying his command by viewing his sleeping body during one of his nightly visits:

> . . . she saw his golden hair drenched with fragrant ambrosia; his neck whiter than milk . . . and though his wings were at rest, the tender down of their edges was aquiver. His limbs were so smooth and so soft that Venus must be proud to have borne such a child.

Curious about her husband's weapons, she withdraws an arrow from its case, accidentally pricks her finger, and "[falls] in love with Love."

A drop of hot oil falls from her lamp and awakens Cupid, who flies away without a word. Psyche clings to his thigh, is carried into the clouds, but grows weary and falls back to earth. Crazed with sorrow, she tries to drown herself, but the river refuses to harm her and leaves her on the bank.

Psyche wanders the earth in search of Cupid, whom Venus has taken in and cured of his burn. Venus harasses the pathetic girl by giving her impossible tasks to perform. Eventually, Cupid escapes his mother's smothering influence and is reunited with Psyche. They celebrate their union at a celestial banquet:

> Juno [sat] with Jupiter and all the other gods in order: Ganymede, the rustic boy, his own footman, filled Jupiter's cup, and Bacchus served the rest: their drink was nectar, the wine of the gods. Vulcan prepared supper, the Hours decked the house with roses and other blossoms, the Graces tossed fragrant herbs, the Muses sang with sweet harmony, Apollo turned pleasantly to the harp, fair Venus tripped lightly to

the music, and the entertainment was so ordained that while the Muses sang in choir, Satyrs and Pans played on their pipes . . .

Lucius, somewhat relieved of his quandary by the winsome tale, regrets that he lacks paper and pen to record it.

Eventually Lucius locates Isis, the Egyptian goddess and sister/ wife of Osiris, and is restored once more to human form after he snatches a rose from a festal garland:

> . . . my deformed and bestial face abated, and first the rugged hair of my body fell off, my thick skin grew soft and tender, my fat belly became thin, the hoofs of my feet changed into toes, my hands were no more feet but returned again to the work of a man that walks upright, my neck grew short, my head and mouth became round, my long ears were made little, my great and stony teeth were proportional, like the teeth of men, and my tail, which before cumbered me most, appeared nowhere.

Filled with gratitude for his deliverance, Lucius enters the priesthood. After learning the cult of the Egyptian deities, he wanders the world, studying and improving himself. At length, the god Osiris appears to Lucius and commands him to practice law.

ST. JEROME

- **The *Vulgate***

ST. JEROME

LIFE AND BACKGROUND

One of the first four to be designated Doctors of the Church and one of the most influential Christians of his century, Eusebius Sophronius Hieronymus (*ca.* 347–419 A.D.), or St. Jerome, as he is currently referred to, was born in Stridon, Dalmatia, near Aquileia, Rome's winter military headquarters, between modern-day Trieste and Venice. His parents were Christians, but Jerome did not become a baptized believer until he was nearly twenty.

Classically educated in Rome by Aelius Donatus, Jerome studied rhetoric and read Greek and Roman literary masterpieces, but he concentrated his energies exclusively on Christian literature. He was enthralled by the catacombs of the early Christian martyrs and soon divested himself of Roman paganism in order to embrace Christianity.

He traveled widely on the Rhine and in Gaul, where he came under the influence of asceticism. He returned to Aquileia in 370 A.D. and set up a short-lived society of ascetics. In 373 A.D., Jerome settled in Antioch, Syria. It was there that he had a dream in which Christ appeared and accused him of being more Roman than Christian. In the grip of spiritual turmoil, he renounced his pagan learning and withdrew to the desert of Chalcis, where he lived as a hermit for four years.

Purging his spirit of Rome's licentiousness, Jerome took strength from stringent self-denial, mortification of the flesh, rigorous penance, and devotion to the study of Church history, Hebrew, Aramaic, and Greek. Of his experience, he writes:

> I used to sit alone; for I was filled with bitterness. My unkempt limbs were covered in shapeless sackcloth; my skin through long neglect had become as rough and black as an Ethiopian's. Tears and groans were every day my portion, and if sleep ever overcame my resistance and fell upon my eyes, I bruised my restless bones against the naked earth.

Eventually, he devoted himself to biblical scholarship and research. Outraged by local controversy within the sect, he returned to Antioch, was ordained by Bishop Paulinus, and went to Constantinople to study under Bishops Gregory of Nyssa and Gregory of Nazianzus.

After journeying to Rome as a delegate to a Church council, Jerome took the post of adviser and secretary to Pope Damasus, who was impressed by the young man's command of languages. While in Damasus' employ, Jerome wrote exegeses, conducted the Pope's Greek affairs, and revised the Latin text of the Gospels, arranging them in their present order (Matthew, Mark, Luke, John) and refining and upgrading their translation without making radical alterations. Having completed the Gospels about 384 A.D., Jerome turned his attention to the Psalter and in 392 A.D., he produced a thorough revamping, which never earned the acceptance that his earlier work had realized.

Jerome also worked as a teacher for rich Roman matrons in the study of Holy Scripture. Two of his pupils, Paula and Marcella, who supported him financially, sent him theological epistles, which are unusual for their time because they demonstrate the learning and piety of patrician women. After Damasus' death, Jerome, an enemy of Pope Siricius, Damasus' successor, returned to Palestine following a furor over the death of Blesilla, Paula's daughter and one of his converts.

Paula, heiress of the wealthy and distinguished Aemilian clan, and her daughter Eustochium followed Jerome to the East in 386 A.D. There, he established a monastery at Bethlehem, which he administered until his death. He put Paula and Eustochium in charge of his convent. Together they oversaw a church and a hospice for wayfarers who came for spiritual replenishment. Both Paula and Jerome exhausted their inheritances in financing these projects. Despite his duties as administrator and his continuing participation in local religious controversies, Jerome devoted himself to the translation of a Latin version of the Old Testament, which he completed in fifteen years.

Jerome was bothered by increasing irascibility, self-imposed alienation, failing eyesight, and ill health in his last years. He was small and frail, but remarkably resilient, surviving both Paula and Eustochium and recovering from his initial shock at the brutal sack of Rome in 410 A.D. He was buried in the grotto of the Nativity at Bethlehem alongside Paula. In later years, his body was transferred to the Church of Santa Maria Maggiore in Rome, and he is said to have worked many miracles.

Jerome's mental capacities, powered by tremendous intellectual curiosity and a genius for languages, impressed his contemporaries, particularly when he debated minute theological points with quotations from myriad sources. He immersed himself completely in Christian faith; however, his personality was marred by quarrelsomeness, biting sarcasm, long-standing hatreds, and lack of respect for those who differed with his beliefs.

Jerome's letters record the religious and social ferment of his day, giving the modern world a clearer picture of fourth-century Roman society. Two years after the Goths raided Rome, he wrote:

> My voice sticks in my throat, and even as I dictate this letter, sobs choke my utterance. The city which had taken the whole world was itself taken; nay, more, famine anticipated the sword, and but few citizens were left to be made prisoners. In their frenzy the starving people had recourse to hideous food and tore each other limb from limb that they might have flesh to eat. Even the mother did not spare the babe at her breast.

Lashing out with the sting of Martial or Juvenal, he lambasted corruption among priests, whose fastidiousness and dilettantism led him to note that they seemed "rather as potential bridegrooms than as clergymen."

To Eustochium, he wrote encouragement to maintain her virtue amid so many loose, unprincipled women:

> It wearies me to tell how many virgins fall daily, what notabilities the Mother Church loses from her bosom: over how many stars the proud enemy sets his throne, how many hollow rocks the serpent pierces and makes his habitation. . . . Be thou the grasshopper of the night. Wash your bed and water your couch nightly with tears. Keep vigil and be like the sparrow alone upon the housetop. Let your spirit be your harp, and let your mind join in the psalms, 'Bless the Lord, O my soul, and forget not all his benefits . . .'

For Jerome, whose encounters with secular life in Rome were enough to color his outlook on all humankind with grim suspicions, propriety was a simple matter of withdrawal and dedication to the faith through strict control of desires and fervent reading of the scriptures.

Jerome's works, which fill eleven volumes, include Bible translations and commentaries, scholarly works about the Bible, *Lives of the
Hermits, The Book of Illustrious Men,* dialogues and arguments, history,
and extensive correspondence.

THE *VULGATE*

Jerome's greatest work is a translation of the Old Testament into
Latin. The *Vulgate,* as it came to be called after the Council of Trent
(1545–63), replaced Hebrew versions and is still a major source for
biblical scholars.

A familiar passage from his translation, the "Dies Irae," found in
Zephaniah 1:14–16, figures in the great liturgical masses of the classical
era. The words, stirring and terrible, lend themselves to dramatic
musical interpretation:

> Iuxta est dies Domini magnus, iuxta est et velox nimis: Vox
> diei Domini amara, tribulabitor ibi fortis. Dies irae, dies illa,
> dies tribulationis et angustiae, dies calamitatis et miseriae, dies
> tenebrarum et caliginis, dies nebulae et turbinis: Dies tubae
> et clangoris super civitates munitas et super angulos excelsos.

As Jerome phrases it,

> The great day of the Lord is at hand, close and hurrying closer:
> on that day, bitter will be the word of the Lord, a mighty
> winnower.

The passage inspired Michelangelo's great fresco *The Last Judgment,*
as well as Mozart's *Requiem Mass* and focuses on the perplexity and
confusion of those souls who doubt the inexorable will of God on
Judgment Day.

ST. AUGUSTINE

- *Confessions*

- *The City of God*

ST. AUGUSTINE

LIFE AND BACKGROUND

The son of Patricius, a Roman bureaucrat and pagan, and Monica, a Christian, Aurelius Augustinus (354–430 A.D.) rose to a position second only to St. Paul in the Christian church. He was born at Tagaste Numidia, south of Sicily on the African coast near Tunisia. He had a brother, Navigius, and a sister, Perpetua. His early training was poor; consequently, he never achieved in Greek, although his learning in Latin literature improved when he enrolled in a school at Madauros at the age of eleven.

At the age of fifteen, Augustine read Cicero's *Hortensius,* which influenced him to study philosophy. The following year, Romanianus paid for Augustine's tuition at a school in Carthage, where the boy took a mistress and produced an illegitimate son named Adeodatus.

Augustine joined the Manichaean sect, which blends the Persian philosophy of Zoroaster with Christian thought, and sought converts in Carthage. For eleven years, he taught grammar and rhetoric, first at Tagaste and then at Carthage, and attempted to establish academies in Rome and Milan. About this time, he abandoned Manichaean beliefs.

In 387 A.D., St. Ambrose, noted neoplatonist and ecclesiast, aroused Augustine's faith through stimulating sermons and baptized him and his son on Easter. Augustine returned to Africa with his family. On the way, his mother died at Ostia. Augustine suffered bouts of poor health, but devoted himself to a strenuous academic regimen of study, prayer, and writing. In his *Confessions,* he credits God with strengthening his will during these arduous days.

Determined to change from his old lifestyle, Augustine denounced his fifteen-year relationship with his mistress, married a young girl, sold his land in Tagaste, and donated the proceeds to a monastic commune. One of his keenest associates was his son.

In 391 A.D., Augustine was ordained by popular demand into the priesthood in Hippo and was henceforth referred to as Augustine of Hippo. He served as the city's bishop, was a zealous proselytizer, and staunchly defended the faith among people of mixed races and religions.

The last years of Augustine's life were filled with challenge. The Vandals, who had sacked Rome in 410 A.D., seized Carthage and moved on to Hippo in 430 A.D. As pagan violence swirled about him, the old man died peacefully, content in his faith. The Vandals destroyed most of the city, but left Augustine's cathedral and library intact. Augustine was buried south of Milan in Pavia, Italy.

Augustine's influence was keenly felt by the thinkers of the Middle Ages, particularly St. Thomas Aquinas. His literary output, contained in two hundred and thirty-two volumes, includes religious commentary, sermons, and correspondence, as well as personal reflection and biography. Some of his best known titles, in addition to his *Confessions* and *The City of God,* include essays on the Trinity, the happy life, order, immortality of the soul, teaching, free will, Faustus, nature, and grace. Primary among his innovations are his emphasis on faith, study of the incarnation and redemption, and the description of the Church as the mystical body of Christ.

_____ *CONFESSIONS* _____

Augustine opens his *Confessions* with repeated paeans and prayers to God and a request that the Holy Spirit guide him in his reminiscences. Recalling his infancy, when he cried for attention and nourishment, Augustine compares that need and struggle with his inner turmoil as a man, still reaching for nutriment for his soul. The person who answered his call was Monica, his mother:

> Because my mother was much disturbed (by whose pure heart and faith she lovingly even gave birth to my eternal salvation), did strive for my conversion and baptism in Your restorative sacraments . . .

He is unable to understand why his conversion was so long delayed, coming, as it did, after a serious illness weakened him severely.

Augustine is quick to confess his faults, particularly his love for Virgil's amorous verse when he studied Roman literature and his subsequent lust for women during his sixteenth year. He concludes:

> But I was too hot upon it (wretch that I was) pursuing the violent course of my desire, having abandoned you completely: yes, I exceeded all your laws; I did not escape your punishments. For what mortal can avoid them? For you were with me at every turn, mildly rigorous, and always besaucing my unlawful pastimes with most bitter discontent . . .

He concludes that his forays into the sinful world enabled him to love God more, having tasted of the separation from sanctity that comes through immersion in carnal pleasures.

A tribute to his dedication and piety, the book ends on a positive note with Augustine's affirmation of faith.

> You, O God, are good and need no good. You are at rest always, because you are yourself rest. And what man shall teach another to understand this? Or what angel teach another angel? Or what angel teach a man? Let it be begged of you, sought in you, knocked for at your door: so shall it be received, so shall it be found, so shall it be opened.

The words echo his repeated reassurances to the reader that God awaits the conversion of each mortal and extends grace and forgiveness for all the waywardness that can lure human beings to their destruction.

THE CITY OF GOD

Begun in 413 A.D. and completed in 426 A.D., Augustine's "great and arduous work" was prompted by the sack of Rome in 410 A.D.

and by a general apprehension that the end of the world was at hand. The philosopher aimed to restore people's faith during a period of schism and doubt. He succeeded, far greater than he anticipated, and produced a ferment among believers that turned fear for the fallen Roman Empire into a triumphant hope for life beyond temporal affairs on earth. To its credit, the work was a favorite of Charlemagne, who read it through repeatedly.

One of Augustine's most famous statements is his assertion that sex is the punishment for Adam and Eve's transgression. Before the Fall, he declares,

> Their love to God was unclouded, their love for each other
> was that of partners living in sincere and faithful union, and
> from this love there flowed a wonderful delight, for the object
> of their love was always theirs to enjoy. Their avoidance of
> sin was tranquil; and so long as it was maintained, no other
> ill could attack them from any quarter and bring sorrow.

In Book X, he makes a similar comment about the corruptibility of the flesh:

> Carnal as we are, weak, liable to sin, and shrouded in the
> darkness of ignorance, assuredly we should be totally unable
> to gain sight of this principle if it did not cleanse and heal
> us by means of the thing that we were and the thing that we
> were not. For we were human, but we were not upright . . .

Yet, to offset the immutable proclivities of human beings, Augustine assures the reader that God is ever the same, knowing neither past, present, or future, and that He, the "perfect craftsman," extends his light to every corner of human habitation.

- **Glossary**
- **Timeline**
- **Roman Emperors**
- **Selected Bibliography**
- **Index**

GLOSSARY

Apuleius (ap u le′ əs)
Augustine (o′ gə stēn)
Catullus (kə tul′ əs)
Cicero (sis′ ə rō)
Ennius (en′ i us)
Epictetus (ep ik te′ tus)
Horace (hor′ əs)
Jerome (je rōm′)
Josephus (jo se′ fus)
Julius Caesar (jū′ lē us se′ zər)
Juvenal (jōō′ ve n′l)
Livy (liv′ i)
Longinus (lon ji′ nəs)
Lucan (lū′ kan)
Lucretius (lū krē′ shi us)
Marcus Aurelius (mar′ kus o rē′ li us)
Martial (mar′ shal)
Ovid (ahv′ id)
Plautus (plō′ tus)
Pliny (plin′ i)
Plutarch (plōō′ tark)
Propertius (pro pur′ shus)
Seneca (sen′ e ka)
Statius (sta′ shi us)
Suetonius (swē tō′ ni us)
Tacitus (tas′ i tus)
Terence (ter′ ens)
Tibullus (ti bul′ us)
Virgil (vur′ jəl)

PRONUNCIATION KEY: ə = *a* in **a**bove, b**a**nan**a**; **a**ct, d**ā**y, d**â**re, f**ä**ther; b**e**t, b**ē**at; t**i**p, **ī**ce; **o**x, b**ō**ne, **oi**l, b**oo**k, b**oo**t; **u**p, r**ü**le.

TIMELINE

I. EARLY ROMAN LITERATURE (514–240 B.C.)

Plautus (ca. 254–184 B.C.)
Menaechmi (The Twin Menaechmi)
Miles Gloriosus (The Boastful Soldier) (ca. 206 B.C.)
Cistellaria (The Casket) (ca. 202 B.C.)
Aulularia (The Pot of Gold)
Amphitryon
Asinaria (The Comedy of Asses)
Stichus (200 B.C)
Pseudolus (191 B.C.)
Truculentus (ca. 187 B.C.)
Captivi (The Captives)

II. THE ROMAN REPUBLIC (240–84 B.C.)

Ennius (239–169 B.C.)
The *Annales* (ca. 170 B.C.)

Terence (ca. 195–159 B.C.)
Andria (The Girl from Andros) (167 B.C.)
Hecyra (Her Husband's Mother) (165 B.C.)
Heautontimorumenos (The Self-Tormentor) (163 B.C.)
The Eunuch (161 B.C.)
Phormio (161 B.C.)
Adelphi (The Brothers) (160 B.C.)

III. THE GOLDEN AGE (83 B.C.–17 A.D.)

Cicero (106–43 B.C.)
De Senectute (On Old Age)
De Amicitia (On Friendship)
De Cataline (Against Cataline)
Ad Atticum (Letters to Atticus)
Ad Familiares (Letters to Friends)
Philippics (Against Antony) (46–44 B.C.)

Julius Caesar (100–44 B.C.)
De Bello Gallico (The Gallic War) (51 B.C.)
De Bello Civile (The Civil War) (47 B.C.)

Lucretius (96–55 B.C.)
De Rerum Natura (On the Nature of Things) (60 B.C.)

Catullus (*ca.* 87–*ca.* 54 B.C.)
Poems (published posthumously)

Virgil (70–19 B.C.)
Eclogues, or *Bucolics* (37 B.C.)
Georgics (30 B.C.)
The *Aeneid* (posthumous, 18 B.C.)

Livy (59 B.C.–17 A.D.)
Ab Urbe Condita (From the City's Foundation) (*ca.* 14 A.D.)

Tibullus (*ca.* 54–*ca.* 18 B.C.)
Elegies (*ca.* 26 B.C.)

Propertius (*ca.* 50–15 B.C.)
Elegies (28, 26, 23, 16 B.C.)

Horace (65–8 B.C.)
Satires (35 B.C.)
Satires II (30 B.C.)
Epodes (30 B.C.)
Odes (23 B.C.)
Epistles (20 B.C.)
Ars Poetica (The Art of Poetry) (20 B.C.)
Carmen Saeculare (19 B.C.)
Odes II (16 B.C.)
Epistles II (15 B.C.)

Ovid (43 B.C.–18 A.D.)
Amores (Love Poems) (22–15 B.C.)
Heroides (Demigoddesses) (15 B.C.)
Ars Amatoria (The Art of Love) (*ca.* 1 B.C.)
Remedia Amoris (Cures for Love) (*ca.* 2 A.D.)
Metamorphoses (Transformations) (8 A.D.)
Tristia (Sadness) (11 A.D.)
Fasti (Holidays) (posthumous, *ca.* 18 A.D.)
Epistulae Ex Ponto (Letters from the Black Sea)
    (posthumous, date unknown)

IV. THE SILVER AGE (14–117 A.D.)

Seneca (*ca.* 4 B.C.–65 A.D.)
Moral Essays
Octavia
Medea
Phaedra
The Mad Hercules

Longinus (*fl.* 1st century A.D.)
On the Sublime

Pliny the Elder (23–79 A.D.)
Naturalis Historia (Natural History) (77 A.D.)

Josephus (37–*ca.* 100 A.D.)
Vita (Autobiography)
Bellum Judaicum (The Jewish War) (76 A.D.)
Jewish Antiquities (94 A.D.)
Against Apion (*ca.* 100 A.D.)

Lucan (39–65 A.D.)
Pharsalia, or *Civil War* (62–63 A.D.)

Martial (*ca.* 40–104 A.D.)
Liber Spectaculorum (Book of Spectacles) (80 A.D.)
Xenia (Guest Gifts); Apophoreta (Party Favors)
(84–85 A.D.)
Epigrammata (Epigrams) (86–102 A.D.)

Plutarch (*ca.* 45–*ca.* 120 A.D.)
Parallel Lives
Morals

Statius (45–96 A.D.)
Thebaid (Deeds of the Seven Against Thebes) (91 A.D.)
Silvae (Forest Books) (*ca.* 95 A.D.)
Achilleid (The Death of Achilles) (posthumous, 96 A.D.)

Tacitus (*ca.* 55–*ca.* 117 A.D.)
Germania (98 A.D.)
Agricola (98 A.D.)
Dialogue on Orators (*ca.* 105 A.D.)
Histories (*ca.* 107 A.D.)
Annals (117 A.D.)

Epictetus *(ca.* 55–135 A.D.)
   Discourses (posthumous)

Juvenal *(ca.* 60–*ca.* 140 A.D.)
   Satires (ca. 127 A.D.)

Pliny the Younger *(ca.* 62–*ca.* 112 A.D.)
   Panegyric on Trajan
   Epistulae (Letters) (posthumous, 114 A.D.)

Suetonius *(ca.* 69–*ca.* 140 A.D.)
   De Viris Illustribus (Illustrious Men) (113 A.D.)
   De Vita Caesarum (Lives of the Caesars)
     (ca. 121 A.D.)
   De Grammaticis
   De Rhetoribus

V. THE LATE EMPIRE (117–395 A.D.)

Marcus Aurelius (121–180 A.D.)
   Meditations (posthumous, *ca.* 180 A.D.)

Apuleius *(ca.* 125–*ca.* 171 A.D.)
   On the God of Socrates; On Plato and his Dogma
   Florida (Bouquet)
   Apologia (Apology)
   Metamorphoses, or *The Golden Ass*

St. Jerome *(ca.* 347–419 A.D.)
   The *Vulgate (ca.* 405 A.D.)
   Letters

St. Augustine (354–430 A.D.)
   Confessions (400 A.D.)
   The City of God (426 A.D.)

ROMAN EMPERORS

Augustus (Octavian)	27 B.C.–14 A.D.
Tiberius	14–37
Caligula (Gaius Caesar)	37–41
Claudius I	41–54
Nero	54–68
Galba	68–69
Otho	69
Vitellius	69
Vespasian	69–79
Titus	79–81
Domitian	81–96
Nerva	96–98
Trajan	98–117
Hadrian	117–138
Antoninus Pius	138–161
Lucius Aurelius Verus	161–169
Marcus Aurelius, surnamed Antoninus	161–180
Commodus	180–192
Pertinax	193
Didius Julianus	193
Septimius Severus	193–211
Geta	211–212
Caracalla (Marcus Aurelius Antoninus)	211–217
Macrinus	217–218
Heliogabalus (Elagabalus)	218–222
Alexander Severus	222–235
Maximinus, surnamed Thrax	235–238
Gordianus I	238
Gordianus II	238
Pupienus Maximus and Balbinus	238
Gordianus III (Gordianus Pius)	238–244
Philip (called the Arabian)	244–249
Decius	249–251
Gallus	251–253

Western Roman Emperors

Eastern Roman Emperors

SELECTED BIBLIOGRAPHY

ROMAN LITERATURE

BROWN, CALVIN S., gen. ed. *The Reader's Companion to World Literature.* New York: New American Library, 1973.

COPLEY, FRANK O. *Latin Literature: From the Beginnings to the Close of the Second Century A.D.* Ann Arbor: University of Michigan Press, 1969.

DUFF, JOHN WIGHT. *A Literary History of Rome: From the Origins to the Close of the Golden Age.* New York: Barnes & Noble, 1953.

_____. *A Literary History of Rome in the Silver Age.* New York: Barnes & Noble, 1960.

GUINAGH, KEVIN, and ALFRED P. DORJAHN, eds. *Latin Literature in Translation.* Philadelphia: Century Bookbindery, 1983.

HAIGHT, ELIZABETH HAZELTON. *Essays on Ancient Fiction.* Freeport, New York: Books for Libraries Press, Inc., 1966.

HERBERT, PETER E. *Selections from the Latin Fathers with Commentary and Notes.* Norwood, Pennsylvania: Telegraph Books, 1981.

LUCE, T. JAMES, editor-in-chief. *Ancient Writers: Greece and Rome* (Volume II, *Lucretius to Ammianus Marcellinus*). New York: Charles Scribner's Sons, 1982.

LYTTELTON, MARGARET, and WERNER FORMAN. *The Romans: Their Gods and Their Beliefs.* London: Orbis Publishing, 1985.

MACKENDRICK, PAUL, ed. *Classics in Translation, Volume II: Latin Literature.* Madison: University of Wisconsin Press, 1966.

PYM, DORA. *Readings from the Literature of Ancient Rome*. Philadelphia: R. West, 1975.

VENABLES, FRANCIS, ed. *The Early Augustans*. Portsmouth, New Hampshire: Heinemann, 1972.

WARR, GEORGE C. W. *Teuffel's History of Roman Literature*. New York: Burt Franklin, 1967.

ROMAN POETRY

BUTLER, HAROLD E. *Post-Augustan Poetry*. New York: Garland, 1977.

CAIRNS, FRANCIS, ed. *Papers of the Liverpool Latin Seminar*. Wolfeboro, New Hampshire: Longwood, 1983.

COLEMAN, DOROTHY. *The Gallo-Roman Muse*. Cambridge, 1979.

CONTE, GIAN B. *The Rhetoric of Imitation: Genre and Poetic Memory in Virgil and Other Latin Poets*. Ithaca, New York: Cornell University Press, 1986.

COPLEY, FRANK. *Exclusus Amator: A Study in Latin Love Poetry*. Decatur, Georgia: Scholars Press, 1981.

CORRIGAN, FELICITAS, ed. *More Latin Lyrics*. New York: Norton, 1977.

CRUMP, MARY M. *The Epyllion from Theocritus to Ovid*. New York: Garland, 1978.

GRIFFIN, JASPER. *Latin Poets and Roman Life*. Chapel Hill, North Carolina: University of North Carolina Press, 1986.

HORNSBY, ROGER. *Reading Latin Poetry*. Norman, Oklahoma: University of Oklahoma Press, 1969.

ISBELL, HAROLD, tr. *The Last Poets of Imperial Rome*. New York: Penguin, 1983.

KENNEDY, E. C., and A. R. DAVIS. *Two Centuries of Roman Poetry.* London: Macmillan & Company, 1965.

LEMBKE, JANET. *Bronze and Iron: Old Latin Poetry from Its Beginnings to 100 B.C.* Berkeley: University of California Press, 1973.

MALTBY. *Latin Love Elegy.* Oak Park, Illinois: Bolchazy Carducci, 1985.

MENDELL, CLARENCE W. *Latin Poetry: The New Poets and the Augustans.* New Haven, Connecticut: Yale University Press, 1965.

RICHARDSON, LEON J. *A Guidebook of Latin Poetry.* Albuquerque, New Mexico: Foundation for Classical Reprints, 1984.

SIKES, EDWARD E. *Roman Poetry.* Westport, Connecticut: Hyperion, 1980.

WENDER, DOROTHEA, tr. *Roman Poetry from the Republic to the Silver Age.* Carbondale, Illinois: Southern Illinois University Press, 1980.

WILLIAMS, GORDON. *Figures of Thought in Roman Poetry.* New Haven, Connecticut: Yale University Press, 1980.

_____. *The Nature of Roman Poetry.* Oxford: Oxford University Press, 1983.

_____. *Tradition and Originality in Roman Poetry.* Oxford: Oxford University Press, 1986.

WOODMAN, TONY, and DAVID WEST, eds. *Poetry and Politics in the Age of Augustus.* Cambridge, 1984.

ROMAN AUTHORS

APULEIUS

BIRLEY, A. *Septimius Severus: The African Emperor.* New York, 1972.

CHAMPLIN, EDWARD. *Fronto and Antonine Rome.* Cambridge, 1980.

HAIGHT, ELIZABETH H. *Apuleius and His Influence.* Norwood, Pennsylvania: Telegraph Books, 1983.

HIJMANS, B. L., JR., and R. T. VAN DER PAARDT, eds. *Aspects of Apuleius' "Golden Ass."* Philadelphia: John Benjamins, North American, Inc., 1978.

HIJMANS, B. L., JR., *et al. Apuleius Madaurensis Metamorphoses.* Philadelphia: John Benjamins, North American, Inc., 1981.

REGEN, F. *Apuleius Philosophus Platonicus.* New York, 1971.

SCHLAM, C. C. *Cupid and Psyche: Apuleius and the Monuments.* University Park, Pennsylvania, 1976.

TATUM, J. *Apuleius and "The Golden Ass."* Ithaca, New York, 1979.

WALSH, PATRICK G. *The Roman Novel: The "Satyricon" of Petronius and the "Metamorphoses" of Apuleius.* Cambridge University Press, 1970.

AUGUSTINE, SAINT

BECHTEL, PAUL, ed. *The Confessions of St. Augustine.* Chicago: Moody, 1981.

BOGAN, MARY INEZ. *Vocabulary and Style of the Soliloquies and Dialogues of St. Augustine.* Cleveland, Ohio: Zubal, Inc., 1984.

BURKE, VERNON J. *Wisdom from St. Augustine.* South Bend, Indiana: University of Notre Dame, 1984.

GIBB, JOHN, and WILLIAM MONTGOMERY. *The Confessions of St. Augustine.* New York: Garland, 1980.

GILSON, ETIENNE. *The Christian Philosophy of St. Augustine.* New York: Hippocrene Books, 1983.

LAWLESS, GEORGE P. *Augustine of Hippo and His Monastic Rule.* Oxford University Press, 1987.

O'DALY, GERARD. *Augustine's Philosophy of the Mind.* Berkeley: University of California Press, 1987.

ULANOV, BARRY, tr. *The Latin Prayers of St. Augustine: A Contemporary Anthology.* New York: Harper & Row, 1984.

CAESAR, JULIUS

BLITS, JAN H. *The End of the Ancient Republic: Essays on Julius Caesar.* Durham, North Carolina: Carolina Academic Press, 1983.

BRADFORD, ERNLE. *Julius Caesar: The Pursuit of Power.* New York: Morrow, 1984.

GARDNER, JANE F., tr. *Civil War.* New York: Hippocrene Books, 1985.

GELZER, MATTHIAS. *Caesar: Politician and Statesman.* Cambridge, Massachusetts: Harvard University Press, 1985.

GIANAKARIS, C. J. *Julius Caesar.* New York: Garland, 1985.

HANSEN, WILLIAM P., and JOHN HANEY, eds. *Caesar.* Edgemont, Pa.: Chelsea House, 1987.

ROBIN, MAY. *Julius Caesar and the Romans.* New York: Watts, 1984.

YAVETZ, ZWI. *Julius Caesar and His Public Image.* Ithaca, New York: Cornell University Press, 1983.

CATULLUS

ADLER, EVE. *Catullan Self-Revelation.* Salem, New Hampshire: Ayer Company, 1981.

FERGUSON, JOHN. *Catullus.* Lawrence, Kansas: Coronado Press, 1985.

FORSYTH, PHYLLIS Y. *The Poems of Catullus: A Teaching Text.* Classical Association Atlantic, 1986.

JENKYNS, RICHARD. *Three Classical Poets: Sappho, Catullus, and Juvenal.* Cambridge, Massachusetts: Harvard University Press, 1982.

SMALL, STUART G. *Catullus: A Reader's Guide to the Poems.* Lanham, Maryland: University Press of America, 1983.

WISEMAN, T. P. *Catullus and His World: A Reappraisal.* Cambridge University Press, 1985.

CICERO

BAILEY, D. R., ed. *Select Letters.* Cambridge University Press, 1980.

BENNETT, CHARLES E., ed. *"On Old Age"–"De Senectute": Cicero.* Oak Park, Illinois: Bolchazy-Carducci, 1980.

ENOS, RICHARD. *The Literate Mode of Cicero's Legal Rhetoric.* Carbondale: Southern Illinois University Press, 1987.

GOULD & WHITELEY. *Cicero de Amicitia.* Oak Park, Illinois: Bolchazy-Carducci, 1983.

MITCHELL, THOMAS N. *Cicero.* Yale University Press, 1979.

MOLES, J. L. *Plutarch: "Life of Cicero."* Oak Park, Illinois: Bolchazy-Carducci, 1986.

RAWSON, ELIZABETH. *Cicero: A Portrait.* Ithaca, New York: Cornell University Press, 1983.

SONKOWSKY, ROBERT P. *Selections from Cicero.* Guilford, Connecticut: J. Norton Publishers, 1985.

WOOTEN, CECIL W. *Cicero's "Philippics" and Their Demosthenic Model: The Rhetoric of Crisis.* Chapel Hill, North Carolina: University of North Carolina Press, 1983.

ENNIUS

JOCELYN, H. D. *Ennius.* Cambridge, 1967.

MACKEY, L. A. "In Defence of Ennius," *Classical Review.* December, 1963.

EPICTETUS

EPICTETUS. *The Echiridion.* Albuquerque, New Mexico: Foundation for Classical Reprints, 1986.

STADTER, P.A. *Arrian of Nicomedia.* Chapel Hill, North Carolina: University of North Carolina Press, 1980.

WHITE, NICHOLAS P. *Handbook of Epictetus.* Indianapolis, Indiana: Hackett Publications, 1983.

XENAKIS, J. *Epictetus, Philosopher-Therapist.* The Hague, 1969.

HORACE

KILPATRICK, ROSS S. *The Poetry of Friendship: Horace, Epistle I.* Lincoln, Nebraska: University of Nebraska Press, 1986.

KNIGHT, R. C. CORNEILLE. *Horace.* Wolfeboro, New Hampshire: Longwood Publishing Group, 1981.

MONAGAN, JOHN S. *Horace: Priest of the Poor.* Washington, D.C.: Georgetown University Press, 1985.

MOSKOVIT, LEONARD, tr. *Horace: Twelve Odes.* Boston: Rowan Tree, 1983.

RUDD, NIALL. *The Satires of Horace and Persius.* Berkeley: University of California Press, 1982.

SHACKLETON, BAILEY. *A Profile of Horace.* Cambridge, Massachusetts: Harvard University Press, 1982.

JEROME, SAINT

BERSCHIN, WALTER. *Greek Letters and the Latin Middle Ages: From Josephus to Nicholas of Cusa.* Washington, D.C.: Catholic University Press, 1988.

BREWER, JAMES W., JR. *Jerome.* Tucson, Arizona: Southwest Parks and Monuments Association, 1976.

FELDMAN, LOUIS, and GOHEI HATA, eds. *Jerome, Judaism, and Christianity.* Detroit: Wayne State University Press, 1987.

FELDMAN, LOUIS. *Jerome and Modern Scholarship.* Hawthorne, New Jersey: De Gruyter, 1984.

RAJAK, TESSA. *Jerome: The Historian and His Society.* Philadelphia: Fortress, 1984.

RICE, EUGENE F., JR. *St. Jerome in the Renaissance.* Baltimore, Maryland: Johns Hopkins, 1985.

JOSEPHUS

COHEN, SHAY. *Josephus in Galilee and Rome.* Leiden, 1979.

STERN, M., ed. *Greek and Latin Authors on Jews and Judaism.* 3 vols. Jerusalem, 1980.

ULRICH, EUGENE C., JR. *The Qumran Text of Samuel and Josephus.* Decatur, Georgia: Scholars Press, 1983.

JUVENAL

GREEN, PETER, tr. *Juvenal:* The Sixteen Satires. New York: Penguin, 1979.

JENKYNS, RICHARD. *Three Classical Poets: Sappho, Catullus, and Juvenal.* Cambridge, Massachusetts: Harvard University Press, 1982.

RUDD, N., and E. C. COURTNEY. *Juvenal's* Satires. Oak Park, Illinois: Bolchazy-Carducci, 1984.

LIVY

BRISCOE, JOHN. *A Commentary on Livy, Books 31–33.* Oxford University Press, 1973.

LIPROVSKY, J. *A Historiographical Study of Livy: Books 6–10.* New York, 1981.

LUCE, T. J. *Livy: The Composition of His History.* Princeton, New Jersey: Princeton University Press, 1977.

LONGINUS

DORSCH, T. S., tr. *Longinus:* On the Sublime. New York: Penguin, 1977.

PRECKARD, A. D., tr. *Longinus on the Sublime.* Westport, Connecticut: Greenwood, 1978.

RUSSELL, D. A., tr. *Longinus, On Sublimity.* Oxford University Press, 1972.

LUCAN

AHL, FREDERICK M. *Lucan: An Introduction.* Ithaca, New York: Cornell University Press, 1976.

DILKE, O. A. W., ed. *Lucan,* De Bello Civili 7. Cambridge, 1970.

GOTOFF, HAROLD C. *Transmission of the Text of Lucan in the Ninth Century.* Cambridge, Massachusetts: Harvard University Press, 1971.

MORFORD, M. P. O. *The Poet Lucan.* Oxford University Press, 1967.

LUCRETIUS

CLAY, DISKIN. *Lucretius and Epicurus.* Ithaca, New York: Cornell University Press, 1983.

DEUTSCH, ROSAMUND E. *The Pattern of Sound in Lucretius.* Steele Commager, ed. New York: Garland, 1979.

HOLLAND, LOUISE A. *Lucretius and the Transpadanes.* Princeton, New Jersey: Princeton University Press, 1979.

LONG, A. A. *Hellenistic Philosophy.* London, 1974.

NICHOLAS, JAMES H., JR. *Epicurean Political Philosophy: The "De Rerum Natura" of Lucretius.* Ithaca, New York: Cornell University Press, 1976.

RIST, J. M. *Epicurus: An Introduction.* Cambridge, 1972.

SANTAYANA, GEORGE. *Three Philosophical Poets.* Totowa, New Jersey: Cooper Square, 1971.

MARCUS AURELIUS

BIRLEY, A. *Marcus Aurelius.* Yale University Press, 1987.

BLANSHARD, BRAND. *Four Reasonable Men: Aurelius, Mill, Renan, Sidgwick.* Middletown, Conn.: Wesleyan University Press, 1984.

BROWN, P. *The World of Late Antiquity, from Marcus Aurelius to Muhammad.* London, 1971.

LAWES, ROY A. *Living Stoically: Selections from Marcus Aurelius.* New York: State Mutual Book and Periodical Service, Ltd., 1985.

MACMULLEN, R. *Enemies of the Roman Order.* Cambridge, 1966.

MILLAR, F. *The Emperor in the Roman World.* London, 1977.

SANDBACH, F. H. *The Stoics.* London, 1975.

WILKINSON, L. P. *The Roman Experience.* London, 1975.

MARTIAL

HOWELL, P. A. *Commentaries on Book I of the Epigrams of Martial.* Atlantic Highlands, New Jersey: Humanities, 1980.

KAY, N. M. *Martial, Book XI.* Oxford University Press, 1986.

POTT, J. A., and F. A. WRIGHT, tr. *Martial, the Twelve Books of Epigrams.* Darby, Pennsylvania: Darby Books, 1981.

SCOTT, K. *The Imperial Cult Under the Flavians.* New York, 1975.

WHIPPLE, T. K. *Martial and the English Epigram from Sir Thomas Wyatt to Ben Jonson.* New York, 1970.

OVID

AHL, FREDERICK. *Metaformations: Soundplay and Wordplay in Ovid and Other Classical Poets.* Ithaca, New York: Cornell University Press, 1985.

GLENN, EDGAR M. *The* Metamorphoses: *Ovid's Roman Games.* Lanham, Maryland: University Press of America, 1986.

HENDERSON, A. A., ed. *Remedia Amoris.* New York: Columbia University Press, 1980.

MYEROWITZ, MOLLY. *Ovid's Games of Love.* Detroit: Wayne State University Press, 1985.

PEARCY, LEE T. *The Mediated Muse: English Translations of Ovid.* Hamden, Connecticut: Shoe String, 1984.

PLATNAUER, MAURICE. *Latin Elegiac Verse: A Study of the Metrical Usages of Tibullus, Propertius, and Ovid.* Hamden, Connecticut: Shoe String, 1971.

VERDUCCI, FLORENCE. *Ovid's Toyshop of the Heart:* Epistulae Heroidum. Princeton, New Jersey: Princeton University Press, 1985.

PLAUTUS

BARSBY, J. A, ed. and tr. *Plautus:* Bacchides. Atlantic Highlands, New Jersey: Humanities, 1986.

LOWALL, GILBERT, and BETTY N. QUINN, eds. *Plautus'* Menaechmi. Oak Park, Illinois: Bolchazy-Carducci, 1981.

ROCHE, PAUL. *Three Plays by Plautus.* Oak Park, Illinois: Bolchazy-Carducci, 1981.

SEGAL, ERICH. *Roman Laughter: The Comedy of Plautus.* Oxford University Press, 1987.

SLATER, NIALL W. *Plautus in Performance: The Theatre of the Mind.* Princeton University Press, 1985.

WRIGHT, JOHN. *Plautus:* Curculio. Decatur, Georgia: Scholars Press, 1982.

PLINY THE ELDER

BURNE, M. A. T. "Pliny's Ideal Roman," *Classical Journal.* March, 1964.

DOWNS, R. B. "The Great Compiler: Pliny the Elder," *Famous Books, Ancient and Medieval.* New York: Barnes & Noble, 1964.

RADICE, B. "Counsel of the Dead," *Harpers.* August, 1980.

_____. "The Eruption of Vesuvius," *Earth Science.* Winter, 1978.

WETHERED, H. N. *The Mind of the Ancient World: A Consideration of Pliny's Natural History.* New York: Longmans, Green, 1937.

PLINY THE YOUNGER

FISHER, M. B., and M. R. GRIFFEN, eds. *Selections from Pliny's Letters Handbook.* Cambridge, New Jersey: Cambridge University Press, n.d.

GREIG, C., tr. *Pliny.* Cambridge, New Jersey: Cambridge University Press, 1979.

PLINY. *Letters of the Younger Pliny.* 2 vols. Philadelphia: Richard West, 1978.

PLUTARCH

BARROW, REGINALD H. *Plutarch and His Times.* New York: AMS Press, 1967.

FROST, F. *Themistocles.* Princeton, New Jersey: Princeton University Press, 1980.

RUSSELL, D. A. *Plutarch.* Wolfeboro, New Hampshire.: Longwood, 1972.

STADTER, PHILIP A. *Plutarch's Historical Methods: An Analysis of the Mulierum Virtutes.* Harvard University Press, 1965.

WARNER, R. *Plutarch: Moral Essays.* Harmondsworth, 1971.

PROPERTIES

HUBBARD, M. E. *Propertius.* Wolfeboro, New Hampshire: Longwood, 1974.

PLATNAUER, MAURICE. *Latin Elegaic Verse: A Study of the Metrical Usages of Tibullus, Propertius, and Ovid.* Hamden, Connecticut: Shoe String, 1971.

STAHL, HANS-PETER. *Propertius: Love and War, Individual and State Under Augustus.* Berkeley: University of California Press, 1985.

WARDEN, JOHN. *Fallax Opus: Poet and Reader in the Elegies of Propertius.* Buffalo, New York: University of Toronto Press, 1980.

SENECA

COSTA, C. D. N., ed. *Seneca: Seventeen Letters.* Oak Park, Illinois: Bolchazy-Carducci, 1986.

FANTHAM, ELAINE. *Seneca's* Troades: *A Literary Introduction with Text, Translation, and Commentary.* Princeton University Press, 1982.

GRIFFIN, MIRIAM T. *Seneca: A Philosopher in Politics.* Oxford, 1976.

HENRY, D., and E. HENRY. *The Mask of Power: Seneca's Tragedies and Imperial Power.* Oak Park, Illinois: Bolchazy-Carducci, 1985.

MOTTO, ANNA L., and J. R. CLARK. *Senecan Tragedy.* Deerfield, Illinois: Coronet, 1986.

MOTTO, ANNA. *Seneca: Selected Moral Epistles.* Decatur, Georgia: Scholars Press, 1986.

SHELTON, JO-ANN. *Seneca's "Hercules Furens": Theme, Structure, and Style.* Göttingen, 1978.

SORENSON, VILLY. *Seneca: The Humanist at the Court of Nero.* University of Chicago Press, 1984.

TARRANT, R. J. *Seneca's* Rhyestes. Decatur, Georgia: Scholars Press, 1985.

STATIUS

DILKE, O. A. W., ed. *Statius:* Achilleid. Cambridge, 1954.

NEWMYER, S. T. *The* Silvae *of Statius: Structure and Theme.* Leiden, 1979.

POYNTON, J. B., tr. *Statius'* Thebaid. 3 vols. New York: Oxford, 1975.

VESSEY, DAVID. *Statius and the* Thebaid. Cambridge, 1973.

SUETONIUS

BALDWIN, B. *Suetonius: The Biographer of the Caesars.* Philadelphia: Coronet, 1983.

TOWNEND, G. B. "Suetonius and His Influence." In T. A. Dorrey, *Latin Biography.* London, 1967.

WALLACE-HADRILL, ANDREW. *Suetonius on the Emperor.* Oxford, 1980.

_____. *Suetonius: The Scholar and His Caesars.* New Haven, Connecticut: Yale University Press, 1984.

TACITUS

BENARIO, HERBERT W. *The Classical World Special Series: Tacitus'* Annals 11 and 12, Volume 3. Washington, D.C.: University Press of America, 1983.

_____. *An Introduction to Tacitus.* Athens, Ga.: University of Georgia Press, 1975.

CHILVER, G. E. *A Historical Commentary on Tacitus'* Histories I & II. Oxford University Press, 1985.

CHILVER, JOHN, and G. B. TOWNSEND. *A Historical Commentary on Tacitus'* Histories IV & V. Oxford University Press, 1985.

GOODYEAR, F. R. D., ed. *The* Annals *of Tacitus.* Cambridge, 1981.

JONES, P. V., ed. *Tacitus'* Histories: *Handbook.* Cambridge, 1975.

SCHELLHASE, KENNETH C. *Tacitus in Renaissance Political Thought.* Chicago: University of Chicago Press, 1977.

SYME, RONALD. *Tacitus.* 2 vols. Oxford University Press, 1980.

WINTERBOTTOM, M., and R. M. OGILVIE, eds. *Cornelii Taciti Opera Minora.* Oxford University Press, 1975.

TERENCE

BOVIE, PALMER, ed. *The Complete Comedies of Terence.* New Brunswick, New Jersey: Rutgers University Press, 1974.

FOREHAND, WALTER E. *Terence.* Boston: G. K. Hall and Co., 1985.

GOLDBERG, SANDER M. *Understanding Terence.* Princeton University Press, 1986.

TIBULLUS

CAIRNS, FRANCIS. *Tibullus: A Hellenistic Poet at Rome.* Cambridge, 1979.

PLATNAUER, MAURICE. *Latin Elegaic Verse: A Study of the Metrical Usages of Tibullus, Propertius, and Ovid.* Hamden, Connecticut: Shoe String, 1971.

PUTNAM, MICHAEL C. *Tibullus: A Commentary.* Norman, Oklahoma: University of Oklahoma Press, 1978.

VIRGIL

BERNARD, JOHN D., and PAUL T. ALESSI, eds. *Vergil at 2000: Commemorative Essays on the Poet and His Influence.* Lawrence, Kan.: AMS Press, 1986.

BLOOM, HAROLD, ed. *Virgil.* Edgemont, Pennsylvania: Chelsea House, 1986.

GARRISON, DANIEL H. *The Language of Virgil: An Introduction to the Poetry of the* Aeneid. New York: Peter Lang Publishing, 1984.

GRANSDEN, K. W. *Virgil's* Iliad: *An Essay on Epic Narrative.* Cambridge, 1985.

HARDIE, PHILIP. *Virgil's* Aeneid: *Cosmos and Imperium.* Oxford, 1986.

JOHNSON, W. R. *Darkness Visible: A Study of Vergil's* Aeneid. Berkeley: University of California Press, 1976.

LEE, M. OWEN. *Fathers and Sons in Virgil's* Aeneid. Albany: State University of New York Press, 1981.

LETTERS, F. J. *Virgil.* Norwood, Pennsylvania: Telegraph Books, 1981.

MILES, GARY B. *Virgil's* Georgics: *A New Interpretation.* Berkeley: University of California Press, 1980.

POSCHL, VIKTOR. *The Art of Virgil: Image and Symbol in the* Aeneid. Westport, Conn.: Greenwood, 1986.

SPOFFORD, EDWARD W. *The Social Poetry of the* Georgics. Salem, New Hampshire: Ayer Company, 1981.

WILLIAMS, GORDON. *Technique and Ideas in the* Aeneid. New Haven, Connecticut: Yale University Press, 1985.

WILLIAMS, R. D., and T. S. PATTIE. *Virgil: His Poetry Through the Ages.* Wolfeboro, New Hampshire: Longwood, 1982.

INDEX

Abelard, Peter, 210
Ab Urbe Condita, 147–49
Acca, 133
Accius, Lucius, 41
Acerra, 252
Acestes, 107, 121
Achaemenides, 107, 119
Achates, 107, 114–15, 123, 128
Achilleid, 303
Achilles, 110, 114, 116, 128, 132–33,
    135, 188, 200, 303
Adam, 334
Addison, Joseph, 168, 217, 286
Adelphi, 49–53
Adeodatus, 331
Adonis, 188
Aelia, 252
Aelius Caesar, Lucius, 311
Aemilian family, 326
Aeneas, 34, 67, 87, 103, 105, 107–35,
    145, 147, 188, 197–99
Aeneid, 34, 103–35, 160, 293
Aeolus, 111, 114
Aeschinus, 51–52
Aesculapius, 319
Aesop, 175
Aesopus, 45
Aetna, 102
Against Apion, 238, 244–46
"Against Cato," 69
Agamemnon, 45, 200
Agricola, 268
Agricola, Gnaeus Julius, 267–68
Agrippa, Marcus, 128
Agrippa, Menenius, 128, 149
Agrippa, Simonides, 238
Agrippina, 209–10, 270–71
Ajax, 190
Alcaeus, 167
Alcinous, 115
Alcmena, 25–27

Alexander the Great, 229, 258,
    261–63
Alexandrine school, 93, 95, 160
Alexis, 136
Aliturus, 239
Allecto, 126
Amata, 107, 109–10, 126, 134–35
Ambrose, St., 331
Ammonius, 257
Amores, 93, 183, 189–93
Amphitryon, 25–27, 212
Amphitryon (Molière), 18
Amphitryon (Plautus), 25–27
Amulius, 198
Anchises, 107, 117, 119, 121–22, 124,
    198
Andria, 40, 49
Andromache, 45, 107–10, 118, 212
Andronicus, Lucius Livius, 10, 39
Anna, 108, 119–20
Annales, 34–35
Annals, 268–72
Anthrax, 23
Antiochus, 59, 149
Antoninus Pius, 311
Antony, Mark, 45, 61, 63, 69, 103,
    128, 148, 160, 165, 229, 243, 245,
    261, 296–97
Antony and Cleopatra, 258
aphorisms, 69, 281, 314
Apion, 238, 245
Apollinaris, 9, 267
Apollo, 118, 123, 132, 167, 257, 321
Apollodorus, 40, 49
Apophoreta, 250
Appendix Vergiliana, 102
Appian Way, 149
Appius Pulcher, 61
Apuleius, 319–22
Aquinas, St. Thomas, 332
Argius, 273

This is the TITLE INDEX, indexing the over 200 titles available by Series, by Library and by Volume Number for both the BASIC LIBRARY SERIES and the AUTHORS LIBRARY SERIES.

TITLE	SERIES	LIBRARY	Vol
Black Like Me	Basic	American Lit	6
Bleak House	Basic	English Lit	3
	Authors	Dickens	1
Bourgeois Gentleman, The (in <u>Tartuffe....</u>)	Basic	European Lit	1
Brave New World	Basic	English Lit	5
Brave New World Revisited (in <u>Brave New World</u>)	Basic	English Lit	5
Brothers Karamozov, The	Basic	European Lit	3
	Authors	Dostoevsky	2
Caesar and Cleopatra (in Shaw's Man and Superman....)	Basic	English Lit	6
	Authors	Shaw	11
Call of the Wild, The	Basic	American Lit	3
Candide	Basic	European Lit	1
Canterbury Tales, The	Basic	Classics	3
"Cask of Amontillado, The" (in Poe's Short Stories)	Basic	American Lit	1
Catch-22	Basic	American Lit	6
Catcher in the Rye, The	Basic	American Lit	6
Choephori (in <u>Agamemnon</u>)	Basic	Classics	1
Clouds, The (in <u>Lysistrata....</u>)	Basic	Classics	1
Color Purple, The	Basic	American Lit	6
Comedy of Errors, The	Basic	Shakespeare	1
	Authors	Shakespeare	8
Connecticut Yankee in King Arthur's Court, A	Basic	American Lit	2
	Authors	Twain	13
Count of Monte Cristo, The	Basic	European Lit	1
Crime and Punishment	Basic	European Lit	3
	Authors	Dostoevsky	2
Crito (in <u>Plato's Euthyphro....</u>)	Basic	Classics	1
Crucible, The	Basic	American Lit	6
Cry, the Beloved Country	Basic	English Lit	5
Cyrano de Bergerac	Basic	European Lit	1
Daisy Miller	Basic	American Lit	2
	Authors	James	6
David Copperfield	Basic	English Lit	3
	Authors	Dickens	1
Day of the Locust, The (in <u>Miss Lonelyhearts....</u>)	Basic	American Lit	5
Death of a Salesman	Basic	American Lit	6
Deerslayer, The	Basic	American Lit	1
"Delta Autumn" (in <u>Go Down, Moses</u>)	Basic	American Lit	4
Demian	Basic	European Lit	2
Diary of Anne Frank, The	Basic	European Lit	2
"Displaced Person, The" (in O'Connor's Short Stories	Basic	American Lit	7
Divine Comedy I: Inferno	Basic	Classics	3
Divine Comedy II: Purgatorio	Basic	Classics	3
Divine Comedy III: Paradiso	Basic	Classics	3
Doctor Faustus	Basic	Classics	3
Doll's House, A (in <u>Ibsen's Plays I</u>)	Basic	European Lit	4
Don Quixote	Basic	Classics	3
Dr. Jekyll and Mr. Hyde	Basic	English Lit	3

TITLE	SERIES	LIBRARY	Vol
Red and the Black, The	Basic	European Lit	1
Red Badge of Courage, The	Basic	American Lit	2
Red Pony, The	Basic	American Lit	5
	Authors	Steinbeck	12
Republic, The (in Plato's The Republic)	Basic	Classics	1
Return of the Native, The	Basic	English Lit	4
	Authors	Hardy	4
Richard II	Basic	Shakespeare	3
	Authors	Shakespeare	10
Richard III	Basic	Shakespeare	3
	Authors	Shakespeare	10
Robinson Crusoe	Basic	English Lit	2
Roman Classics	Basic	Classics	2
Romeo and Juliet	Basic	Shakespeare	2
	Authors	Shakespeare	9
Scarlet Letter, The	Basic	American Lit	1
Secret Sharer, The (in Heart of Darkness)	Basic	English Lit	5
Separate Peace, A	Basic	American Lit	7
Shakespeare's Sonnets	Basic	Shakespeare	3
	Authors	Shakespeare	10
Shane	Basic	American Lit	7
Shaw's Man and Superman & Caesar and Cleopatra	Basic	English Lit	6
Shaw's Pygmalion & Arms and the Man	Basic	English Lit	6
Shelley (in Keats and Shelley)	Basic	English Lit	1
Siddhartha (in Steppenwolf & Siddhartha)	Basic	European Lit	2
Silas Marner	Basic	English Lit	4
Sir Gawain and the Green Knight	Basic	Classics	4
Sister Carrie	Basic	American Lit	3
Slaughterhouse Five (in Vonnegut's Major Works)	Basic	American Lit	7
Sons and Lovers	Basic	English Lit	6
Sound and the Fury, The	Basic	American Lit	5
	Authors	Faulkner	3
Steppenwolf	Basic	European Lit	2
Stranger, The	Basic	European Lit	1
Streetcar Named Desire, A (in The Glass Menagerie....)	Basic	American Lit	6
Sun Also Rises, The	Basic	American Lit	5
	Authors	Hemingway	5
T.S. Eliot's Major Poems and Plays	Basic	English Lit	6
Tale of Two Cities, A	Basic	English Lit	4
	Authors	Dickens	1
Taming of the Shrew, The	Basic	Shakespeare	1
	Authors	Shakespeare	8
Tartuffe	Basic	European Lit	1
Tempest, The	Basic	Shakespeare	1
	Authors	Shakespeare	8
Tender is the Night	Basic	American Lit	5
Tess of the D'Urbervilles	Basic	English Lit	4
	Authors	Hardy	4

TITLE	SERIES	LIBRARY	Vol
Three Musketeers, The	Basic	European Lit	1
To Kill a Mockingbird	Basic	American Lit	7
Tom Jones	Basic	English Lit	2
Tom Sawyer	Basic	American Lit	2
	Authors	Twain	13
Treasure Island	Basic	English Lit	4
Trial, The	Basic	European Lit	2
Tristram Shandy	Basic	English Lit	2
Troilus and Cressida	Basic	Shakespeare	1
	Authors	Shakespeare	8
Turn of the Screw, The (in Daisy Miller....)	Basic	American Lit	2
	Authors	James	6
Twelfth Night	Basic	Shakespeare	1
	Authors	Shakespeare	8
Two Gentlemen of Verona, The (in Comedy of Errors...)	Basic	Shakespeare	1
	Authors	Shakespeare	8
Typee (in Billy Budd & Typee)	Basic	American Lit	1
Ulysses	Basic	English Lit	6
Uncle Tom's Cabin	Basic	American Lit	2
Unvanquished, The	Basic	American Lit	5
	Authors	Faulkner	3
Utopia	Basic	Classics	4
Vanity Fair	Basic	English Lit	4
Vonnegut's Major Works	Basic	American Lit	7
Waiting for Godot	Basic	European Lit	1
Walden	Basic	American Lit	1
Walden Two	Basic	American Lit	7
War and Peace	Basic	European Lit	3
"Was" (in Go Down, Moses)	Basic	American Lit	4
"Waste Land, The" (in T.S. Eliot's Major Poems and Plays)	Basic	English Lit	6
White Fang (in Call of the Wild & White Fang)	Basic	American Lit	3
Who's Afraid of Virginia Woolf?	Basic	American Lit	7
Wild Duck, The (in Ibsen's Plays II)	Basic	European Lit	4
Winesburg, Ohio	Basic	American Lit	3
Winter's Tale, The	Basic	Shakespeare	1
	Authors	Shakespeare	8
Wuthering Heights	Basic	English Lit	4

This is the AUTHOR INDEX, listing the over 200 titles available by author and indexing them by Series, by Library and by Volume Number for both the BASIC LIBRARY SERIES and the AUTHORS LIBRARY SERIES.

AUTHOR	TITLE(S)	SERIES	LIBRARY	Vol
Aeschylus	Agamemnon, The Choephori, & The Eumenides	Basic	Classics	1
Albee, Edward	Who's Afraid of Virginia Woolf?	Basic	American Lit	7
Anderson, Sherwood	Winesburg, Ohio	Basic	American Lit	3
Aristophanes	Lysistrata * The Birds * Clouds * The Frogs	Basic	Classics	1
Aristotle	Aristotle's Ethics	Basic	Classics	1
Austen, Jane	Emma	Basic	English Lit	1
	Pride and Prejudice	Basic	English Lit	2
Beckett, Samuel	Waiting for Godot	Basic	European Lit	1
Beowulf	Beowulf	Basic	Classics	3
Beyle, Henri	see Stendhal			
Bronte, Charlotte	Jane Eyre	Basic	English Lit	3
Bronte, Emily	Wuthering Heights	Basic	English Lit	4
Brown, Claude	Manchild in the Promised Land	Basic	American Lit	7
Buck, Pearl	The Good Earth	Basic	American Lit	4
Bunyan, John	The Pilgrim's Progress	Basic	English Lit	2
Camus, Albert	The Plague * The Stranger	Basic	European Lit	1
Carroll, Lewis	Alice in Wonderland	Basic	English Lit	3
Cather, Willa	My Antonia	Basic	American Lit	3
Cervantes, Miguel de	Don Quixote	Basic	Classics	3
Chaucer, Geoffrey	The Canterbury Tales	Basic	Classics	3
Chopin, Kate	The Awakening	Basic	American Lit	2
Clark, Walter	The Ox-Bow Incident	Basic	American Lit	7
Conrad, Joseph	Heart of Darkness & The Secret Sharer * Lord Jim	Basic	English Lit	5
Cooper, James F.	The Deerslayer * The Last of the Mohicans	Basic	American Lit	1
Crane, Stephen	The Red Badge of Courage	Basic	American Lit	2
Dante	Divine Comedy I: Inferno * Divine Comedy II: Purgatorio * Divine Comedy III: Paradiso	Basic	Classsics	3
Defoe, Daniel	Moll Flanders	Basic	English Lit	1
	Robinson Crusoe	Basic	English Lit	2
Dickens, Charles	Bleak House * David Copperfield * Great Expectations * Hard Times	Basic	English Lit	3
	Oliver Twist * A Tale of Two Cities	Basic	English Lit	4
	Bleak House * David Copperfield * Great Expectations * Hard Times * Oliver Twist * A Tale of Two Cities	Authors	Dickens	1

AUTHOR	TITLE(S)	SERIES	LIBRARY	Vol
Dickinson, Emily	Emily Dickinson: Selected Poems	Basic	American Lit	2
Dostoevsky, Feodor	The Brothers Karamazov * Crime and Punishment * Notes from the Underground	Basic	European Lit	3
	The Brothers Karamazov * Crime and Punishment * Notes from the Underground	Authors	Dostoevsky	2
Dreiser, Theodore	An American Tragedy * Sister Carrie	Basic	American Lit	3
Dumas, Alexandre	The Count of Monte Cristo * The Three Musketeers	Basic	European Lit	1
Eliot, George	Middlemarch * The Mill on the Floss * Silas Marner	Basic	English Lit	4
Eliot, T.S.	T.S. Eliot's Major Poets and Plays: "The Wasteland," "The Love Song of J. Alfred Pru-frock," & Other Works	Basic	English Lit	6
Ellison, Ralph	The Invisible Man	Basic	American Lit	7
Emerson, Ralph Waldo	Emerson's Essays	Basic	American Lit	1
Euripides	Electra * Medea	Basic	Classics	1
Faulkner, William	Absalom, Absalom! * As I Lay Dying * The Bear * Go Down, Moses * Light in August	Basic	American Lit	4
	The Sound and the Fury * The Unvanquished	Basic	American Lit	5
	Absalom, Absalom! * As I Lay Dying * The Bear * Go Down, Moses * Light in August The Sound and the Fury * The Unvanquished	Authors	Faulkner	3
Fielding, Henry	Joseph Andrews	Basic	English Lit	1
	Tom Jones	Basic	English Lit	2
Fitzgerald, F. Scott	The Great Gatsby	Basic	American Lit	4
	Tender is the Night	Basic	American Lit	5
Flaubert, Gustave	Madame Bovary	Basic	European Lit	1
Forster, E.M.	A Passage to India	Basic	English Lit	6
Fowles, John	The French Lieutenant's Woman	Basic	English Lit	5
Frank, Anne	The Diary of Anne Frank	Basic	European Lit	2
Franklin, Benjamin	The Autobiography of Benjamin Franklin	Basic	American Lit	1
Gawain Poet	Sir Gawain and the Green Night	Basic	Classics	4
Goethe, Johann Wolfgang von	Faust - Parts I & II	Basic	European Lit	2
Golding, William	Lord of the Flies	Basic	English Lit	5
Greene, Graham	The Power and the Glory	Basic	English Lit	6
Griffin, John H.	Black Like Me	Basic	American Lit	6

AUTHOR	TITLE(S)	SERIES	LIBRARY	Vol
Haley, Alex	The Autobiography of Malcolm X	Basic	American Lit	6
see also Little, Malcolm				
Hardy, Thomas	Far from the Madding Crowd * Jude the Obscure * The Mayor of Casterbridge	Basic	English Lit	3
	The Return of the Native * Tess of the D'Urbervilles	Basic	English Lit	4
	Far from the Madding Crowd * Jude the Obscure * The Mayor of Casterbridge The Return of the Native * Tess of the D'Urbervilles	Authors	Hardy	4
Hawthorne, Nathaniel	The House of the Seven Gables* The Scarlet Letter	Basic	American Lit	1
Heller, Joseph	Catch-22	Basic	American Lit	6
Hemingway, Ernest	A Farewell to Arms * For Whom the Bell Tolls	Basic	American Lit	4
	The Old Man and the Sea	Basic	American Lit	7
	The Sun Also Rises	Basic	American Lit	5
	A Farewell to Arms * For Whom the Bell Tolls The Old Man and the Sea The Sun Also Rises	Authors	Hemingway	5
Herbert, Frank	Dune & Other Works	Basic	American Lit	6
Hesse, Herman	Demian * Steppenwolf & Siddhartha	Basic	European Lit	2
Hilton, James	Lost Horizon	Basic	English Lit	5
Homer	The Iliad * The Odyssey	Basic	Classics	1
Hugo, Victor	Les Miserables	Basic	European Lit	1
Huxley, Aldous	Brave New World & Brave New World Revisited	Basic	English Lit	5
Ibsen, Henrik	Ibsen's Plays I: A Doll's House & Hedda Gabler * Ibsen's Plays II: Ghosts, An Enemy of the People, & The Wild Duck	Basic	European Lit	4
James, Henry	The American * Daisy Miller & The Turn of the Screw * The Portrait of a Lady	Basic	American Lit	2
	The American * Daisy Miller & The Turn of the Screw * The Portrait of a Lady	Authors	James	6
Joyce, James	A Portrait of the Artist as a Young Man * Ulysses	Basic	English Lit	6
Kafka, Franz	Kafka's Short Stories * The Trial	Basic	European Lit	2
Keats & Shelley	Keats & Shelley	Basic	English Lit	1
Kesey, Ken	One Flew Over the Cuckoo's Nest	Basic	American Lit	7
Knowles, John	A Separate Peace	Basic	American Lit	7

AUTHOR	TITLE(S)	SERIES	LIBRARY	Vol
Lawrence, D.H.	Sons and Lovers	Basic	English Lit	6
Lee, Harper	To Kill a Mockingbird	Basic	American Lit	7
Lewis, Sinclair	Babbit * Main Street	Basic	American Lit	3
	Babbit * Main Street	Authors	Lewis	7
Little, Malcolm see also Haley, Alex	The Autobiography of Malcolm X	Basic	American Lit	6
London, Jack	Call of the Wild & White Fang	Basic	American Lit	3
Machiavelli, Niccolo	The Prince	Basic	Classics	4
Malamud, Bernard	The Assistant	Basic	American Lit	6
Malcolm X	see Little, Malcolm			
Malory, Thomas	Le Morte d'Arthur	Basic	Classics	4
Marlowe, Christopher	Doctor Faustus	Basic	Classics	3
Marquez, Gabriel Garcia	One Hundred Years of Solitude	Basic	American Lit	6
Maugham, Somerset	Of Human Bondage	Basic	English Lit	6
Melville, Herman	Billy Budd & Typee * Moby Dick	Basic	American Lit	1
Miller, Arthur	The Crucible * Death of a Salesman	Basic	American Lit	6
Milton, John	Paradise Lost	Basic	English Lit	2
Moliere, Jean Baptiste	Tartuffe, Misanthrope & Bourgeois Gentleman	Basic	European Lit	1
More, Thomas	Utopia	Basic	Classics	4
O'Connor, Flannery	O'Connor's Short Stories	Basic	American Lit	7
Orwell, George	Animal Farm	Basic	English Lit	5
	Nineteen Eighty-Four	Basic	English Lit	6
Paton, Alan	Cry, The Beloved Country	Basic	English Lit	5
Plath, Sylvia	The Bell Jar	Basic	American Lit	6
Plato	Plato's Euthyphro, Apology, Crito & Phaedo * Plato's The Republic	Basic	Classics	1
Poe, Edgar Allen	Poe's Short Stories	Basic	American Lit	1
Remarque, Erich	All Quiet on the Western Front	Basic	European Lit	2
Rolvaag, Ole	Giants in the Earth	Basic	European Lit	4
Rostand, Edmond	Cyrano de Bergerac	Basic	European Lit	1
Salinger, J.D.	The Catcher in the Rye	Basic	American Lit	6
Sartre, Jean Paul	No Exit & The Flies	Basic	European Lit	1
Scott, Walter	Ivanhoe	Basic	English Lit	1
Shaefer, Jack	Shane	Basic	American Lit	7
Shakespeare, William	All's Well that Ends Well & The Merry Wives of Windsor * As You Like It * The Comedy of Errors, Love's Labour's Lost, & The Two Gentlemen of Verona * Measure for Measure * The Merchant of Venice * Midsummer Night's Dream * Much Ado About Nothing * The Taming of the Shrew * The Tempest *	Basic	Shakespeare	1

AUTHOR	TITLE(S)	SERIES	LIBRARY	Vol
Shakespeare, William	Troilus and Cressida * Twelfth Night * The Winter's Tale	Basic	Shakespeare	1
	All's Well that Ends Well & The Merry Wives of Windsor * As You Like It * The Comedy of Errors, Love's Labour's Lost, & The Two Gentlemen of Verona * Measure for Measure * The Merchant of Venice * Midsummer Night's Dream * Much Ado About Nothing * The Taming of the Shrew * The Tempest * Troilus and Cressida * Twelfth Night * The Winter's Tale	Authors	Shakespeare	8
	Antony and Cleopatra * Hamlet * Julius Caesar * King Lear * Macbeth * Othello * Romeo and Juliet	Basic	Shakeapeare	2
	Antony and Cleopatra * Hamlet * Julius Caesar * King Lear * Macbeth * Othello * Romeo and Juliet	Authors	Shakespeare	9
	Henry IV Part 1 * Henry IV Part 2 * Henry V * Henry VI Parts 1,2,3 * Richard II * Richard III * Shakespeare's Sonnets	Basic	Shakespeare	3
	Henry IV Part 1 * Henry IV Part 2 * Henry V * Henry VI Parts 1,2,3 * Richard II * Richard III * Shakespeare's Sonnets	Authors	Shakespeare	10
Shaw, George Bernard	Man and Superman & Caesar and Cleopatra * Pygmalion & Arms and the Man	Basic	English Lit	6
	Man and Superman & Caesar and Cleopatra * Pygmalion & Arms and the Man	Authors	Shaw	11
Shelley, Mary	Frankenstein	Basic	English Lit	1
Sinclair, Upton	The Jungle	Basic	American Lit	3
Skinner, B.F.	Walden Two	Basic	American Lit	7
Solzhenitsyn, Aleksandr	One Day in the Life of Ivan Denisovich	Basic	European Lit	3
Sophocles	The Oedipus Trilogy	Basic	Classics	1
Spenser, Edmund	The Faerie Queen	Basic	Classics	4
Steinbeck, John	The Grapes of Wrath *	Basic	American Lit	4
	Of Mice and Men * The Pearl * The Red Pony	Basic	American Lit	5

AUTHOR	TITLE(S)	SERIES	LIBRARY	Vol
Steinbeck, John	The Grapes of Wrath * Of Mice and Men * The Pearl * The Red Pony	Authors	Steinbeck	12
Stendhal	The Red and the Black	Basic	European Lit	1
Sterne, Lawrence	Tristram Shandy	Basic	English Lit	2
Stevenson, Robert Louis	Dr. Jekyll and Mr. Hyde *	Basic	English Lit	3
	Treasure Island & Kidnapped	Basic	English Lit	4
Stoker, Bram	Dracula	Basic	English Lit	3
Stowe, Harriet Beecher	Uncle Tom's Cabin	Basic	American Lit	2
Swift, Jonathan	Gulliver's Travels	Basic	English Lit	1
Thackeray, William Makepeace	Vanity Fair	Basic	English Lit	4
Thoreau, Henry David	Walden	Basic	American Lit	1
Tolkien, J.R.R.	The Lord of the Rings & The Hobbit	Basic	English Lit	5
Tolstoy, Leo	Anna Karenina * War and Peace	Basic	European Lit	3
Turgenev, Ivan Sergeyevich	Fathers and Sons	Basic	European Lit	3
Twain, Mark	A Connecticut Yankee * Huckleberry Finn * The Prince and the Pauper * Tom Sawyer	Basic	American Lit	2
	A Connecticut Yankee * Huckleberry Finn * The Prince and the Pauper * Tom Sawyer	Authors	Twain	13
Virgil	The Aeneid	Basic	Classics	1
Voltaire, Francois	Candide	Basic	European Lit	2
Vonnegut, Kurt	Vonnegut's Major Works	Basic	American Lit	7
Walker, Alice	The Color Purple	Basic	American Lit	7
Warren, Robert Penn	All the King's Men	Basic	American Lit	6
West, Nathanael	Miss Lonelyhearts & The Day of the Locust	Basic	American Lit	5
Wharton, Edith	Ethan Frome	Basic	American Lit	3
Whitman, Walt	Leaves of Grass	Basic	American Lit	1
Wilder, Thornton	Our Town	Basic	American Lit	5
Williams, Tennessee	The Glass Menagerie & A Streetcar Named Desire	Basic	American Lit	6
Woolf, Virginia	Mrs. Dalloway	Basic	English Lit	5
Wordsworth, William	The Prelude	Basic	English Lit	2
Wright, Richard	Black Boy	Basic	American Lit	4
	Native Son	Basic	American Lit	5

INDEX OF SERIES

BASIC LIBRARY (24-0)

THE SHAKESPEARE LIBRARY: 3 Volumes, 26 Titles (25-9)
  - V. 1 - The Comedies 12 titles (00-3)
  - V. 2 - The Tragedies, 7 titles (01-1)
  - V. 3 - The Histories; The Sonnets, 7 titles (02-X)

THE CLASSICS LIBRARY: 4 Volumes, 27 Titles (26-7)
  - V. 1 - Greek & Roman Classics, 11 titles (03-8)
  - V. 2 - Greek & Roman Classics, 2 titles (04-6)
  - V. 3 - Early Christian/European Classics, 7 titles (05-4)
  - V. 4 - Early Christian/European Classics, 7 titles (06-2)

ENGLISH LITERATURE LIBRARY: 6 Volumes, 55 Titles (29-1)
  - V. 1 - 17th Century & Romantic Period Classics, 7 titles (07-0)
  - V. 2 - 17th Century & Romantic Period Classics, 7 titles (08-9)
  - V. 3 - Victorian Age, 11 titles (09-7)
  - V. 4 - Victorian Age, 10 titles (10-0)
  - V. 5 - 20th Century, 10 titles (11-9)
  - V. 6 - 20th Century, 10 titles (12-7)

AMERICAN LITERATURE LIBRARY: 7 Volumes, 77 Titles (33-X)
  - V. 1 - Early U.S. & Romantic Period, 11 titles (13-5)
  - V. 2 - Civil War to 1900, 11 titles (14-3)
  - V. 3 - Early 20th Century, 9 titles (15-1)
  - V. 4 - The Jazz Age to W.W.II, 11 titles (16-X)
  - V. 5 - The Jazz Age to W.W.II, 10 titles (17-8)
  - V. 6 - Post-War American Literature, 13 titles (18-6)
  - V. 7 - Post-War American Literature, 12 titles (19-4)

EUROPEAN LITERATURE LIBRARY: 4 Volumes, 29 Titles (36-4)
  - V. 1 - French Literature, 12 titles (20-8)
  - V. 2 - German Literature, 7 titles (21-6)
  - V. 3 - Russian Literature, 7 titles (22-4)
  - V. 4 - Scandinavian Literature, 3 titles (23-2)

AUTHORS LIBRARY (65-8)

  - V. 1 - **Charles Dickens** Library, 6 titles (66-6)
  - V. 2 - **Feodor Dostoevsky** Library, 3 titles (67-4)
  - V. 3 - **William Faulkner** Library, 7 titles (68-2)
  - V. 4 - **Thomas Hardy** Library, 5 titles (69-0)
  - V. 5 - **Ernest Hemingway** Library, 4 titles (70-4)
  - V. 6 - **Henry James** Library, 3 titles (71-2)
  - V. 7 - **Sinclair Lewis** Library, 2 titles (72-0)
  - V. 8 - **Shakespeare** Library, Part 1 - The Comedies, 12 titles (73-9)
  - V. 9 - **Shakespeare** Library, Part 2 - The Tragedies, 7 titles (74-7)
  - V. 10 - **Shakespeare** Library, Part 3 - The Histories; Sonnets, 7 titles (75-5)
  - V. 11 - **George Bernard Shaw** Library, 2 titles (76-3)
  - V. 12 - **John Steinbeck** Library, 4 titles (77-1)
  - V. 13 - **Mark Twain** Library, 4 titles (78-X)

Moonbeam Publications ISBN Prefix: 0-931013-

HARDBOUND LITERARY LIBRARIES

INDEX OF LIBRARIES

This is the INDEX OF LIBRARIES, listing the volumes and the individual titles within the volumes for both the BASIC LIBRARY SERIES (24 Volumes, starting below) and the AUTHORS LIBRARY SERIES (13 Volumes, see Page 6).

BASIC LIBRARY SERIES (24 Volumes)

THE SHAKESPEARE LIBRARY: 3 Volumes, 26 Titles

Vol 1 - The Comedies (12 titles)
*All's Well that Ends Well & The Merry Wives of Windsor * As You Like It * The Comedy of Errors, Love's Labour's Lost, & The Two Gentlemen of Verona * Measure for Measure * The Merchant of Venice * A Midsummer Night's Dream * Much Ado About Nothing * The Taming of the Shrew * The Tempest * Troilus and Cressida * Twelfth Night * The Winter's Tale*

Vol 2 - The Tragedies (7 titles)
*Antony and Cleopatra * Hamlet * Julius Caesar * King Lear * Macbeth * Othello * Romeo and Juliet*

Vol 3 - The Histories; The Sonnets (7 titles)
*Henry IV Part 1 * Henry IV Part 2 * Henry V * Henry VI Parts 1,2,3 * Richard II * Richard III * Shakespeare's Sonnets*

THE CLASSICS LIBRARY: 4 Volumes, 27 Titles

Vol 1 - Greek & Roman Classics Part 1 (11 titles)
*The Aeneid * Agamemnon * Aristotle's Ethics * Euripides' Electra & Medea * The Iliad * Lysistrata & Other Comedies * Mythology * The Odyssey * Oedipus Trilogy * Plato's Euthyphro, Apology, Crito & Phaedo * Plato's The Republic*

THE CLASSICS LIBRARY (cont'd)

Vol 2 - Greek & Roman Classics Part 2 (2 titles)
Greek Classics * Roman Classics

Vol 3 - Early Christian/European Classics Part 1 (7 titles)
Beowulf * Canterbury Tales * Divine Comedy - I. Inferno * Divine Comedy - II. Purgatorio * Divine Comedy - III. Paradiso * Doctor Faustus * Don Quixote

Vol 4 - Early Christian/European Classics Part 2 (7 titles)
The Faerie Queene * Le Morte D'Arthur * New Testament * Old Testament * The Prince * Sir Gawain and the Green Knight * Utopia

ENGLISH LITERATURE LIBRARY: 6 Volumes, 55 Titles

Vol 1 - 17th Century & Romantic Period Classics Part 1 (7 titles)
Emma * Frankenstein * Gulliver's Travels * Ivanhoe * Joseph Andrews * Keats & Shelley * Moll Flanders

Vol 2 - 17th Century & Romantic Period Classics Part 2 (7 titles)
Paradise Lost * Pilgrim's Progress * The Prelude * Pride and Prejudice * Robinson Crusoe * Tom Jones * Tristram Shandy

Vol 3 - Victorian Age Part 1 (11 titles)
Alice in Wonderland * Bleak House * David Copperfield * Dr. Jekyll and Mr. Hyde * Dracula * Far from the Madding Crowd * Great Expectations * Hard Times * Jane Eyre * Jude the Obscure * The Mayor of Casterbridge

ENGLISH LITERATURE LIBRARY (cont'd)

Vol 4 - Victorian Age Part 2 (10 titles)
*Middlemarch * The Mill on the Floss * Oliver Twist * The Return of the Native * Silas Marner * A Tale of Two Cities * Tess of the D'Urbervilles * Treasure Island & Kidnapped * Vanity Fair * Wuthering Heights*

Vol 5 - 20th Century Part 1 (10 titles)
*Animal Farm * Brave New World * Cry, The Beloved Country * The French Lieutenant's Woman * Heart of Darkness & The Secret Sharer * Lord Jim * Lord of the Flies * The Lord of the Rings * Lost Horizon * Mrs. Dalloway*

Vol 6 - 20th Century Part 2 (10 titles)
*Nineteen Eighty-Four * Of Human Bondage * A Passage to India * A Portrait of the Artist as a Young Man * The Power and the Glory * Shaw's Man and Superman & Caesar and Cleopatra * Shaw's Pygmalion & Arms and the Man * Sons and Lovers * T.S. Eliot's Major Poems and Plays * Ulysses*

AMERICAN LITERATURE LIBRARY: 7 Volumes, 77 Titles

Vol 1 - Early U.S. & Romantic Period (11 titles)
*Autobiography of Ben Franklin * Billy Budd & Typee * The Deerslayer * Emerson's Essays * The House of Seven Gables * The Last of the Mohicans * Leaves of Grass * Moby Dick * Poe's Short Stories * The Scarlet Letter * Walden*

AMERICAN LITERATURE LIBRARY (cont'd)

Vol 2 - Civil War to 1900 (11 titles)

*The American * The Awakening * A Connecticut Yankee in King Arthur's Court * Daisy Miller & The Turn of the Screw * Emily Dickinson: Selected Poems * Huckleberry Finn * The Portrait of a Lady * The Prince and the Pauper * Red Badge of Courage * Tom Sawyer * Uncle Tom's Cabin*

Vol 3 - Early 20th Century (9 titles)

*An American Tragedy * Babbitt * Call of the Wild & White Fang * Ethan Frome * The Jungle * Main Street * My Antonia * Sister Carrie * Winesburg, Ohio*

Vol 4 - The Jazz Age to W.W.II Part 1 (11 titles)

*Absalom, Absalom! * As I Lay Dying * The Bear * Black Boy * A Farewell to Arms * For Whom the Bell Tolls * Go Down, Moses * The Good Earth * The Grapes of Wrath * The Great Gatsby * Light in August*

Vol 5 - The Jazz Age to W.W.II Part 2 (10 titles)

*Miss Lonelyhearts & The Day of the Locust * Native Son * Of Mice and Men * Our Town * The Pearl * The Red Pony * The Sound and the Fury * The Sun Also Rises * Tender is the Night * Unvanquished*

Vol 6 - Post-War American Literature Part 1 (13 titles)

*100 Years of Solitude * All the King's Men * The Assistant * The Autobiography of Malcolm X * The Bell Jar * Black Like Me * Catch-22 * The Catcher in the Rye * The Color Purple * The Crucible * Death of a Salesman * Dune and Other Works * The Glass Menagerie & A Streetcar Named Desire*

AMERICAN LITERATURE LIBRARY (cont'd)

Vol 7 - Post-War American Literature Part 2 (12 titles)

*The Invisible Man * Manchild in the Promised Land * O'Connor's Short Stories * The Old Man and the Sea * One Flew Over the Cuckoo's Nest * The Ox-Bow Incident * A Separate Peace * Shane * To Kill a Mockingbird * Vonnegut's Major Works * Walden Two * Who's Afraid of Virginia Woolf?*

EUROPEAN LITERATURE LIBRARY: 4 Volumes, 29 Titles

Vol 1 - French Literature (12 titles)

*Candide * The Count of Monte Cristo * Cyrano de Bergerac * Les Miserables * Madame Bovary * No Exit & The Flies * The Plague * The Red and the Black * The Stranger * Tartuffe, Misanthrope & Bourgeois Gentlemen * The Three Musketeers * Waiting for Godot*

Vol 2 - German Literature (7 titles)

*All Quiet on the Western Front * Demian * The Diary of Anne Frank * Faust Pt. I & Pt. II * Kafka's Short Stories * Steppenwolf & Siddhartha * The Trial*

Vol 3 - Russian Literature (7 titles)

*Anna Karenina * The Brothers Karamozov * Crime and Punishment * Fathers and Sons * Notes from the Underground * One Day in the Life of Ivan Denisovich * War and Peace*

Vol 4 - Scandinavian Literature (3 titles)

*Giants in the Earth * Ibsen's Plays I: A Doll's House & Hedda Gabler * Ibsen's Plays II: Ghosts, An Enemy of the People & The Wild Duck*

AUTHORS LIBRARY SERIES (13 Volumes)

AUTHORS   LIBRARY

Vol 1 - Charles Dickens Library (6 titles)
*Bleak House * David Copperfield * Great Expectations *
Hard Times * Oliver Twist * A Tale of Two Cities*

Vol 2 - Feodor Dostoevsky Library (3 titles)
*The Brothers Karamazov * Crime and Punishment *
Notes from the Underground*

Vol 3 - William Faulkner Library (7 titles)
*Absalom, Absalom! * As I Lay Dying * The Bear * Go
Down, Moses * Light in August * The Sound and the Fury
* The Unvanquished*

Vol 4 - Thomas Hardy Library (5 titles)
*Far from the Madding Crowd * Jude the Obscure * The
Major of Casterbridge * The Return of the Native * Tess
of the D'Urbervilles*

Vol 5 - Ernest Hemingway Library (4 titles)
*A Farewell to Arms * For Whom the Bell Tolls * The Old
Man and the Sea * The Sun Also Rises*

Vol 6 - Henry James Library (3 titles)
*The American * Daisy Miller & The Turn of the Screw *
The Portrait of a Lady*

Vol 7 - Sinclair Lewis Library (2 titles)
*Babbitt * Main Street*

AUTHORS LIBRARY SERIES

Vol 8 - Shakespeare Library, Part 1 - The Comedies (12 titles)
*All's Well that Ends Well & The Merry Wives of Windsor
* As You Like It * The Comedy of Errors, Love's Labour's
Lost & The Two Gentlemen of Verona * Measure for
Measure * The Merchant of Venice * A Midsummer
Night's Dream * Much Ado About Nothing * The Taming
of the Shrew * The Tempest * Troilus and Cressida *
Twelfth Night * The Winter's Tale*

Vol 9 - Shakespeare Library, Part 2 - The Tragedies (7 Titles)
*Antony and Cleopatra * Hamlet * Julius Caesar * King
Lear * Macbeth * Othello * Romeo and Juliet*

**Vol 10 - Shakespeare Library, Part 3 - The Histories; The
Sonnets (7 titles)**
*Henry IV Part 1 * Henry IV Part 2 * Henry V * Henry VI
Parts 1,2,3 * Richard II * Richard III * Shakespeare's The
Sonnets*

Vol 11 - George Bernard Shaw Library (2 titles)
*Pygmalion & Arms and the Man * Man and Superman &
Caesar and Cleopatra*

Vol 12 - John Steinbeck Library (4 titles)
*The Grapes of Wrath * Of Mice and Men * The Pearl *
The Red Pony*

Vol 13 - Mark Twain Library (4 titles)
*A Connecticut Yankee in King Arthur's Court * Huckle-
berry Finn * The Prince and the Pauper * Tom Sawyer*